# GRAPE EXPECTATIONS

GRAPE EXPECTATIONS



Summersdale Publishers Ltd
46 West Street
Chichester
West Sussex
PO19 1RP
UK

www.summersdale.com

Printed and bound in Great Britain by CPI Group (UK) Ltd, Croydon, CR0 4YY

ISBN: 978-1-84953-257-0

# GRAPE EXPECTATIONS

## A Family's Vineyard Adventure in France

Caro Feely

summersdale

# About the Author

Caro Feely worked as a project manager and IT strategy consultant in Ireland and South Africa before trading it all in to pursue her dreams. She now runs a successful organic wine estate with wine school and gîte rental business in the Dordogne Valley in France with her husband, Sean.

# Note from the Author

This is a true life story; however, some characters, events and place names have been changed to protect the privacy of the people concerned.

Dedicated to our new friends in Saussignac, our loyal customers and my family, Sean (SF), Sophia and Ellie, without whom this adventure would not have been possible.

*Wine in itself is an excellent thing.*

Pope Pius XII

# Contents

# Prologue

I took a deep draught and swirled it around, feeling the warming sensation of alcohol on the back of my throat. The wine filled my mouth with plum and blackberry. The finish had a hint of spice and an attractive saline minerality.

'Delicious.' I licked my lips. The wine filled me with joy. A picture of a vineyard drenched in sunlight formed in my mind. Séan drew me rudely back to the lounge of our semi-d.

'Did you get the spice?'

I nodded.

'How can they be in liquidation if they make wine this good?' I asked.

We should have stopped right there. We were driven by something that went beyond logic: a decade-long dream that took us to places we could not have imagined.

# Chapter 1
# Beware the Dream

'I think this wine is like an ageing dancer. Her moves are slow and supple. Then she performs a pirouette just like she did when she was younger.'

Pierre-Jacques dipped the pipette into the wine-stained oak barrel, transferring tastes swiftly to our outstretched glasses. We stood in the entrance to his cellar, a cave hewn out of the chalky cliffs, captivated by the softening sun and his sensuous descriptions. The wine was smooth and serene across my tongue before fresh raspberries twirled at the finish.

'The wines are grown. I am not a winemaker. I merely help the grapes' transformation.'

Pierre-Jacques, a compact man with dark curly hair and a twinkle in his eye, chronicled the weather of the vintage, the monthly progress in the vineyard, the gentle shepherding of the harvest. Something stirred in our blood. No longer was wine just wine, but a living liquid bright with memory. We had caught a glimpse of the soul of winemaking and were smitten.

After that revelation, we had sought out artisanal wines from French vignerons, people whose lives were expressed in what they bottled. Sean took night classes in wine. I took French. We both dreamed.

Now I was leaning on the kitchen counter, staring at grey drizzle, grabbing a few moments of peace between baby feeds and thinking back to our first visit to that French vineyard. I reflected on how our lives had developed since that fateful day. Every spare cent went into our vineyard fund. We researched, studied and saved. I was an IT-strategy-consultant-turned-early-stage-venture-capitalist and Sean, an investment writer for the asset management business of a large bank. We were typical yuppies but with a long-term mission to change our lives.

Then our first daughter Sophia was born. A malformation of her oesophagus led to five hours of life-critical surgery at less than a day old. It was a time of extreme feeling: powerful love as a first-time mother, fear that she would be taken from us and desperate hope that she would stay. For a year we thought of nothing but her health. She survived – more than that, she glowed with vitality. With Sophia healed, our thoughts returned to a vineyard of our own. We searched the Internet for our dream vineyard most evenings and weekends but had found nothing.

The dream was in fact seeded long before Pierre-Jacques. Sean's grandfather, long dead, was a winegrower. In our mid-twenties we had nearly bought a vineyard but a career opportunity with the large technology multinational I worked for put the vineyard on hold. Now, ten years later, here we were, confirmed city dwellers living on M&S dinners.

It was still raining. I dragged myself away from the window and opened my laptop. Even on maternity leave I logged in every day to see what was going on at work. Ellie, our second daughter, had arrived safely and was exactly six weeks old. I felt vaguely like a super-mum having given birth with no epidural thanks to a few white lies from the midwives: 'You're only minutes away.' Yeah, right.

As I flicked through work emails a property newsletter popped up on the screen. It was filled with tantalising images of cottages in France... And a vineyard: it was the closest to perfect I had seen. The property matched our criteria: 25 acres of vines, a large house, a winery and equipment, and within our price range. In a frenzy of excitement I emailed Sean then read the description again. It seemed too good to be true. Patrick Joseph, the agent, answered my call. I explained the property we were interested in and asked for more details. He hesitated before extinguishing my excitement.

'I'm really sorry, it's been sold.'

Disappointment enveloped me like a wet blanket. He tried to sell me the other vineyard in the newsletter but it was way out of our price range. He could tell we were on a mission and wanted to help. I had to remind myself and him that if our dream ever was to succeed we had to keep to our financial reality. The phone rang again as I hung up and it was Sean.

I announced the bad news; we both knew that properties like this one were like hen's teeth. Through years of searching, the vineyards that matched what we wanted were always out of our price bracket. This was the first that looked right and that we could afford, but it was sold. I was gutted.

'It must have been a fake announcement to get people like us in contact. It probably didn't even exist,' I said bitterly.

'Maybe. We'll have to keep looking,' said Sean sagely. 'I've got to go.'

That last phrase meant someone had arrived at Sean's desk. Our search was in stealth mode. We couldn't let on to his work that he was on a mission to completely change his life.

Trying to take my mind off the lost vineyard, I started unloading the dishwasher. Now was not the time anyway. Ellie was too young. It was a crazy idea. We had no experience working in a vineyard or winery. Sean's night wine classes were just theory. We had thought about taking a few weeks' leave to go and work on a vineyard but it hadn't worked out. A cry from the lounge stopped my internal debate. I grabbed a nappy, picked Ellie up, snuggled her tiny body close to mine, and climbed the stairs to the changing station.

A few weeks later there was a message on the answering machine.

'Caro, it's Patrick Joseph. That vineyard is back on the market. The buyer couldn't get a mortgage. You should move quickly, it will sell fast at this price.' Patrick was a Frenchman living in Nottingham. He helped people like us, with limited French, manage their way through the confusion of French property law.

I was thrilled and scared.

'Are we ready for this?' asked Sean when we spoke a few minutes later.

'I don't know, SF. It would be better if Ellie was older... but it seems so perfect.'

'We'll kick ourselves if we don't view it. I can't take another year in the rat race,' said Sean.

Sean left home before dawn and got back after dark. Investment management was stressful and city traffic hell. They were taking their toll. Sophia, now two years old, missed him. I did too, especially at 5 p.m. with a toddler and a newborn to placate. This vineyard was the answer. We would pursue our passion and get away from the rat race... and the rain.

'You'll have to go on your own,' I said. 'We won't get a passport for Ellie fast enough for me to go. Even if it doesn't work out it will be good for our research.'

Research was a good word to keep the property at arm's length. Sean booked his flight.

With absolutely no experience in vineyards and winemaking we needed someone to help us assess the property. An Internet search offered up the agricultural organisation Société d'Aménagement Foncier et d'Établissement Rural, or SAFER. They looked like the experts we needed.

To call them I had to use my French, which, for all my lessons, was pitiful. I had done a few years of basic French at school then a few years of night classes with the Alliance Française. I wrote down what I wanted to say and made the call. A woman answered and my brain froze. I stammered out the first sentence on the page in front of me.

*'Je ne parle pas beaucoup français. Parlez très lentement s'il vous plait.'*

After several repeats of words that made no sense to me I realised Madame was saying someone would call me back. My investment in night classes was not delivering what I hoped.

A Monsieur Dupont called at 7 a.m. the next morning from something called La Sa Furr. I assumed he had the wrong number and was about to hang up when it dawned on me that this was the pronunciation of SAFER. No wonder I'd been confused the day before. With Ellie latched onto my breast and Sophia jammed into the high chair, I rolled out my 'please speak very slowly' again and tried to concentrate. After spelling his name three times and repeating his phone number ad infinitum, I could tell his patience was wearing thin. A five-minute discussion about what *quinze heures* meant drained what little of it remained but I had a rendezvous between him and Sean at what I hoped was 3 p.m. the following day at the vineyard.

Sean left for Bordeaux. While on the outside I calmly went through my daily routine, inside, my mind was racing. At last, the phone rang.

'*C'est Jean*.' He had already changed his name to the French version.

'Tell all.' I was so excited I couldn't keep still. I paced and Sophia toddled round the room after me while Ellie, lying in a bouncy chair on the floor, looked on bemused.

'It's been some afternoon,' said Sean. 'When Monsieur Dupont arrived, the sellers looked rattled, then he announced that the place is in liquidation. The French agent didn't even know. Sweet divine. Lucky you phoned SAFER. But *bellissima*, it's beautiful, Carolinus.'

Beautiful was one thing, liquidation was another. The French agent was from the local property agency that had the property on their books. Patrick was a go-between for us, offering help and advice, particularly on the legal aspects of the transaction. It was looking like we were really going to need him.

'We don't want to get into a complicated transaction. We've seen how badly things can go wrong buying property in France,' I said. We had been avid viewers of *No Going Back* and similar shows.

'We won't make an offer until we've done our homework,' he said reassuringly. 'The house is in bad shape. We'll have to learn to renovate.'

Liquidation, a ruin of a house; perhaps this wasn't it after all. We had never done more than a coat of paint between us. Part of me was in denial and another part desperately wanted this property to be the one. We had been dreaming of this for so long.

'Patrick gave me the name this morning: Château Haut Garrigue. It's near Bergerac in the Dordogne, an hour east of Bordeaux.'

I had never been to the Dordogne.

'The house has incredible views,' continued Sean. 'You can see Bergerac cathedral, twenty kilometres away. Saussignac village is five minutes' walk through the vineyards. It has a primary school and a restaurant.'

'The girls could walk to school,' I said. 'We wouldn't even have to commute for the school run.' This property was looking more attractive. 'What about the land?'

'Apart from the vineyards it has peach, hazelnut, cherry and fig trees.'

'It was made for us, SF!' I shouted. I love figs.

'Calm down, Carolinus! The place is totally rundown. The figs are nice to have for personal consumption. I don't know... it needs a lot of investment.'

'What about the vineyard? How much money do they make?'

'They sell everything in bulk to a *négociant*. Based on the numbers they gave me they gross about twenty thousand a year. If that's true, after costs, they make nothing with two of them working full-time.'

A *négociant* buys wine in bulk then blends it with other wines and bottles it for sale. We knew they paid low prices for wine but this income sounded wrong, far too low. We had to be missing a zero. We agreed that Sean had misheard and moved on, ignoring the harsh reality of the wine crisis.

'And the winery?'

'The winery needs investment.'

We avoided discussing where this 'investment' was going to come from. Based on rough calculations, with the money from selling our house, after paying off the mortgage, we'd have just enough to buy this property. We'd be throwing everything we had into it and there wouldn't be any left over for renovation or 'investment'. There was a long pause where both our minds churned silently over the financial elements.

'Did you taste the wines?' I asked.

'The sauvignon blanc and the red. They're surprisingly good given the state of the place. The vineyard slopes are steep and well drained. Monsieur Dupont says it's a good vineyard but it needs renovation. The soil is similar to what we saw on the grand crus classés plateau and slopes in St Émilion; clay and limestone. I think it can produce great wines.'

That was it: great wines. Our dream was more than a vineyard, it was creating great wines. I went to bed but couldn't sleep. My body tossed and my mind thrashed in all directions. It was what we wanted and I was excited but the prospective upheaval was immense. The mere logistics of making the move were turning me into an insomniac; the idea of what we would do when we got to that foreign land and had to create our wine was beyond me.

When Sean got home we spent an exhilarating afternoon arguing the pros and cons of Château Haut Garrigue. That evening he presented me with a bottle of vintage 2000 red from the vineyard. He poured tasting amounts into our Riedel glasses.

Riedel makes what some believe are the finest lead crystal wine glasses. They are crafted to bring out the best in wine through their shape and design. We thought Riedels were only for wine snobs, then our closest friends gave us a pair for Christmas. Drinking wine from them was like listening to a symphony on a serious sound system compared to a portable CD player.

I took the glass from Sean and lifted the mahogany liquid to my nose, inhaling a melody of dark fruit with a clean mineral streak through the centre. Desire drew me forward and I tilted the glass to my lips.

'Hang on,' said Sean. 'What did you get on the nose?'

Sean wanted analysis. I wanted to drink. 'Blackberry,' I said, eager to get on with my first swig.

'What else?'

'Mineral.'

'OK, now you can taste.'

I took a deep draught and swirled it around, feeling the warming sensation of alcohol on the back of my throat. The wine filled my mouth with plum and blackberry. The finish had a hint of spice and that attractive saline minerality.

'Delicious.' I licked my lips. The wine filled me with joy. A picture of a vineyard drenched in sunlight formed in my mind. Sean drew me rudely back to the lounge of our semi-d.

'Did you get the spice?'

I nodded.

'It's probably the oak, the wine was barrel-aged.'

'How can they be in liquidation if they make wine this good?' I asked.

'I got the impression they have bigger problems than their finances. Maybe their subsequent vintages weren't this good.'

We found a Bergerac-based *notaire* who was described as a specialist in vineyards and liquidations. The combination sounded ominous but was exactly what we needed.

A *notaire* is an all-powerful state lawyer who does not litigate but rather deals with property, commercial and inheritance law. He assured us that we would be protected from the current owner's debts if we bought the property, rather than their business. It was excellent news. Now we could seriously consider buying the property. Then he outlined the process for buying a property in liquidation.

It was complicated. We would be buying the land and house from the owners, the equipment and stock from the liquidator and negotiating the possibility of all of this through the French government agency SAFER. SAFER and the liquidator would consider multiple offers before making a decision on who to sell to. There would be multiple decision makers. I still didn't fully understand the process but at least I knew we weren't putting ourselves at risk to the previous owner's debts.

This wasn't just a purchase for us; it was a massive life decision. To buy the property we had to sell our house. There was no halfway.

'What are we going to do, SF?' I asked as we debated the purchase that evening.

Sean had been playing it cool. He didn't want me to feel influenced but I knew what he wanted. For me, the quality of the wine had sealed it. Now that we knew the liquidation was not a problem it was obvious we should make an offer.

Patrick, the agent, called the next day before I had a chance to call him. Although I had only spoken to him a few times he felt like a confidante; he knew more about our dream than our closest family and friends.

'A person who viewed the place after Sean has offered the full price,' he said. 'What do you want to do?'

This put a new aspect of risk on the purchase. It was not as simple as our decision to go ahead or not. There was no certainty that it would be ours. Over the previous few days I had slowly been making this vineyard my new home.

Patrick was convinced a slightly higher price would clinch the deal so we agreed. Minutes later he confirmed the seller had accepted our bid. I flew up onto cloud nine, revelling in my sun-drenched vineyard image. Sophia, rolling around on her Winnie the Pooh car, and Ellie, lying in the bouncy chair, both looked up at my yell of triumph. When Sean got home we toasted our new venture with butterflies of excitement and fear intertwined with the fine bubbles of the champagne. It seemed like it was really happening... I had already forgotten that the *notaire* had said it was not only the seller's decision.

The following evening Patrick shattered our dream.

'Caro, you won't believe this, but everything's off. In French law, once the asking price has been accepted on a place it's closed to other bids so they can't take your offer even though they want to. Gazumping isn't allowed.'

I had spent a week setting my sights on this property as our new home, the place to settle for good, and now we couldn't even bid. My vineyard vision fizzled away like a sparkler doused in water. I felt aggressive.

'The *notaire* said the liquidator would consider multiple offers,' I snapped.

'Sorry, Caro, this is what the agent in France told me. This is a bit different to a standard sale. I'll query it and get back to you as soon as I can. In the meantime, consider everything on stop.'

Sometimes Patrick's French came through in the English he used, like saying everything is on 'stop'. If he didn't know what was going on, what hope was there for us?

'Don't worry, Carolinus,' soothed Sean in his frustratingly calm manner when I called him with the latest twist. 'There will be other places.'

'But will they be as perfect? Walking distance to a school, views, the right grape varieties?' I could see our dream slipping away.

We were in limbo. The combination of the anxiety about the vineyard and broken nights created by a newborn guaranteed insomnia. I called Jacky, our pharmacist, to ask for sleeping pills I could take while breastfeeding. She sent me a homeopathic lifesaver that arrived the morning Patrick called back.

'Caro, you were right. You can make an offer. It's all on again.'

I was beginning to understand that in France, nothing was a straight line, neither the walls of our potential new home nor the negotiations to get there.

'So what do we need to do?'

Patrick started with a long 'Well' in his signature Gallic style. 'You need to send in a signed *promesse d'achat* and a business plan laying out all the details: finance, experience, strategy and anything else you feel will make your proposition a viable one. It should be in French and they need it by Monday.'

In my sleep-deprived state this sounded insurmountable; my French wasn't good enough to write a business document. I felt like crying.

'Why do they need all of that? They should only be interested in whether we can pay.'

'Usually, yes, but this is an agricultural property in liquidation so the mandatory liquidator will look at all the angles. He will compare the price offered, financing and viability before choosing the buyer. It could take a few weeks. I'll check over the French for you.'

Patrick had read my mind. Sean and I spent the weekend discussing the costs and potential revenues. We knew horrifyingly little of what we needed. The Internet was a great source of information but how realistic American state extension office vineyard costs and revenues were for France was anybody's guess. By the end of the weekend we knew that this venture was a massive risk. It would be hard to make ends meet. We should have stopped right there but our journey had already taken us beyond the bounds of logic.

I contacted an accountant who specialised in vineyards for a sense check on our plan. He increased many of our costs but thought the revenue seemed reasonable. We submitted our plan and signed offer.

The next week flew by in a blur as we prepared to sell our house. In two weeks the nebulous idea of changing our lives had become high-definition reality and homeopathic sleeping pills had become my best friend.

Sean arranged to go to France for a two-week intensive French course. If this property came through he would need some language skills *tout de suite*. The day he left I went to the O'Briens', our closest friends, for lunch. This was the first time I'd been able to talk to them about our move. I was excited but nervous.

'What? You're buying it without seeing it?' asked Aideen as she served up a portion of roast chicken, our regular Sunday treat and Sophia's favourite. Aideen was my best friend and had been a rock for me through Sophia's first year. A professional coach in a technology company by day and a breastfeeding consultant by night, Aideen had supported me with the difficult circumstances of breastfeeding a newborn recovering from life-critical surgery, which in itself helped me cope emotionally, offering me a concrete way to contribute to Sophia's recovery.

'We had to make the decision. I couldn't go without Ellie and she didn't have a passport. It all happened so quickly. We still don't have a firm answer on the property but we've decided to sell the house anyway. If it doesn't come through we'll find another one. We've decided this is the right thing for us.'

'I'm gobsmacked.'

We hadn't told anyone about our plans. We worked in a tight-knit technology and finance community and had decided that our careers would be seriously impaired if there was any inkling of our move. Until we were sure that it was going ahead we wouldn't say a word to anyone, not even our closest friends and family.

'The "for sale" sign goes up tomorrow so I have to talk to all our neighbours this afternoon.'

The finality of what we were doing hit me.

'It's so sudden,' she said.

I couldn't have said it better myself. Though we had been thinking about this dream for more than a decade, now it was happening too fast. Tears welled up. I would miss Aideen.

We spent hours talking over lunch then over a long walk through the park. By the time Aideen and Barry invited us to stay on for a light supper they were as excited about our move as I was. They had had an inkling of our 'back to the land' dream but just like ourselves had no idea how far we were willing to take it. Two weeks before if someone had asked me if we were really going to pursue this crazy dream I would have said 'unlikely'. Something had clicked.

I felt torn; part of me was thrilled and wanted to go, the other part was terrified, and wanted to stay. We would be leaving our friends. We would be leaving successful careers and their associated income. I would be changing from a responsible job that had me networking with famous entrepreneurs and analysing leading-edge technology to looking after kids full-time in rural France.

When I got home there was a message on the answering machine.

'Hi Caro and Sean, it's Patrick. The sellers have decided to take your offer but they want to know how quickly you can proceed.'

I felt elated, then went into a state of panic. My mind flooded with what we would have to do in the coming weeks and my adrenaline sky-rocketed. It was too late to call him back. Sean rang from Paris in time to stop me spinning completely out of control.

'Calm down, Carolinus. You can call Patrick in the morning. It is Sunday, after all. Take a deep breath. It's good news but nothing is sure until we have a signed agreement. Take your sleeping pills and get some rest.'

Between getting up to feed Ellie and thinking about what Patrick's message meant for us, I slept little in spite of the pills. In the morning our agent assured me we would have our house sold in two weeks. I called Patrick, expecting it to be the final call in this long negotiation process.

'You won't believe this,' he said, 'the seller just called and they have accepted another offer. A third party offered three thousand more than you, they are taking the offer and they don't want a counter offer from you. They don't want a price war.'

I felt like a jilted lover. After putting our hearts and souls into the business plan it was even more personal. We had shared our dream with the decision makers. 'What can we do?' I said eventually.

'Nothing right now. I told them you would match the offer but they were adamant they didn't want to hear it. We're going to try to influence the decision through the mandatory liquidator and SAFER. The other party is a retired couple who want it for a holiday house and will sell off the vines.'

I didn't need any more information, I hated them already. They were stealing our dream to turn it into a retirement house. I felt like vomiting.

'Patrick, we can't go much higher. The place needs a lot of work. You saw the architect's estimate: €50,000 to make the house liveable. There's serious investment required in the vineyard and winery. One minute we have the property, the next minute we don't. One day it's the mandatory liquidator making the decision, the next it's the owners; one day they can't take a gazumping offer, the next they can. The uncertainty is killing me. I am not sure how much more of this I can take.'

'I know, Caro. This is a very difficult transaction but the property is a great buy. If this doesn't work then I think it will be time to walk away.'

I hung up feeling nauseous and texted Sean. For the sellers to refuse more money when they were in financial trouble didn't make sense. Ellie gave me a huge smile and latched onto my breast, blissfully oblivious to the turmoil in our lives.

# Chapter 2

# Goodbye Pay Cheques, Hello Château

'Good morning, Caro. How are you today?' said Patrick chirpily. 'The other offer has gone away and the seller wants to accept your initial offer.'

'What happened?' I asked, feeling a cautious prickle of elation.

'Well, the offer was never formalised. Perhaps there was persuasion by Sa Furr. Our agent will get a *promesse de vente* signed by the seller this afternoon so that they can't change their minds again.'

I texted Sean then tried to contact the *notaire*. After calling seven times I spoke to him. He assured me our verbal offer was accepted and he would call me back later in the day to arrange a formal signing. It looked like it was really going to happen.

I caught Sean on a break from his French class and filled him in on the final episode of our limbo nightmare, ending with the *notaire* who still had not called me back to arrange the formal signing.

'I am sure this *notaire* is doing something funny. Maybe his brother is trying to buy the vineyard.'

Sean laughed and told me I was paranoid then went back to the calm of his class. By the evening, the import of the acceptance had sunk in and I felt like I had jumped out of a plane without a parachute.

Fortunately a safety net was developing: the bidding on the house we were selling went beyond our agent's estimate. We closed the sale with a critical boost to our budget. We knew from reading about moves to France that the rule of thumb was to double your renovation estimate. We would learn that even this was not enough.

At last we could talk about our move. In jubilance, I called an old friend in Oxford.

'Saucy Jack?' said Mike.

'Not Saucy Jack. Saussignac. It's famous for its wines. Haven't you heard of it?'

'No. We'll have to come and try it.'

No one had heard of the wine appellations Saussignac and Bergerac but it was too late to change our minds. A signed copy of the contract to purchase arrived. It was accompanied by a letter stating that a previous owner, Monsieur Battistella, was due 200 litres of our wine every year. There were two sales of the property separating us and him. We debated contesting it but decided Monsieur Battistella might prove a useful ally. We didn't want to land up like Jean in *Jean de Florette*; thwarted at every step by the locals. We were foreigners planning to settle in rural France and take on a métier that was an icon of France. It could spell trouble.

I felt like I was in a dream and would wake up at any moment. This was not what a normal person like me did. It was far too risky, it was not rational, but it was also intoxicatingly exciting.

We moved out of our home. The sale had proceeded even faster than the agent forecast. Ellie slept and Sophia watched packing operations while Sean and I cleaned cupboards.

'Don't take my chair!' yelled Sophia as her high chair disappeared into the back of the van.

Before I could explain, she spied her polar bear going the same way and shouted: 'They're putting Floppy on the truck!' I promised we would see the chair and Floppy at our new house in France in a few weeks.

Sophia was a very composed young lady. I explained what we were doing again and she nodded sagely. We had already talked about the move but she had no frame of reference for it. She was only two and had never known anything but that house. It was our first real home, where both our daughters were born, the place where we felt truly settled for the first time in our married lives. She knew something big was up.

Sean and I tried not to look too far ahead, focusing on moving to our rental house that would be our home for four weeks while we worked out our notice at our respective jobs, participated in numerous planned farewells with work and friends and held Ellie's christening. Although everything was official with the vineyard purchase, we had read that nothing was certain until the final transaction went through, at which point we would be installed in France with no turning back. A few hours later the moving truck, jam-packed with our belongings, pulled away from the driveway and we locked our house for the last time. We were leaving our friends and familiar comforts. We drove to our furnished weekly rental armed with survival rations of clothes, baby equipment and paperwork. I choked back my sobs. I didn't want to upset the girls but a river of sadness flowed over me. I swallowed hard.

That evening Sophia looked worried.

'We forgot my sandpit,' she said, large tears forming in her eyes.

I assured her it would be delivered to us in France. She looked doubtful. Thinking it would give her something concrete about where we were going, I showed her an ancient map that included our vineyard, Château Haut Garrigue. Then we looked up the meaning of '*garrigue*': herbal scrubland populated with lavender, thyme, rosemary and scrub oak; commonly found in Provence. In old French it also meant chalky hill which must have been the origin of the name since our new home was five hours' drive from Provence.

The weeks of farewell parties and tying up loose ends flew by. Colleagues and friends were incredulous. Our GP said, 'You're brave... or mad... or both.' An accounting friend said, 'That's risk with a capital "R".' Both were right. The excitement was mounting but so was the stress. On the eve of our move to France, Sean ignored me, drank too much and watched television instead of packing.

'How can you watch TV when we are making the most important move of our lives?' I yelled. I had been packing and cleaning non-stop for what seemed like days. 'There is still a mountain to pack!'

'It's my life. If I want to watch this film I will,' he said, turning back to the TV.

'It's not only your life,' I screamed. 'It's all our lives. We're moving country in a few hours.'

It ignited one of the severest fights we had ever had. We yelled stinging insults at each other until Sean said dismissively, 'Just go to bed.' I decided to bow out before things turned even more nasty. Sean continued to watch his movie and I stomped upstairs to check on Ellie and Sophia.

Was this the way Sean would handle our new life? How could we possibly get through our first harvest if we couldn't keep our heads while packing our cases?

Sean was the love of my life. I had known from the moment we met fifteen years before. Back then, he was a handsome journalist covering the momentous political change in South Africa. Creative and tall, with long, blonde, wavy hair, he was my ideal man. I was besotted. He took me to parts of Johannesburg I had never heard of, to jive to African reggae in colourful rooms thick with marijuana and hope. He helped me to see life through a wider lens. He never accepted the status quo.

Sean was happier as a journalist than as the financial writer he had been for the last eight years. He had committed himself to it and succeeded, acquiring the coveted and gruelling certified financial analyst title. In the last year, along with a full-time job and a very young family, he held down a second part-time job lecturing to Masters in Finance students in the evenings at a local university. It had meant more pressure and less time at home but it added to our savings and helped realise our dream – that was rapidly turning into a nightmare...

The girls were sleeping peacefully despite our screaming match. I got into bed exhausted and switched off the light. My mind continued to churn. If this move was going to jeopardise our relationship, I did not want to go through with it. Sean was more important to me than following this dream.

But it was too late. The high-pitched beep of our alarm clock exploded through my brain and I scrambled to switch it off. In a few hours we would be on French soil.

Still smarting from our fight I jabbed Sean aggressively in the ribs then went downstairs to brew strong tea. The kitchen was pristine and everything was packed. Sean must have stayed up almost all night after his film ended. I felt contrite.

Soon we were staring blearily over mountains of luggage at a timid dawn through a taxi window. Sophia and Ellie looked remarkably wide-eyed, despite our best attempts to keep them asleep. As we passed familiar streets filled with memories from almost a decade of our life, tears welled up in my eyes.

We arrived at the airline counter with our two-storey trolley of luggage. The airline representative looked at us with mild amusement and I muttered something about moving country. Her eyes flicked over the stratospheric total on the scale and she handed us our boarding cards. She hadn't charged a cent for excess. Soon we were in France, navigating our luggage mountain out of Bordeaux airport.

'I think we should go straight to Haut Garrigue,' said Sean.

'I want to go to the B&B. We'll see it in a few days,' I replied.

I had booked a B&B on a local vineyard that was a few kilometres from Haut Garrigue. It looked authentic and clean but most importantly I hoped that staying with winegrowers meant we could learn something.

'But it's on the route.'

Sean was naturally desperate to show me our new abode. But I was in denial. I wanted to go home.

I was scared. I didn't want to be disappointed. By the time we reached the Bergerac exit on the Bordeaux ring road, thanks to Sean's persuasion and my own curiosity I capitulated. Before long we were climbing the hill into Saussignac. It was a postcard-perfect French village with a magnificent château looking onto the main *place*, or square, with a restaurant on the opposite side and a second square with a small park, post office, bread shop and church. A few houses later we passed the school and a few vineyards and took a well-worn road past the cemetery and three new-looking houses. Then Château Haut Garrigue was in front of us. No warning, no avenue of trees, no signs, just a bunch of dishevelled buildings at the end of a short, bumpy dirt road.

The owners' dogs thrashed around the car. There was broken equipment lying around the yard. The house looked worse than the photos had promised. The shutters were eaten away by rot and termites.

We got out of the car and were offered a tour of the property. The fence around the 3-metre-high terrace was rusted away, making it a deathtrap for children. The place was thoroughly rundown. I looked at the date, 1737, etched above the cellar and thought 'Oh my God, what have we done?' then swallowed back a wave of tears and tried to concentrate on the view. The natural splendour of the valley sprawling below, decked out in the bright greens of summer, was breathtaking.

The owner continued the tour inside. It was beyond a nightmare. The main house was filthy. The renovation required was terrifying. The potential of the place, with its views and deep history, was clear, but the prospect of living in it with Ellie a mere five months old filled me with horror. After the visit we sat at the outdoor table to talk through the final details for the property transaction that was due to take place the following week. The dogs rollicked over to Ellie's buggy and slavered on her tiny hands. I grabbed a wipe and cleaned them before she could put them into her mouth. On my way into the kitchen to throw away the wipe, I saw a pack of gastroenteritis dog medicine on the table. I sprinted back out and lifted Ellie from her pram well out of the dogs' reach, wiping her hands frantically. We couldn't risk Ellie's health another second.

I made an excuse about needing to feed the kids and strapped Ellie into her car seat, motioning to Sean to leave urgently. 'Sweet divine, it's much more rundown and dirty than I recall from my visit,' said Sean as we took off.

'I liked the doggies,' said Sophia.

I filled Sean in on the gastroenteritis tablets I had seen, a small ball of angst for Ellie forming in my stomach. It was clear to both of us that the first priority once we moved in was cleaning and disinfecting the house.

As we drove to the B&B that would be our home for ten days as we waited for the property transaction to complete we discussed plans for the coming weeks. Despite the horrors we'd seen we were remarkably upbeat. While the filth and renovation were more daunting than I imagined, the natural beauty, views and history of the property created magic that far exceeded my expectations. We were embarking on the adventure of our lives and we were both excited.

The B&B was run by a family who had a vineyard the same size as the one we were about to purchase. We arrived at our apartment on their farm and found it to be the perfect antidote: spotless and with everything we needed including delightful toys for Sophia. She was developing a nurturing instinct and took great pleasure in looking after the baby dolls complete with accessories – cots, pushchairs, baby bath and clothes.

When we sat down to dinner that night with our hosts, Bernard and Myriam Barse and their teenage daughter Élodie, I explained in halting French why we were there.

'We are buying Château Haut Garrigue in Saussignac. The purchase goes through next week so we are staying here while we wait for that to happen. We left our city jobs and moved country today. We saw on the website that you have twenty-five acres like we will have so we thought it would be useful to stay with you to hear what it is like.'

Their eyes popped out on stilts.

'*C'est très dur,*' (It's very hard) said Bernard.

Myriam could not believe that we had chosen to swap the comforts of city life for the tough life of winegrowing. She explained that they both had day jobs off the vineyard, Bernard as an electrician and she as a teacher's aide at the local *école maternelle*, to make ends meet.

Bernard, a quiet, compact man, considered our story a little longer then added: 'Prudence. You must be very careful. Costs are high and sales are difficult.'

He was a man of few words and not given to offering advice lightly. Perhaps our financial plan wasn't a reflection of reality.

Four delicious courses ensued, helping to remind us why we were here: baguette and *rillettes de canard*, a local delicacy of cold shredded duck in its fat, matched with the Barses' Saussignac dessert wine; lamb chops from their own herd of sheep, cooked to perfection with rosemary and matched with their red; then home-grown green salad with a selection of fine *fromage*, finished off with a home-made fruit compote. It was a local feast *extraordinaire*.

'Would you like anything else?' asked Myriam as we finished.

'No thank you, that was delicious, *je suis pleine*,' I replied, using the only French words for 'I have had enough' that I could think of.

Élodie, the Barses' teenage daughter, almost fell off her chair laughing.

Myriam giggled politely. 'Used like this, *"Je suis pleine"* means "I am drunk",' she explained.

That evening Sean and I sat outside our apartment enjoying the warm evening air once the girls had fallen asleep. The first major step had been taken: we had moved country. The fight we had the night before was a result of stress and fatigue and while we were still raw from it we had begun to forgive each other. If we were going to take on the challenges that the Barses had indicated were to come, our relationship had to be strong.

This move was a chance to put down roots and to pursue our passion together. Since meeting in Johannesburg we had lived in Vancouver, Cape Town and Dublin and worked even further afield. Our longest sojourn so far had been Dublin and with our ancestry – we grew up in South Africa but Sean's grandparents were Irish and my great grandmother too – we had felt very at home there... but there were no vineyards.

I made a list of what we needed to do over the next few days. We drifted onto our dreams for our new life and our vineyard, our fight almost erased from our memories. I would have stayed up later had I not known I would be woken to breastfeed Ellie within a few hours.

The next day, warned by Myriam and Bernard, but undaunted, we tackled the practicalities of setting up our new life: getting an operational bank account; registering Sophia with a local *école maternelle*, the pre-primary school; buying supplies and purchasing the necessary furniture and equipment to survive at Haut Garrigue while we waited for our belongings to arrive. The heat was extreme. Sean found me sobbing in the supermarket car park. A few minutes at 44 degrees and I was in meltdown. Little wonder. Back home a heatwave was anything over 24 degrees.

Ellie got her first tooth complete with vomiting and fevers. Our apartment didn't have a washing machine so Myriam offered me the use of theirs. In the evenings when the temperature eased we revelled in the warmth, sitting at our outdoor table eating picnics and waving at Bernard's ancient uncle feeding their sheep. Each day we got another brick of our new lives in place. On our moving-in day Myriam kindly offered to take Sophia, Ellie and me to our new home while Sean collected newly purchased furniture from Bergerac. We had formed a bond over the ten days, discovering that they had had a similar experience when Élodie was born to the one we had with Sophia. They were generous and big-hearted.

Myriam loaded us up with gifts, hand-me-down toys for Sophia and bottles of fig jam. We arrived at Château Haut Garrigue and hauled our luggage inside.

'*Bon courage,*' called Myriam as she left. I felt mine fail.

The dark, shuttered house didn't feel like home. It felt empty and rundown. There was dirt everywhere. The shower hadn't been cleaned in decades. It had black fungus centimetres deep down the back corners and up the sides. Opening the shutters to let in the sun and air helped immediately. Ellie, settled in her bouncy chair, watched Sophia buzz around settling her baby dolls from Myriam into their new place.

I started cleaning the kitchen. The sink had brown gunk ingrained into the supposedly stainless steel. After an hour the sink was stainless and I was feeling better. The view out of the kitchen window offered much needed succour, raised as it was above vineyards plunging down towards the Dordogne valley: a picture postcard of green vines, golden sunlight and a village in the distance with a classic French church spire and beautiful tones of local stone. Just as the dirt was starting to drag me down, my hero, Sean, looking like a happy cowboy in his leather Stetson, drove into the courtyard in a large truck hired for the half-day. We heaved our newly acquired double bed, fridge-freezer, washing machine and dishwasher inside and Sean left to return the truck. An hour later he was back installing the equipment.

By the end of our first day we were exhausted but we had a makeshift table and chairs, beds made with fresh linen, cupboards clean enough for our new crockery and a working washing machine, dishwasher and fridge. Sophia fell asleep instantly but Ellie, despite my efforts with her new travel cot, would not settle. She had been sleeping in her bouncy chair instead of a cot since this life-changing purchase started. I moved her into the chair and her little leg started kicking, offering her the soothing bounce that helped ease the tumultuous change. Minutes later she was asleep.

Relieved, Sean and I sat down and drank a toast to our new home with a bottle of our Château Haut Garrigue red. It tasted great. Thank God, since we'd bought 4,000 bottles of it with the property.

We had done it. Tired as we were, we took a few moments to soak in the atmosphere of the 300-year-old room with its enormous beams and metre-thick walls, to appreciate the silence of our new surroundings, and to enjoy a selection of fine cheeses that were becoming a daily habit. Creamy Camembert, nutty Comté and salty Bleu d'Auvergne with slices of apple tasted like heaven. Through the window the light of the moon highlighted the contours of the vines, reminding us why we were here. An owl hooted in the barn across the courtyard. Our city life felt a world away, although it was only ten days since we left.

I fell asleep as my head hit the pillow. At three that morning I woke to the lashing rain of a summer storm and found Sean running around the kitchen placing pots and potties in strategic places. Our one-day-old home was a leaking ship.

The next morning droppings in Ellie's pram confirmed a mouse infestation. We soon realised they were everywhere, eating our food and Ellie's milk-stained clothes in the washing bag. My days became consumed with the Mouse War. I opened the bin and they leapt out at me, bungee-jumping over the edge. They woke us at night. Each time a grey blur streaked across the floor I jumped three feet in the air and screamed. I couldn't bring myself to pick up a dead one let alone deal with a live one; so much for a less stressful life.

At first we encouraged them to leave with expensive sonic devices. When it became clear that they would not take the hint we moved on to other methods. As the week progressed we deployed mousetraps, rat traps and mouse 'chocolate', a supposedly irresistible but lethal mouse snack, carefully placed behind skirting boards where we were sure that Sophia could not get them. In between trips to France Telecom to try to get our phone connected I bought all the mouse-killing devices I could find. My French was improving as fast as my blood pressure was rising. France Telecom wouldn't connect us because the previous owners didn't officially disconnect their phone line.

As a counterbalance to these stresses of our new life I found chocolate in the supermarket which offered *une touche de sérénité*, a touch of serenity. This dark chocolate, filled with bits of cherry, promised to aid the fight against daily stress thanks to high levels of magnesium. Two 100-gram slabs were all that was required for my daily dose.

For more healthy fare I discovered the Gardonne market 4 kilometres away, its stalls groaning with vegetables and fruit, farm-raised chickens and more. I relished the seasonal produce, loading up on the bounty of late summer: punnets of plump tomatoes dressed with large sprigs of basil, myriad different lettuces from purple and smooth to bright green and frizzy, ruby plums and early apples. There was something therapeutic about shopping there, enjoying the banter between stallholders and the care they took with finding exactly what I was looking for.

Fortunately the two girls were taking the mice and the move in their stride and I wasn't even sharing my cherry delight with them. Sophia started school two days after we moved in. She walked confidently into the classroom, delighted to find her name above a coat hook especially for her. Despite speaking no French she settled in remarkably smoothly. The smooth entry was not to last. On the fourth day, as we arrived at school, she started sobbing inconsolably but bravely went into the classroom despite tears pouring down her little cheeks. I choked back my tears as I got back into the car, anxious not to upset Ellie who was strapped into her car seat in the back. Sophia was a courageous little character. Given the start she had it was no wonder.

That night, worrying about her having too much change to cope with at such a young age, I overdosed on stress-buster chocolate. Still bleary-eyed from my bad night, I took her to school the next day expecting another difficult morning. As we arrived, a brave voice in the back of the car declared, 'I am not going to cry today.'

Sophia was handling a new country, new language and school for the first time in her life while I wasn't coping with a mouldy shower, mice and a leaking roof. At least the roof was about to be fixed.

*'Quelle vue,'* (What a view) said the roofer, looking over the terrace that wrapped around most of the house. The late summer sun glowed down on the hillside, highlighting the contours of the vine rows. The Dordogne River, meandering towards Bordeaux, twinkled in the distance.

He climbed the ladder and ranged across the roof like a mountain goat while we waited anxiously below. After pushing a few tiles into position he leapt expertly off the ladder.

'It's fixed. You need to realign the tiles when they get out of line.' He quickly showed Sean how to do it and wouldn't take any payment. 'It will need to be completely renovated in time. You can probably get away with it like this for another couple of years,' he added as he left.

It was a gesture of unexpected generosity that left me grateful and humble but I couldn't help my mind racing ahead to consider the costs required in a year or two. Through my roof-budgeting haze I heard Sophia shouting, 'Ellie's got that! Ellie's got that!' I ran to find Ellie chewing on the toilet-cleaning brush. I was failing as a mother. I couldn't find my way to the supermarket without getting lost, opening a tin of paint was a serious challenge and I missed my work and my friends. I said a prayer asking God to protect Ellie from the germs of the toilet bowl, moved the toilet brush out of her reach and told myself to get a grip.

Some small but significant successes helped me do that. Two weeks of constant harassing brought France Telecom to their senses and they agreed to connect our phone line based on a certificate of residence provided by our mayor. Having a telephone and access to the Internet was like stepping out of the dark ages.

The mice were proving more stubborn. I was on the brink of moving out when they met their match. The local one-man hardware store sold the world's most sensitive mousetraps. At 95 cents each they were the cheapest remedy so far and they took the entire hoard of rodents down. Sean was my hero. He valiantly removed the dead bodies as they succumbed, mouse by mouse. I almost missed them once they were gone. With these time-consuming challenges solved we turned our attention to the renovations and the farm.

# Chapter 3

# Homesick

I wanted the glamorous part of owning a vineyard, not the hard work. Sean was to do the vineyard work and I would look after the kids, do light renovation and eventually the marketing. At the time there was little that could be called glamorous in what we had purchased save perhaps the view.

What we had bought was a large old house that had originally been two houses, numerous ragged outbuildings including the fermentation winery or *pressoir*, the storage winery and a very large barn, and a chunk of about 30 acres of surrounding land of which 25 acres were vineyards in different stages of disrepair. One small part of the house was liveable: a large bedroom where we had installed our entire family, a kitchen where we had a makeshift set-up that included our new equipment and a very old hob, and a large bathroom that once thoroughly cleaned was passable but miles from glamorous. Looking after a very young family in a kitchen that rated just above camping was a full-time job. The gas hob had two working plates and we had no oven. We were scared stiff of spending any more money.

The winery and its renovation were on the long finger – we might have to put them off for a while. It would be a year before we turned our attention to our first harvest and it seemed far, far away. Just coping with daily life in this new environment was enough; my mind could not take in the idea of making our own wine.

Decades of garbage had to be removed from Château Haut Garrigue: fridges and ovens that didn't work, beds that hadn't been used in generations and mounds of unidentifiable detritus. Soon the dreadlocked young man at the dump was greeting me like a friend.

We lived in one large room together while we worked on our first project – a bedroom for the girls. It was lightweight renovation, decorative rather than structural, and meant we would at last get a bit of parental privacy. It had a dirty neon light and walls covered with brown, flowery wallpaper that was peeling badly and stained dark yellow with nicotine. The window in the corner was black with mould. Below it were several fist-size holes that had been the main entrance for our late friends, the mice. The concrete floor was covered with filthy linoleum curling up at the edges like old tobacco. The door had several large vertical cracks running down the upper half and didn't close. We started by removing the linoleum. Once we had cleared the room I tackled the wallpaper while Sean took on the window. I steamed and scraped until my arms ached. Drops of boiling water, molten nicotine and soggy paper fell incessantly onto my arms and hair. I geared up in waterproofs with goggles and hood regardless of the heat. The wallpaper was beyond tenacious. An Internet search affirmed that what we had was not normal. Clearly something more serious than standard wallpaper glue had been used to attach it.

Weeks later, my arms were toned but the room was still in an awful state. I was more at home with a keyboard than a screwdriver and found myself a reluctant renovator.

'We're getting nowhere, SF,' I said, bursting into tears. Completing this room alone before Sean started pruning the vineyard was looking unlikely. I envisioned trying to do the renovations on my own and dissolved into further floods of tears.

'Feck it, Carolinus, we have moved country,' said Sean, trying to cheer me up, but only making me cry harder. The stress of our move was taking its toll. We'd moved country before but not like this: then it was in the same language and with the security of the large multinational for which I worked. It wasn't just getting familiar with physically hard work. We hadn't made love in months – living in a room with our daughters didn't help. Romance was forgotten in change overload. We were spending more time together than ever, but I had never felt so estranged from Sean.

That afternoon, a neighbour we met in passing at the village fête dropped in. Jamie was an impressive character who had worked his way up to being vineyard manager of one of the largest wine estates in our region. He had spent half his life in England and half in France and the speed of his French when he talked on his mobile left me breathless and envious. We had a chat then he looked uncomfortable.

'I've got a favour to ask of you,' he said. 'I need a *chai*. We've got problems with some of our vats. This year will be a catastrophe if we don't find somewhere else to make our wine and since you're not using yours this year I thought of you.'

A winery is called a *chai*, pronounced 'shay'. We hadn't worked up the courage to venture into ours.

We leapt at Jamie's proposal which provided the opportunity to watch a harvest in our own winery and to get to know the equipment. A week later we rose early to see him bringing in the first of his grapes with François, his colleague. The weather was changing, autumn had arrived and with it that morning a chilly five degrees. With Ellie wrapped in blankets in her pram and Sophia bundled up in her winter coat we watched, enthralled, as the dawn poked long gold fingers through the vines. The harvest machine was already motoring up and down the rows and soon the trailer loads were arriving every half-hour. Jamie explained the idiosyncrasies of our winery as he and François worked frenetically to move their machine-harvested grapes from the trailer into a vat. He had to yell above the noise of the tractor that drove a pump in the trailer to push the grapes into a massive pipe oriented into the vat. I hung onto Sophia, anxious to keep her out of the way of the large machinery.

A few hours later the harvest machine left and there was a moment of peace before I had to take Sophia to school. Jamie offered us cups of fresh, pure sauvignon blanc. It was super-sweet grape juice but with the classic aromas of lime and gooseberry and a delicious zesty finish. We had learned these terms in textbooks and tasting finished wine; now we were getting to apply them in the process of winemaking. This was why we were here. It raised us out of our renovation rut and made our dream feel real.

Jamie was a regular visitor from then on, arriving at the winery at least once a day and sometimes twice a day. His arrival would often be accompanied by noise as he pumped liquids from one vat to another or heated or cooled them with our heat exchanger. Just moving the heat exchanger and associated pumps and pipes to the different zones of the winery was heavy work. We exchanged few words most days, but having him come by made me feel less lonely. We were also getting an idea of how much physical work went into making wine.

Jamie did a lot more than rent our *chai*. He taught Sean how to drive the tractor and was an infinite source of advice, encouragement and contacts. One of the contacts was the Chamber of Agriculture; we were the right side of forty to get some free help and perhaps some financial aid under the *jeune agriculteur*, young farmer, banner.

One of the chamber's representatives, Monsieur Ducasse, suggested we meet. I took copious notes on the phone about how to get to his office and he remained remarkably restrained as I asked him to repeat everything many times.

Without a single wrong turn we arrived on time, and clean – Ellie was still in the habit of throwing up on me. Monsieur Ducasse was chunky and dark with serious eyes framed by bushy eyebrows. He welcomed us politely, clearly taken aback by the arrival of a seven-month-old to the meeting. I wedged Ellie's buggy between Sean and myself, gave her a bottle of milk, then explained our situation. Sean's French wasn't up to participating so he left it all to me.

Monsieur Ducasse's severe look darkened with each word.

'We want to know what help we can get from you since we are new to this business,' I said.

'What farming experience do you have?' he asked.

'None really... But we both grew up in a rural environment,' I said helpfully.

Monsieur Ducasse's Gallic eyebrows rose.

'But you must have some practical farming experience?' he pressed.

'Well, we had a small organic vegetable patch in our city garden,' I replied.

The eyebrows shot up.

'We had two grape vines in the garden,' I added quickly.

His eyes popped out.

'What about an agricultural degree?' he asked.

'No, we have masters degrees in economics and finance,' I said.

Ellie watched him suspiciously, sensing his discomfort, while he made urgent notes on the page in front of him.

'How many employees do you have helping in the vineyard and winery?' he asked at last.

'None. We can't afford employees. Anyway, the property is small enough for Sean to farm on his own.'

'Not even part-time?' he gasped, wedging his hand under his chin to stop his mouth from gaping open.

'No... But we have a neighbour who is giving us lots of useful advice,' I said hoping to save him from cardiac arrest. 'He told us to contact you.'

His eyebrows were now within a whisker of his hairline. There were a few minutes of silence wherein he sought to regain control of his facial parts. Ellie watched him intently, finding the drama of his expressions very entertaining.

'There is nothing we can do to help you,' he said eventually, delivering a massive blow to our hopes of aid money to help keep our leaking ship afloat.

Seeing my dismay he tried to explain his position.

'You need an agricultural degree from a French university to get onto the young farmer aid programme, or you need to do a university equivalent programme in Périgueux.'

I started to ask something about the programme.

'It's in French,' he said, stopping me in my tracks and making it clear he didn't consider my language skills up to the level required.

'I thought your organisation was here to help farmers, especially new farmers, like us,' I said bitterly.

'I think there is someone who can help you in the vineyard. I'll give you the number for Cécile Bernard, she's our vineyard advisor for your area.'

We thanked him despite feeling that we got nothing from the exchange except depression at our lack of farming credentials. The young farmer programme opens the door to layer upon layer of aid, something he didn't explain. By not being on it at the start, we were excluded from benefits that multiplied through the system.

Fortunately, we got more than we realised when Cécile Bernard became our advisor.

Cécile was a wonderful woman with a heart of gold, brown, curly hair, and a ready smile. She was in her thirties and knew vineyards. When she arrived to meet us a few weeks later Sean dragged me out despite my reluctance to get involved in vineyard work. His lack of French meant that I already knew more about tractors and other farm equipment than I wanted to.

With Ellie on my hip we walked the vineyards with Cécile. She and Sean made good progress despite the language barrier. I tuned out and busied myself with eating the delectable botrytis sauvignon blanc that had been left on the vines. Botrytis is a miraculous 'noble' rot that develops on late-harvest grapes under special conditions. It concentrates the flavours and sugars to produce the most heavenly taste. The way the late-harvest grapes develop is unique, and hence considered worthy of a special designation, giving the wine of Saussignac its commune appellation.

Appellation is an ancient concept developed in France to denote a quality food or drink from a geographic area. The first food to gain the pre-cursor to appellation d'origine contrôlée (AOC) was Roquefort cheese back in the 1400s. Wine appellations were relative latecomers, only officially initiated in 1935. Our reds, rosés and dry whites fell under the Bergerac appellation, one of the original areas to gain AOC status. Saussignac was made a commune appellation in 1982 but its dessert wines were famous as early as the 1500s. At the time all I knew was that those grapes were so good I could not stop myself.

As I stuffed the fifth bunch into my mouth, I noticed that Sean was having difficulty understanding something Cécile was saying. Cécile repeated herself. Sean turned to me.

'I think she's trying to ask us a question.'

'I know, but I didn't catch what it was.'

Cécile looked at us as if we were aliens from outer space.

'Are you trying to ask Sean something?'

Cécile cracked up and all three of us roared with laughter while Ellie looked on in mild amusement. I think she had realised just how little we knew about how to farm vines. Here we were trying to learn something completely new and complex – winegrowing – in a language we didn't even understand. If we didn't laugh we would have cried. I felt like I was Alice in Wonderland. We had a long way to go.

---

My birthday card from our closest friends, Barry and Aideen, arrived with the caption: 'The road to a friend's house is never long.' I dissolved into tears. There was a silver lining inside the card; they were coming to visit us in a few weeks.

The night they arrived we set up camp for them in the second half of the house where renovations we still seriously required. Cillian, their nine-year-old son, and Juliette, their seven-year-old daughter, were ecstatic; it was a real adventure being in an abandoned semi-ruin. Mattresses, sleeping bags and boxes as side-tables offered simple comfort. We put the kids to bed early and settled down to catch up, starting with an aperitif of the Saussignac dessert wine we bought with the property.

'This is fantastic,' said Barry.

Aideen followed with more superlative comments. She grabbed my notebook and took tasting notes. Then we tasted the reds.

'You must sell these wines direct this Christmas,' said Barry.

We had been enjoying the wines but we didn't feel confident enough to sell them. Sean had taken samples to a *négociant* nearby who had voiced interest – but at outrageously low prices.

'Are they good enough to market to our future customer base?' I asked.

'You have to. If you wait, people will forget you. Get the offer out there.'

'But how will we do it in time for Christmas? It's nearly November.'

'It can't be that hard,' said Barry. 'Do the sales over the Internet.'

We had worked on large-scale transactional Internet projects, Sean for the bank and myself for diverse clients, but that seemed far away in the past, although it was a mere three months since we'd moved. The bottles we bought were 'nude' so we needed labels and capsules, the covers that go over the corks, then we'd need a shipping partner and approval from the customs authorities to ship the wine.

Undaunted by the logistical problems, we spent the evening coming up with labels and tasting notes for the sales campaign which in a few hours had become a reality. 'Ho Ho Haut Garrigue' became our Christmas tag line, but 'Sassy Saussignac' in bold gold with lurid pink lips underneath didn't look quite as appealing the following morning when we all got up to participate in our first ever hand-harvest of 'sassy' dessert wine.

We arrived at the Barses', the family that had hosted us at their B&B. Their ancient uncle was in the winery and didn't recognise us. When we'd stayed in the B&B we visited his half of the Barse house, which was like stepping back in time. Medieval cobbles on the floor were cracked and worn from centuries of use and, opposite the door, a huge fireplace with hooks and pots hanging over it was still in use as the primary cooking facility. He greeted us warily and escorted us to where the extended family was picking grapes. To him, after a lifetime of working this vineyard, anyone offering to help hand-harvest for fun was regarded with suspicion.

Sun filtered through the vines highlighting pickers in a honeyed haze. Mist, part of the secret of the unique Saussignac botrytis which creates these sweet wines from heaven, was painted in golden airbrush strokes over the scene. All was quiet save for a few bird calls and chatter between pickers. Bernard greeted us warmly and gave us a succinct lesson which I endeavoured to translate as succinctly for our friends. He handed round harvest secateurs and baskets with a brief warning about taking care. A few minutes later he passed by my basket and removed a bunch whose botrytis was less developed than the rest. Without saying a word he had set the level for me.

Cillian quickly copped on, removing grapes that were a bit green or the ones that had gone too far. Juliette nicked her finger but after a plaster and a kiss was back picking more eagerly than before. The magic and excitement of harvest time spread a unique energy through us. Even Sophia gathered some bunches, while Ellie looked on from her all-terrain buggy. '*Les enfants* are often the best at picking Saussignac,' said Myriam. 'Their senses are much finer than ours.' Back in the *chai*, Bernard passed round cups of juice as it came out of the press. It was thick as honey and as sweet but with layers of flavour: apricot, almond and orange. Standing in the winery surrounded by the noises and smells of harvest I felt joy and excitement mingled with a little fear. Making wine, for all the hard work, created a deep resonance inside me. I was spellbound. We had witnessed our first harvest of the miraculous Saussignac wine.

When the O'Briens left, we tackled the Christmas sales campaign with vigour. It seemed impossible but within a few weeks Sean had provisional approval from the authorities, our labels ready to print and a shipper lined up.

We sent personal emails to our friends and former colleagues, not expecting to sell more than twenty cases. We watched the orders come in through our new website with a mixture of excitement and trepidation. We passed the twenty-case mark overnight. By the deadline we had 115 orders and more promised including an order for corporate Christmas gifts from a close friend.

Sean contacted the shipper to let them know we would be sending three pallets. He emailed back to say the customs official would not accept the shipment. We were horrified. The official had given Sean the go-ahead as long as we prepaid the taxes before the shipment left our property. What had gone wrong? Sean called our customs contact on the speaker phone.

'We gave you the go-ahead for this delivery because it was a shipment to friends, not 1,800 bottles,' said the official.

I felt a rush of nausea but Sean remained calm.

'You are right. When I spoke to you I estimated three to six hundred bottles, which was what we were expecting, but we have been amazed at the response.'

'Are you sure this was an email offer to friends? You didn't have any advertising in a newspaper or magazine?'

'No, this was an email to friends and colleagues.'

'We'll let you do it this time,' he said. 'For next time you will have to have completed your registration and have your tax representative approved.'

I danced a jig around our rustic temporary office in the boiler room, while the customs official explained the concept of a tax representative: an administrative project for another day.

Overnight the weather changed to freezing. The 1,800 bottles had to be lovingly washed in icy water before being 'dressed'. With frozen fingers we revelled in the exhilaration of our first order and the rich aromas of wine and oak that surrounded us in our ancient barn.

After washing, the wine moved to capsuling, fixing the metal cap over the top of the bottle to cover the cork. To seal the capsule, the bottle is fed into an exceptionally noisy, rocket-shaped apparatus, called a *capsuleuse*. The right amount of pressure must be applied: too little pressure and the capsule comes out like a skirt, frilly and ruffled at the base; too much pressure and the top of the capsule is pierced. After a few hours of practice Sean was an expert and the capsules were smooth. Ellie was remarkably good-natured despite the noise, wrapped in five layers of blankets in her buggy, calmly watching the progress.

For days we listened to U2 and labelled cases with familiar addresses feeling cold, happy and homesick at the same time. The order represented a critical start for our wine business. When the transporter collected we felt inordinately proud; we hadn't made the wine but it came from our vineyard.

The vines changed colour. Their leaves fell. At night we froze despite still being huddled together in one room. I struggled on with the renovations, learning to wield a screwdriver and a paint roller like a pro. The local building supplies man greeted me with glee whenever I appeared. My hands were calloused. I wore the same paint-splattered working clothes for weeks on end. It was a shock change from our city lives of business suits, cappuccinos and heated offices.

Early December we were wracked with coughing, vomiting and fevers. I could barely drag myself out of bed to attend to Sean and our sick daughters. There was a mountain of washing and we didn't have a tumble dryer. Phil Collins' lyrics about the roof leaking and the wind howling kept rolling around in my head. After doing another round of nursing I went to see our local doctor in desperation. I needed to be well to care for everyone.

'There is a mild chest infection but you can fight it off yourself with a week of rest,' he said.

'I want an antibiotic. Someone has to look after the sick children.'

'Isn't there someone who can help you? Your *belle-mère*?'

I explained that there was no mother-in-law and there would be no rest.

Minutes later I walked into the pharmacy armed with my prescription. With two young children, I was already well known to them. A large promotion stand at the entrance announced the launch of a new deodorant with 48-hour effectiveness. I giggled despite my throbbing headache. Who would advertise not washing every day? To my 'cleanliness next to Godliness' upbringing it was incomprehensible. Little did I know that a week later, when the real cold of winter set in, I would be back for some of my own. Our erratic heating system couldn't match the deep freeze. Bathing every two days was as much as I could stand. I left the pharmacy armed with my medicine and returned to my sick household.

Just when it seemed it would never end, we woke up feeling well, the sun was shining and a huge rainbow hung over the Dordogne valley. We ate our favourite lunch of baguette and Brie and stared at the view. Ellie smiled benevolently from her high chair and Sophia tucked in with relish. Food never tasted so good and we revelled in the magic of feeling well.

I could not fault our new community. People were generous and warm. Bernard Barse did the electrical work for our new kitchen as a gift. Even the notorious French civil servants were friendly and helpful. Sophia started singing in French, proving our worries about her settling in unfounded. I agonised about our precarious financial future but the success of the Christmas offer filled me with hope. Ellie started crawling and putting her tiny hands into my paint and other undesirable substances. Meanwhile Sean's thoughts turned in earnest to the vineyard: a place bristling with unknown danger.

# Chapter 4

# Six Tons of Chicken Poo and No '*Épandeur*'

Sean commissioned a soil analysis so we could gauge the state of the vineyard. The soil consultant took us through the diagnostic, explaining that, in his opinion, the vineyard needed a serious fertility boost.

'By my calculations you need six tons of fertiliser. It must be ordered and spread as soon as possible,' he declared.

I asked how long it would take to spread that amount of fertiliser.

'For Sean, since he's new to it, about three days but rain is forecast in three days so you must do it now.'

Since the fertiliser was not ordered, this seemed optimistic.

Sean shelved his other plans for the day and went out to investigate the machinery in the hangar. The 'hangar' was a rusted corrugated iron lean-to around the side of the *pressoir* where old agricultural equipment that we had acquired with the farm was stored. He found a fertiliser spreader and connected it to the tractor only to discover it was broken. In the intervening hour I got an express order of organic fertiliser delivered. Now we were the proud owners of 6 tons of compressed chicken manure with no way to spread it.

Sean postulated that we could spread the poo using our back packs with some minor adjustments. It involved piercing holes into the bottom of the packs and running tubes from the holes, then filling the packs with extremely noxious material and walking up and down each side of each vineyard row aiming the issue from the tubes at the base of the vines. I carefully explained with the aid of calculations related to the weight, distance and smell why we should reject this notion out of hand. I was beginning to doubt whether my husband's sense of practicality was a match for farming. We moved on to the next option, to repair the spreader, and decided it would take too long and probably be more costly than buying another one.

'Phone around to find out prices for a new one then,' said Sean.

'What is it called and where would I get one?' I replied, reaching for the phone.

'I don't know. You'll have to phone Jamie.'

A few minutes later, thanks to our lifesaver Jamie, I had what I thought was the name – an *'epondre anglais'*. I didn't know exactly what it meant – *pondre* is to lay eggs, I knew that, which seemed a little strange – but I had the numbers for three places that supplied them. I called the list ending off with Monsieur Bonny, who was rapidly becoming our local mechanical genius.

Monsieur Bonny had one of the happiest, friendliest faces I had ever encountered. He was a small fellow with boundless energy. In his late fifties, although he didn't look it, he had been working as a mechanic in his family workshop in Coutures since he was thirteen years old. He had a wonderful, strong Dordogne accent. *Maintenant*, *justement* and other similar words ending in 'ent' or 'ant' become 'ain' and take on the most beautiful sing-song ring when he says them. *Besoin*, the word for need, also ends more softly, sounding more like *'beswain'*. We made his acquaintance soon after moving in and had been regular visitors to his workshop ever since.

Monsieur Bonny explained that it was an *épandeur d'engrais*, a fertiliser spreader, and nothing to do with English or laying eggs. Several machinery sales people in the Dordogne were having a good laugh on me. Monsieur Bonny had a second hand one that would be perfect for us. A few hours later Sean was spreading chicken manure as fast as he could. Ellie and I watched from the kitchen window laughing as he and the strange machine with its awkward wagging tail sped up and down the rows leaving a smelly trail in their wake.

Sean was getting neurotic about machinery. He smashed the back window of the tractor with the fertiliser spreader. Days later he drove under a tree and dislodged the exhaust. His number of visits to Monsieur Bonny in Coutures was travelling in the opposite direction to our bank balance. Soon Sean was back with Monsieur Bonny buying electric secateurs in preparation for the pruning season. This automatic pruning apparatus could take your finger off in a second. I eyed them warily, relieved that he would be wielding them and not me.

Sean had learnt the basics of pruning on the vines in our back garden in Dublin: now he had to prune 25,000 of them. Pruning is one of the most important jobs in the vineyard and physically demanding. Jamie spent the afternoon with Sean helping him get familiar with this new task.

While Sean learnt the practical details of pruning I tried to get the plumber, the tall, dark and handsome Monsieur Lombere, to commit to a date for fitting the new shower and toilet into the broken bathroom in our house. I had been waiting for months for him to do the promised work. We had family arriving for Christmas and I was agitated. When I signed his formal *devis* for the work – a quotation that becomes binding on both parties once signed – I'd included the statement that the work had to be completed before the end of November, which was now a sniff away. The charming but unresponsive Monsieur Lombere was taking no heed. I explained my worries to Jamie when he came up from the vineyard, showing him the name of the plumber as I had written it down when a friend in the village gave me the number. Jamie cracked up. 'Mr Lambert!' he said, writing down the correct spelling. 'I'll call him for you. He's doing all the renovation work at our place.' I went red, feeling like the village idiot. Despite years of classes I still had no clue about French spelling and pronunciation.

Jamie's powers of persuasion were epic. Within hours, Monsieur Lambert called to say Jean-Marc would start the bathroom on Monday. He arrived on cue: a muscular fellow with a clean-shaven head and an upbeat attitude that remained even when he had to look into the bowels of old toilets. I showed him the renovation target. The bathroom had bright multi-coloured mosaic tiles on the floor, pink-flowered tiles on the walls, a broken basin, a broken toilet and a black depression in the wall where a shower had once been. I asked him what the white box behind the broken toilet was.

'It's a *broyeur*. A *broyeur* is a chopper that minces the waste into a smooth mixture so that it can travel down a small waste water pipe instead of a large sewage pipe.'

I interrogated him about whether this was acceptable sanitary practice and he assured me it was. The only alternative was to rebuild the main wall of the house so we could replace the small pipe with a large sewage pipe. The wall was close to a metre thick and three hundred years old.

'You will have to use a *broyeur* in your new bathroom,' he concluded. 'You can use this one, it works perfectly.'

He flushed the broken toilet and I heard the signature chopping sound of the *broyeur*. I was horrified by the whole idea but reluctantly accepted his suggestion, although I had a feeling it would be trouble.

A few days later, after the new floor tiles were installed by our tiler, Jean-Marc reappeared to fit the new bathroom. I had worked until past midnight the night before removing the old pink flower wall tiles from the shower area. I was adamant that such an unskilled job had to be done by me to save money. The tile removal took much longer than anticipated but there was no way I was going to be the reason for a delay in the work after the pressure we had put on Lambert. I planned to cunningly paint the rest of the tiles with a tile primer followed by a coat of cream paint. Removing more of them was out of the question.

When we bought the new shower tray Sean and I struggled to move it a few feet so I told Jean-Marc to let us know when he needed some help to get it upstairs. Before I knew it he had the tray upstairs without a murmur. Within a day he had finished the new bathroom. The following day our tiler tiled the shower walls while I painted the primer over the remaining pink flowers.

Once my final coat was complete it was a total transformation. The bathroom was gleaming cream, white, glass and chrome. Between my paintwork on the wall tiles, the new floor and Jean-Marc's fitting of the bathroom components that I had searched Bordeaux for, it looked like something that would happily pass in a stylish boutique hotel. Jean-Marc stopped by to fit the last element: the taps on the shower.

'It's very pretty,' I said.

'*Ça fonctionne,*' declared Jean-Marc, making it clear that in the world of plumbing, function was far more important than form.

Sean got on with the pruning, key to the health of the vine and to excellent grapes. The vines looked like scraggly bundles of dead twigs attached to small tree trunks. The first step was to prune each vine from this unruly state down to one or two carefully selected canes that would be the bearers of next year's bounty. Canes are the young branches that grow from the main trunk of the vine. There are many and selecting the right ones for the following year is a skilled job requiring concentration, judgement and stamina. Sean lost weight, gained muscle and looked healthier despite the harsh weather. In their hibernating state the vines were becoming his friends.

When we arrived, the farm was a large chunk of land distinguished by obvious markers like buildings and tracks. Now it was becoming familiar, each part of the vineyard had a name and a personality. In front of the house looking down into the Dordogne valley was the merlot vineyard we called Lower Garrigue. Running away from the *pressoir*, the part of the winery where the grapes are pressed at harvest time, were the vineyards we called Hillside, consisting of young sauvignon blanc, ancient sémillon and merlot. Beyond Lower Garrigue heading down to the valley floor were a set of vineyards called Lenvège which originally belonged to the Château Les Tours de Lenvège, a half-kilometre from us.

The original medieval tower of Les Tours de Lenvège was built in the twelfth century for protection. It contrasted dramatically with the main château in the village built in the late seventeenth century in a more decorative style. Our farm was the look-out. This was particularly important during the period of English rule of Aquitaine, and also in the wars of religion when the powerful merchants of Bergerac were Protestant but most of the surrounding villages, like ours, were Catholic. We were slowly getting to know our new place.

It was not just vines that Sean met while pruning; he regularly saw deer, hares and pheasant. One day he came face to face with a giant wild boar. The boar blew several smoky breaths into the cold morning air then sauntered off without causing any trouble. Still, when he didn't come in at the expected time I was thrown into a state of panic. The electric secateurs gave me a chill every time I looked at them. When Sean was out pruning I kept checking to see that he wasn't a blob of blood on the frost.

Sophia was in great form and loving school. At first she struggled to say her teacher's whole name, Mademoiselle Fournier, and would regularly call her 'Fournier' which sounded hilarious and unwittingly insolent.

A week before the annual Christmas outing a pressurised letter appeared in Sophia's notebook demanding proof of her school insurance. School insurance is obligatory and covers damage or personal injury caused to your child or that caused by your child to others on outings of extra-curricular activities. I had given them the number of the policy several months before so I couldn't understand what the problem was. Mademoiselle Fournier explained patiently that we needed an official letter from the insurance company as proof. Thereafter she spoke to me as if I was one of her students, slowly and with great enunciation, but in a kind rather than 'school marm' way. She regularly checked I had understood the messages in Sophia's schoolbook by asking the same thing in several different ways. She was delightful, as was Martine, her assistant.

Martine was a fifty-year-old woman with long blonde hair, a good physique and incredible enthusiasm for life. She was always dressed impeccably and I wondered how she looked so good with a horde of three-year-olds to look after. I couldn't keep clean for longer than a few minutes each morning before having something thrown over or thrown up on me.

Martine was a wonder and she had a soft spot for Sophia, greeting her every morning with a huge smile, the obligatory kisses on each cheek and a cry of 'Ma Kiki!' Each time Sophia wore a dress she exclaimed, *'Oh, si belle, si jolie, cette petite robe!'* On hearing Martine's compliment about her pretty dress, Sophia's face would light up and she would skip into the classroom. Even the more austere *maîtresse* would furnish kisses to the kids in the morning.

Not only was Sophia learning to speak French like a native, she was also learning to eat like a native. Every day at school she had a three-course lunch consisting of, for example, *salade d'endives*, *boeuf bourguignon* and *tarte aux pommes*. Sean and I would salivate over her menu which was dutifully copied to the parents at the start of the month on a single-page calendar meal-planner, presumably to make sure we didn't feed them the same gourmet feast that evening. There was little chance of that.

Ellie was ecstatic to fetch Sophia from school each day with me. We'd arrive at school and they would greet each other with glee.

'Mummy, I don't love Ellie,' said Sophia one day on our way home.

'What do you mean?' I asked.

'If we love each other then we'll make babies,' said Sophia.

I explained that this was incorrect. It was only when two grown-ups like a mum and a dad loved each other in a very special way that this amazing feat could take place. She looked dubious. When I got home I told Sean about our strange conversation.

'Whoa!' said Sean. 'That's my fault. Sophia asked me where babies come from yesterday. I explained that it happens when two people love each other.'

We agreed he should follow up with some clarification on his rather broad explanation.

Mike, the one who called Saussignac 'Saucy Jack', Bev, his wife, and their two young sons arrived to visit for a few days' holiday. Mike and Bev were old university friends of mine and we were looking forward to catching up… we also hoped that the extra help would accelerate the renovations.

While Bev and I kept the children occupied, Mike and Sean set to preparing the ancient kitchen for the new one we had ordered. This involved some tile removal and a minimal amount of plumbing, which they vowed would be done in half a day.

Every time we walked past, Mike and Sean were deep in discussion surrounded by myriad tools, books and countless plumbing supplies. A few hours later the car would roar off on yet another visit to the *quincaillerie*, our local hardware store. Later, the discussion would continue even more earnestly over a beer or two. Five days and countless bags of plumbing equipment later, not a tile had been removed and the plumbing job was complete but leaking.

The next time Jean-Marc came round I asked him to fix the work they had done. He took a look, shook his head, then ran out to his van for a toolbox.

Five minutes later he declared: *'Ça fonctionne!'*

Mike and Bev left as my parents and the hoar frost arrived. It transformed our farm into a scene from *The Lion, the Witch and the Wardrobe*. White ice crystals hung delicately off telephone wires, trees and vineyard trellising, and covered the ground like shimmering snow. In the sun it was like necklaces of diamonds; stunning but extremely cold; the coldest winter in living memory.

Mum and Dad were in a state of shock. Not only were they finding it hard to accept that we had left our successful city careers for a very risky rundown farm, they were new to grandchildren and they were frozen. Their modern house maintained a comfortable 20 degrees no matter the weather. We were maintaining an uncomfortable 10 degrees with the heating on full blast... until the heating packed up.

It was 29 December and there was no answer from the office of Lambert the Handsome. Fortunately, Jamie had Jean-Marc's mobile number.

To help my parents stay warm during the emergency I encouraged them to remove the old wallpaper in the salon. Working with a steamer and climbing up and down ladders to remove streams of nicotine-laden, velvet-flocked, burgundy wallpaper soon increased their body heat. By the time Jean-Marc arrived the salon was like a sauna.

After half an hour he emerged from the boiler room covered from head to toe in a thick layer of black soot.

*'Ça fonctionne,'* he declared triumphantly.

'You must have the heating off each time the tank is filled and for a minimum of six hours afterwards,' he scolded. I nodded and showed him to the basin. I kicked myself for not remembering that Jamie had mentioned this handy tip on one of his winery visits. This was the first time we had filled the fuel tank and it had slipped my mind. All these small errors were costing us money we didn't have.

At least it gave a critical boost to the renovations: my parents were so exhilarated by removing the foul wallpaper that they steamed on regardless that the heating was now *'en fonction'*. Once the paper was off they were so taken with the room's potential, they painted it. By the time they left the salon was transformed.

The charming *broyeur* that had been reinstalled in our brand new bathroom developed a leak. I called Monsieur Lambert, since except in emergencies everything had to go through *le patron*, and Jean-Marc appeared.

*'Qu'est-ce que vous m'avez cassé aujourd'hui?'* (What have you broken for me today?) he asked with a twinkle in his eye. This became his first question each time he saw me, providing much merriment.

These breakages in the house were due to lack of foresight on my part and were beginning to rival Sean's in the vineyard. The *broyeur* was blocked by debris from a past era. I kicked myself again for not having cleaned it when Jean-Marc removed it for the bathroom fitting. Too many trips to Monsieur Bonny and visits from Jean-Marc were making our bank balance look sick. We were guzzling through our savings and we hadn't tackled a full winemaking cycle or any investment expenses yet.

After the cutting, the next job in the pruning cycle was pulling the discarded canes off the trellising. In our region the vines grow on a vertical trellising system with three rows of wire running between upright poles that run the length of the vine row. The vines grow up this vertical surface so there is as much sun exposure as possible for their leaves in the growing season. Once the winegrower has cut the canes they don't fall to the ground since the vine has attached itself to the trellising during the growing season using little tendrils. The tendrils that looked so delicate holding the canes onto the trellis in summer became hard and tough as wire in the winter. Pulling the canes off the trellising was tough and sometimes dangerous work as the canes could whip back unexpectedly. Protective eye gear was obligatory.

With the pressure of spring's arrival mounting I asked our neighbour, Sonia, to look after Ellie so I could help. Sonia had a son named Alane of a similar age to Ellie and a daughter of a similar age to Sophia, plus she had trained to look after young children. Sonia and her husband Fred's house was the nearest of the new houses on the road that took us into the village, a mere hundred metres away. We could not have wished for a more ideal neighbour. Ellie was two months away from her first birthday. The outing to Sonia would give her some light relief from her usual entertainment of watching me roll paint or sand old wood windows.

Donning goggles, winter rain gear and large rubber boots, I waddled out like the Michelin man. After two rows I was exhausted.

'Get on with it or we'll never finish in time!' Sean snapped. He was focused. I never wanted to do vineyard work and now I was out there, an unwilling helping hand.

Cécile, our vineyard advisor, inspected Sean's pruning, pronounced it *'très bonne'*, and wanted to know where he had done his training. Sean nearly kissed her. He didn't own up to being largely self-taught on two vines in our back garden. I felt bad about my unwilling attitude. Sean was facing the real transformation, responsible for growing our livelihood, learning new skills in a language he was only starting to grasp. Seeing the look on his face at Cécile's compliment, I felt a deep empathy for him and realised his rough attitude since we arrived was partly due to this subtle but intense stress.

Cécile convinced Sean to sign up for a two-day course she was running on managing vineyard pests and diseases. At the last minute he decided he wasn't confident enough in his French and asked me to go. I walked into the training room several minutes late after dropping Sophia at school.

'Please give me a brief introduction: your name, the size of your vineyard, how long you have been installed and your viticultural experience,' said Cécile. My heartbeat pounded in my cranium. I hate group introductions and in a room full of local farmers, I felt totally out of my depth.

'Nicolas Demetier, seventy-five acres in Monbazillac, installed since birth, fourth generation *viticulteur*,' said the first.

I withered into my seat as the rest of the men followed in a similar vein. My turn, the last, came around too fast.

'Caro Feely, twenty-five acres in Saussignac. My husband has been installed since September,' I said, feeling the lack of several generations of vineyard knowledge.

A day of rapid-fire French followed. The less I concentrated on the words, the more I understood. The minute I tried to 'understand', the words became a torrent of incomprehensible sounds. Cécile took us through endless slides of photos of pests and diseases and how to combat them. We went for lunch and I tried not to make a fool of myself. Seated beside me was a farmer from Saussignac, Pierre Sadoux, a thin rake of a fellow who smoked rolled cigarettes and had a ready smile. He repeated the name of his property but I didn't recognise it. I could barely say Haut Garrigue, the name of our own farm. Understanding and pronouncing the names of those around us remained impossible.

At the end of the first day I was bushwhacked by language difficulties but also terrified by what was lurking in our vineyard. *Ravageurs* lay around every corner and the sprays required to slay them were more frightening. Even the sprays for organic producers like us weren't too appetising. I spent the evening showing Sean the photos of the monsters resident in our vines, terrifying creatures ranging from red and dragon-like to spotted and horned. Fortunately, most were invisible to the naked eye.

I was convinced the following day could bring nothing as gruesome but Cécile distributed an innocent-looking booklet called 'Risk Evaluation' to take home. Sean and I read it in horror. The winery was more petrifyingly dangerous than all the *ravageurs* in the vineyard put together. It was home to four killers which regularly took their toll on winemakers: carbon dioxide asphyxiation, mechanical accidents, falling from height and electrocution.

Jamie warned us that the electricity in the winery was far from robust. We resolved to get it replaced and to put a security barrier around the top of the vats in the main winery. There were certain things that, even with security measures, remained dangerous, like carbon dioxide and some pieces of machinery. Ellie got her fifth tooth that night and between getting up to administer paracetamol I had nightmares about winery killers.

In late winter or early spring the trellising posts that have rotted at the base must be replaced. Some farmers had moved to metal posts, which lasted longer but had a propensity to attract and conduct electric and radio waves, creating 'noise' in the vineyard. Regardless of the type of post, it needed to be bashed into the ground. Sean checked out the prices of mechanical post-bashers and concluded that, while an attractive idea, it was not an option for us.

Stephan Ranzato, a 7-foot-tall, solidly built local winegrower who was also a part-time salesman for trellis posts and accessories, offered to lend us his 50-kilogram manual post-basher; a massive *cloche*, or bell, used to bash the trellising posts into the ground. He delivered it, unfolding himself awkwardly out of his tiny Renault. I felt he was doing us a huge favour lending us his equipment when he barely knew us. I leapt forward to grab it.

'*Merci beaucoup,*' I said. 'Don't worry, I'll take it in.'

'Ah *non*, *non*, it's very heavy,' he said picking up the *cloche* with two fingers as easily as if it were delicate china. He deposited it in the barn. When he left a few minutes later, I went to the barn to see if I could pick it up: not a millimetre.

Despite having a sore throat and threatening worse, Sean replaced 150 rotten trellis poles using the lead *cloche* in cold and rain. A few days later he had a raging fever. The doctor diagnosed a chest infection and prescribed an antibiotic. The antibiotic didn't work and Sean's chest infection turned into pneumonia. He was feeling grim and stressed about the work in the vineyard going undone. Despite a second antibiotic Sean's pneumonia worsened. The third antibiotic was so strong it made Sean nauseous for several hours after each dose. At least it worked. A week later Sean was well again but we were seriously behind with the vineyard work.

The buds started to swell on the vines and Sean raced to finish tying the canes onto the trellising. Once the buds develop there is a chance of damaging them, but it's a fine balance. To minimise harm that can be caused by a late frost it's best not to tie down too soon. We were under intense pressure, so I asked Sonia to look after Ellie again and took a break from renovating the wooden shutters to help Sean. Now that the weather was improving I had moved from painting inside to outside. My days were a round of cooking, feeding, cleaning and renovating. I took great satisfaction from the renovations as the interior of the house was significantly transformed but I was lonely. I filled the gap of missed colleagues and friends with slabs of cherry chocolate. It would take time to find good girlfriends.

We revelled in the greening beauty of springtime but I was slow at tying down. I blamed it on being left-handed but Sean blamed it on lack of will. He expected me to keep pace and yelled at me to hurry up. Soon my fingers were blistered and I was even slower.

'Come on Carolinus, get on with it!' he shouted as I lagged behind yet again.

Our relationship was better than it had been in winter but Sean was a different person to the one I had known. He was stressed and hostile like he used to be at the end of each quarter when he worked for the bank. Back then it was for a couple of days once a quarter. Now it was constant. I could understand it since everything was new, unfamiliar and dangerous but I didn't know how long I could live with it. An error in his analysis would have been dire but not as bad as if he misplaced his finger and it was chopped off by the electric secateurs. In the back of our minds we also had the ever-present pressure of worrying about our finances. With no income for the foreseeable future and constant outgoings, they were not pretty.

Those few days were our first taste of the headlong rush that spring, summer and autumn would be for us. We finished tying down as the buds turned from hard little green nodules into pink lumps. Within a day or two, tiny, fluffy, pink and lime-green leaves appeared like tiny fairies standing on the canes. It was swift and magical.

# Chapter 5
# Tangling with Red Tape

Alongside spring growth I had some administrative challenges to face in our new country famed for bureaucracy. A local winemaker was shipping a container of wine to North America and they had space for ten cases. We decided to take the space to ship samples to friends and family. The winemaker gave me a list of paperwork that the importer had to have in advance.

Top of the list was the *agrément* that the wine was certified AOC Bergerac. We had been sold the wine as such by the Bergerac town liquidator under the guidance of our wine specialist *notaire* when we bought the property. We had to have this document. I scoured the property transaction paperwork and found nothing that matched the description. Jamie advised me to call the Conseil Interprofessionnel des Vins de la Région de Bergerac (CIVRB), who were responsible for things like this.

Juggling Ellie in one arm and the phone in the other I called the CIVRB. I explained my story while trying to stop Ellie from grabbing the phone. Madame listened patiently and told me to phone the Institut National de l'Origine et de la Qualité (INAO) Bergerac who were responsible for managing the AOC.

Soon I was explaining my dilemma for the second time. The Madame at the INAO said she could only give copies of *agréments* to the person who owned the property at the time.

'You could contact the previous owner. If they contact me I'll be able to release a copy.'

'They have moved to Spain and we don't have contact details for them,' I said. 'Anyway, the Bergerac liquidator sold us the wine, not the previous owners. We own the wine. You must be able to give me a copy of the document.'

Madame was kind but firm; there was no way. In any case, they only kept the last four years of *agréments*. Our wine was more than four years old. My heart sank.

'You could try contacting the INAO *juridique* in Paris,' she threw out as a parting comment.

Perhaps this was a sinister plot to make me practise my French and to test Ellie's patience. I gritted my teeth and called the INAO *juridique* to tell my tale for the third time.

'You must contact the INAO in Bergerac,' said Madame helpfully.

Ellie tried to grab the phone and I couldn't blame her. I was finding it somewhat difficult to control my frustration too.

I explained calmly that the INAO Bergerac had sent me to her. She was apologetic but adamant that they were the only people who could solve my problem.

After settling Ellie into her high chair I called INAO Bergerac again to be told a little more firmly that despite what Paris had said there was nothing she could do.

'Contact the Bergerac liquidator and your *notaire*,' said Madame and put down the phone.

The liquidator was on vacation and the Scarlet Pimpernel, our *notaire*, was unavailable. As a last resort I called Jamie.

'I'll try to grease the wheels for you, Caro, but I can't promise anything. Sometimes there's no logic to these things,' he said.

I visited the *notaire*'s offices in Saussignac and found his assistant in.

'Officially I can't do anything,' she said. Then glancing around to see no one was looking she whispered, 'I'll make a few calls for you.'

Jamie called back a few hours later and said he had got nowhere. If Jamie couldn't swing it, it wasn't possible. I put down the phone, defeated.

Cécile, our vineyard consultant, came to do our weekly tour of the vineyard. Most of her service was free to us as newly installed young farmers, a huge bonus. We started this routine as soon as the first buds appeared. I was the person touring the vineyard each week while Sean looked after *les enfants*. He still wasn't confident enough in the language to take on the weekly meeting. He planned to take a course with a local language school at the end of the growing season when we hoped his work pressure would ease, so I wouldn't have to make all his phone calls and take his meetings for him. Contrary to my initial misgivings, though, I looked forward to my weekly meeting with our vineyard consultant, taking copious notes for debriefing Sean. Cécile was a mine of information. Her knowledge, attention to detail and reliability were refreshing. At the end of her visit we stopped for our usual summary of the position.

'Have you made your vineyard declaration for the Saussignac?' said Cécile.

'I don't think so. What is it?'

'You need to declare Appellation Contrôlée Saussignac and Appellation Contrôlée Côtes de Bergerac vineyards upfront. The deadline for the declaration was yesterday. Didn't you get a form in the post?'

'No,' I replied, feeling nauseous. Both of these appellations were part of our planned range of wines.

'Contact the INAO straight away,' said Cécile. 'They may let you make a late declaration because you didn't get the forms.'

There were four bodies that controlled the lives of the Bergerac winemaker, and I didn't know which was responsible for sending these all-important forms. After more than six months I was still totally confused about where the lines of responsibility lay between the Fédération des Vins de Bergerac (FVB), the CIVRB, the INAO and the *douanes* (customs), who were strangely linked into many processes. Bureaucracy was proving a serious opponent and we hadn't made any wine yet.

I called the INAO Bergerac again, the same people I had been in touch with in my failed hunt for the copies of the *agréments*, and explained my new problem. Madame said she would allow me to do the declaration for AC Saussignac and AC Côtes de Bergerac in person the following morning at their offices. I arrived punctually. When we finished the declarations Madame picked up a folder on her desk and passed it to me.

'I have those copies for you.'

I opened the folder to find the four *agréments* we needed for the sample shipment. I still don't know who convinced her to give us copies of *agréments* that were officially no longer available but I took them home, elated.

A few days later as we prepared the sample shipment two AOC 'police' arrived. One was Joel, a middle-aged farmer with a mass of bob-length greying blonde hair, and the other our old friend Monsieur Ducasse, the Chamber of Agriculture representative, who raised his eyebrows in surprise at seeing us still here. He and Joel had come to count buds and check that the pruning on the Saussignac appellation vineyards met the strict rules. Ellie eyed him suspiciously, maybe wondering if she was in for another dazzling display of facial contortions.

Appellation rules cover everything; from what you plant and how you plant it, to how you make your wine. These rules are outlined in a *cahier des charges* and are so detailed they even define the maximum number of buds allowed per vine; eight in this case. Low yields are necessary for quality and this is a way to restrict yields from the start of the season. The vineyard check went smoothly and they left after offering Sean a few suggestions about managing the yield and de-leafing. I was sure that our quota of administrative skirmishes was over for a while.

The following week we got a letter from the INAO saying they could not grant us the right to do AC Saussignac as we had no white grape vines.

'SF, I think the *notaire* duped us and transferred the white half of the vineyard to his brother,' I said, exasperated.

'No, it's a farce created to keep you practising French,' said Sean.

A few calls to the INAO and a visit to the *douanes* traced the error to a historic rental agreement by the previous owners. It was all straightened out in one afternoon. I was almost disappointed.

With the house renovations in hand thanks to Jamie's intervention with Lambert, we started to look to future building priorities. The winery electricity was a matter of life and death and a tasting room was fundamental to sales success. I called the electrician that Jamie recommended. Jamie was a great colleague to have, always happy to help and knowledgeable not only on winegrowing and winemaking but also bureaucracy and renovation. We didn't get to know him very well socially, he was a bachelor with a busy diary, but I was pleased we'd been able to help him out too in those early days so that I could call on him when needed.

Christophe the electrician, based in Gardonne five minutes away and available 24/7 to his winemaker clients, arrived in a beautiful new Mercedes van.

'*Ce n'est pas aux normes,*' said Christophe, looking around the winery. 'We must take it out and redo it.'

'It's not within regulatory norms' was a phrase I was becoming familiar with. In France everything is regulated down to exactly how bread must be made to be called 'traditional'.

Christophe pointed to uncovered neon lights. 'With liquids being pumped at high pressure winery lights must have waterproof covers. And all this wiring must go.'

Even to my untrained eye the old cables snaking round the roof looked in need of replacement.

Christophe took measurements and disappeared with a desultory wave. The next day the fax spewed out a *devis* for ten thousand euro. I was staggered. The work didn't even include digging up half the courtyard to lay the new electricity cables in the ground, which he said had to be done by someone else.

At that price there was no way we could afford to redo the electricity but we didn't want to wind up another winemaker fatality. Bernard Barse, our old friend with the B&B and a qualified electrician as well as a vigneron, whistled when I mentioned the amount, but when he came round later and had a close look he confirmed the price was right.

Meanwhile, despite the lack of funds I went ahead and asked a local roofer for an estimate for the renovation of the tasting room. He estimated that a quick repair of the roof would be a couple of thousand. Ignoring completely how little money we had to put towards the project he recommended a total replacement of the entire outbuilding roof, as a 'quick' repair would not be guaranteed since it would be attached to structural parts of the old roof that would not be replaced. Soon I was perched in front of his boss looking at a quote for twenty thousand. The tasting room renovation was looking as likely as the electricity. I felt desperate. Our operating budget was disappearing way faster than planned and the renovation budget had been eaten up by the house. There was no way we could afford to do these critical renovations.

A few days later, just after I had resigned myself to potential electrocution and no tasting room, we got a letter from the taxman saying he owed us several thousand from the previous tax year. God clearly wanted us alive. I called Christophe, the electrician, in jubilation and asked him to find a way to halve his quote. He pared it back to the most crucial parts and the electricity work was soon underway.

Through our first heatwave Sean lifted then relaid several tons of concrete for the cable and a drainage course alongside the house. Sweat pouring off his face and ears ringing with the noise of cutting cement, he struggled through blistering 40-degree heat, wishing he was back in an air-conditioned office.

With the underground cable safely installed, Christophe's two electricians appeared in another new Mercedes van, ready to rewire the winery in cool, peace and calm. In the process of doing the winery work they disconnected the lights of the upstairs section of our house. Convinced that they were going to leave the house in darkness, Sean demanded that I verify that the house lights were going to be reconnected before they left.

'Don't worry. We leave a gift of candles when we go. It's all part of the service,' said Manu.

'Oh, and matches too,' said Serge, his partner.

They were both doubled over with laughter by the time my lamentable French caught up with the joke. By late afternoon everything was reconnected. We would have to do the tasting room roof repairs ourselves as there was no way to stretch our tax refund to include that. While the renovation work was coming together, the work in the vineyard was getting away from us. Spring was powering ahead and leaving us behind.

# Chapter 6

# Shark Attack

On supermarket shelves back home almost all baby food was organic. In France, in our area at least, there appeared to be no organic baby food. Bio, short for *biologique*, the term for organic, was far from accepted. Despite this, since coming to France we were even more convinced of the benefits of organic.

The more we read about the toxic chemicals used in conventional farming, the less we liked them. They were bad for the land, the people applying them, the wildlife and the consumers of the result. Labels that stated 'do not enter the vineyard for 48 hours after you have sprayed this product' could not be good. Why would we want to put them onto grapes that were going into the food chain?

On the opposite side of our valley, a couple of kilometres away, was a vineyard that looked like a desert. Sean nicknamed the incumbent 'Napalm Nic'. He sprayed herbicide over the entire vineyard, leaving not a blade of grass standing.

'He does it to save doing the work of mowing the grass and ploughing,' said Cécile. 'It encourages erosion and is bad for the soil. Eventually it will be as lifeless as a desert.'

Up close, the soil looked sick. Later in the season we saw Napalm Nic using a chemical spray for vine shoot removal. He was doing it to cut costs so he could supply cheap wine but also ensuring carcinogenic chemical residues for the consumer.

With spring underway we needed an alternative to herbicide fast if we were to stick to our organic principles. Sean was up to his eyes with work in the vineyard – mowing, ploughing and raising the wires of the trellising – so it was up to me to find a weeding solution. We mow and plough alternating rows to prevent the competition, from plants like grass and weeds that grow between the rows, hampering the vines' growth. The new weeding solution needed to remove these plants from under the trellising and around the vine trunks.

Cécile, my secret weapon, appeared with a yellow book of equipment and supplies for vineyards that included descriptions and price ranges for all available mechanical weeders. At first Cécile had been sceptical about us going organic but now she fully supported our conviction. At the start she was worried we wouldn't cope, even farming conventionally. She had seen how committed we were to learning but also to our organic philosophy.

We liked the look of a relatively simple, hydraulically operated mechanical hoe that attached to the tractor and worked the soil between the vines where a regular plough could not reach. The salesman invited Sean to a demonstration at a nearby farm owned by Thierry Daulhiac. We had never met Thierry but we knew he was the president of the Saussignac appellation union. He probably had a reliable view on machinery. We also heard that he farmed organically. Sean still struggled with French – being an independent winegrower in France was a lonely job – and Thierry's English being little better, they communicated as only fellow farmers can. Sean was desperate for male company. He spent his days farming alone and his nights with his wife and very young daughters. Even his weekends were completely consumed by the vineyard. We had bitten off a lot more change and risk than we expected back in the heady days of planning our move.

Sean saw the machine in operation at Thierry's farm and was impressed. We ordered the hoe and waited. The weeds were growing with more vigour than the vines. Even Cécile was ruffled. The weeds grew. We waited some more. The weeds grew faster.

'Perhaps we should do one pass of a chemical herbicide to keep control of the vineyard,' said Cécile, struggling to see anything but weeds. We hadn't started organic certification yet as we had missed the annual cut-off, but we could not stomach using herbicide. I harassed the supplier again.

In the intervening four weeks since we ordered the hoe Sean had more trips to Monsieur Bonny. The vine sprayer we had bought with the property was broken. Monsieur Bonny estimated that to fix it would cost almost the same as getting a more modern second-hand one. The second-hand one he proposed cost more than Sean had budgeted in equipment costs for the entire year but we needed a working sprayer *tout de suite*. In our region mildew poses a potentially lethal risk to the grape crop and preventative sprays are obligatory. The cash budgeted for our first year's expenses was diminishing much faster than planned. We were way outstripping the costs expected even after the vineyard accountant's judicious adjustments.

We collected the bulbous spraying beast with eight arms from Monsieur Bonny. He was his usual bouncy self, showing Sean how it worked with me listening in for the odd bit of translation while trying to control the girls. I was almost unnecessary; although

Sean's everyday French was pitiful, he already knew far more French agricultural machine terms than I did.

'Be very, very careful to keep the power-take-off shaft in position otherwise it will break because of the height of the connector,' said Monsieur Bonny as we prepared to leave. It meant little to me, but Sean reassured him he'd be fine; all was clear.

I waved goodbye and set off for home. Sean followed with the beautiful sprayer behind the tractor. As he drove into the courtyard at Haut Garrigue I knew something was wrong. I rushed out to find Sean almost in tears.

'I was concentrating so hard, Carolinus. It was a split second of inattention as I drove through Saussignac village and hit a bump.'

The power-take-off shaft was broken.

That evening Sean read the entire tractor manual from cover to cover, discovering in the process that a simple twist of a button would have saved the breakage. Thereafter Monsieur Bonny always checked we had understood by asking the same thing in different ways, but that didn't help the broken shaft. We had so much to learn: I felt inadequate. It was yet another expense we didn't need. We were drowning financially but also in the work in the vineyard.

Our neighbour, Sonia, agreed to look after Ellie for a few days so I could help Sean with shoot removal. Like roses, vines send out sucker shoots at the base of the vine that need to be removed. This can be done by hand, by machine or with chemicals. We didn't have a machine, so hand-work it was. It was tough work but it felt good. We were alone together for the first time in weeks, laughing and making better time than we would have working alone. There was something deeply satisfying about physically demanding work outside in a beautiful place with someone who you love. It wasn't easy but I glimpsed how fulfilling it could be, following this, our passion.

The weeds were so high they were growing into the trellising. At last the hoe arrived but it didn't work. After checking the connection several times the sales guy explained that they needed a hydraulic system different to the one on our tractor. They would have to manufacture a hydraulic oil reservoir to attach to the back of the tractor. It would cost €800 and would take a few days. My face went red with fury.

'We're going to do it for free,' he said stepping back nervously. 'We'll have it ready in two days.'

When the working hoe arrived Sean toiled from dawn to dusk to remove the jungle that had leapt up around our vines. Cécile was delighted to see what he had achieved. At last the vineyard was unencumbered by weeds. As we walked up the third row of Garrigue she turned to me.

'*Je suis impressionnée.* You are doing so well. *C'est vrai*, when you arrived, I didn't think you would make it. Your French has improved so much. You have both adapted so well to the life here. The work Sean is doing in the vineyard is *impeccable*.'

I thought back to our first meeting, me stuffing myself with grapes while Sean looked at Cécile mouthing incomprehensible French at him. Cécile was our lifesaver. Each week she went well beyond advising us on what dose of copper and sulphur to use to beat the mildew and odium. She would check the work Sean was doing, help to plan the week ahead and show us how to do new tasks that were coming up in the vineyard cycle.

'I got the results of the count of the *typhlodromes* and your vineyard has three times the average of the group,' she said. 'It's a good sign and proof of the benefits of organic farming.'

Typhlodromus are tiny mites that eat vine pests, thus helping avoid the use of cancer-causing pesticides. They are a way for nature to keep the balance but are killed by treatments used in chemical farming. To thrive they need a balanced herbal environment, not a monoculture, therefore some weeds are indispensable. At least there was an upside to our award-winning weeds.

'Perhaps we should have the group meeting here next week so we can show the others what is possible with organic,' said Cécile. 'It's good to show people there are alternatives.' Every week there was an hour-long meeting of the group of farmers that she and her colleagues advised. We had been to a few of them and at least twenty farmers would typically attend. Before Sean had a chance to protest, the next group meeting was booked to take place at Château Haut Garrigue.

Sean used the mechanical hoe successfully for another five hours then it stopped working. En route to do the weekly shop with Ellie, I dropped the relevant part into the supplier for repair. It was a minor fix.

'To avoid the same thing happening again, your husband must make sure he tightens the bolt every hour or so,' said the mechanic. I dutifully passed on the message.

We were in the zone of extreme pressure in a winegrower's life when everything needs to be done at once. Late spring and early summer are non-stop. Anti-fungal treatments, ploughing the soil, mowing the grass, shoot removal, elevating the trellising to the next level of growth, trimming the vine canopy and keeping track of the development of the flowers and subsequent grapes. The vines can grow up to 10 centimetres a day. We had around

30,000 of them – you could almost hear the growth on a hot afternoon.

As organic farmers, we needed to protect the vine before the risk rather than after, a preventative rather than curative ethos. This meant constant observation of the vineyard and the weather forecast. Regular low doses of copper and sulphur before rain protect the vines from fungal disease. Sean would start treatments at five in the morning to finish before the heat of the day to avoid leaf-burn.

It wasn't only the leaves that got burned: even with sunscreen loaded on, the roasting sun was a daily challenge. Some days I felt I would explode from the heat. Since we had no pool I would lie in a cold bath to try to recover my sangfroid. A ten-minute soak was what it took to regain a cool, calm demeanour.

Heat and a little humidity are perfect conditions for fungal disease. Trimming the vines can help reduce the development of fungus. The trimmer was a monstrosity, a large metal arch fitted with scores of sharp lawnmower-like blades that whirred around terrifyingly chopping vine tops and sides. Sean hitched it onto the tractor for the first time, attaching and adjusting it perfectly. He came in for lunch having successfully finished a hectare. For once, a tractor job was going smoothly. That afternoon he came back earlier than expected having nicked the trimmer on a trellising pole. It needed straightening before he could use it again.

Sean dismantled the trimmer and I took the offending part to Monsieur Bonny. I had done so many trips I could drive the road to Coutures blindfolded. The part was fixed in an hour and Sean moved the trimmer into the courtyard to reassemble it. He was determined to get it back together and Garrigue vineyard trimmed before Cécile arrived for the group meeting that afternoon.

The trimmer proved more difficult to put together than it had been to dismantle. Without sufficient tightening, the blades could fly off, wreaking destruction. Lunchtime came and went and Sean remained in the roasting courtyard battling with the trimmer. Exhausted, frustrated and soaked in sweat he kept at it. Cécile arrived for the meeting closely followed by twenty farmers. Halfway through the introductions Sean yelled for me and ran to the kitchen holding his arm awkwardly. I bolted after him, saw a trail of blood and shouted for Cécile.

Sean was standing over the sink pouring blood and shouting for clean towels. Cécile, after seeing Sean's arm, yelled out the door for anyone that knew first aid. A young man appeared and quickly took charge.

'No tourniquet, just pressure,' he said, holding a clean cloth tightly over the massive gash on the inside of Sean's arm. He encouraged Sean to lie down. In the meantime Cécile called the ambulance. Sean was shivering with shock and blood loss. I sat down on the step, my head between my legs to stop fainting. This was my husband's blood, and more than I had ever seen in one place. I heard Cécile describing the wound. My head swam again and I lodged it back between my legs. I vaguely heard Sean asking Cécile to check I was OK and tried to pull myself together, admonishing myself about who had been injured. Fifteen long minutes later the ambulance arrived.

The paramedics checked Sean's vital statistics, asked me a few questions, then lifted him onto a stretcher and passed him through the kitchen window to the ambulance. Sean was begging for painkillers and shaking relentlessly. They explained they couldn't give him anything as he needed surgery. I kissed him and they whisked him away to Bergerac Hospital.

'Remember to phone the school and ask Sonia to look after Ellie,' said Sean as the ambulance doors closed.

Two farmers put the tractor and the trimmer away. Others cleared up Sean's tools. Cécile called our social services organisation to notify them that Sean had had an '*accident du travail*' and to find out what assistance we could get. She took the details and explained them carefully to me. I thanked Cécile from the bottom of my heart. She asked if I was sure I would be all right. I wasn't sure but I said I was.

There was a rich trail of blood from where Sean had been working into the kitchen. The kitchen floor was a mass of red and the sink was full of gore. I had to clean it before Ellie woke up. I couldn't afford to pass out but I felt light-headed and outside my body. I stopped every few minutes to put my head between my legs. My mind kept darting ahead to the hospital and what was happening to Sean. I needed to get there fast. Once the sink was clean I mopped the floor. The bucket was red with blood. I felt desperate and anxious.

I packed a few things then woke Ellie and took her to Sonia, who promised to look after Sophia after school as well. Minutes later I was speeding along the D14, the Route des Coteaux. With Sean's accident, nothing seemed urgent except his health. Our vineyard worries were nothing when compared to life and health.

Sean was groggy from pre-surgery drugs and strapped to a gurney waiting to go into theatre. Despite his state he asked me how we would get the vineyard trimmed now that he was in hospital. I told him not to worry, we'd work it out, then an orderly wheeled him away.

The nurse was unable to tell me how serious Sean's injury was but she assured me that he would have to stay overnight at a minimum. I drove home lonely and exhausted with a ball of dread in the pit of my stomach, worried about Sean's health but also about the vineyard. With Sean out of action we could lose our entire harvest. If we had a few downpours and couldn't treat for fungal disease, the grapes would be lost. Trimming the vines was critical to controlling the fungal disease and that was the most urgent vineyard job, regardless of rain.

I collected the girls and explained as simply as possible why their dad was not at home. They were remarkably calm. Jamie arrived to find out how Sean was; he hadn't been at the meeting but had already heard the news.

We walked across the terrace. Jamie pointed to the vineyard, golden under a glorious sunset: the entire expanse was trimmed. At the bottom of Lenvège I saw François trimming the last few rows, highlighted in the glow. I rubbed my eyes partly in disbelief and partly to rub away tears of gratitude and relief. That was the spirit of our new winegrower community. I felt thoroughly humbled.

When I phoned the hospital a little later Sean was still asleep from the anaesthetic and no one was able to give me any information on how the surgery went. I ate several rows of cherry chocolate, took two sleeping tablets and went to bed.

The next morning we heard that the surgery went well and we could fetch Sean. He couldn't remember how the accident had happened, although it was obviously a blade on the trimmer. Sean nicknamed it 'Shark' as the gash and subsequent scar looked exactly like a shark bite. He was lucky: the cut stopped a millimetre from the major tendon in his arm. He would be off for a few weeks but if it had got the tendon it would have been several months. News of his accident spread like wildfire.

Sean had to take it easy and make regular visits to the hospital. I couldn't drive the tractor so we prayed for good weather and no fungal growth. By the next rain, Sean was well enough to get back onto the tractor.

Monsieur Bonny's mechanic, Éric, came over to reconfigure the shark and to check the leak on the sprayer. After looking at them he took me aside.

*'Votre mari est trop musclé.'* (Your husband is too muscly.)

I laughed.

'He is tightening the bolts too tight and that is what broke the casing on the sprayer.'

Machinery was complicated; first the bolts were too loose, now they were too tight. No wonder Sean was getting a complex. He felt he couldn't touch a machine without doing it or himself some damage. Fortunately, Éric offered this news in such a diplomatic manner, Sean smiled when he joined us minutes later.

After Éric's visit, Sean remembered how he had cut his arm. He was tightening the bolt on one of the shark's knives when the spanner slipped and the power he was applying drove his arm down onto the knife below. Éric was right, he was *trop musclé*. The accident made me starkly aware of how dependent we were on Sean. There was no sick leave at Haut Garrigue and no safety net; if Sean was injured, we were in trouble.

We had leapt into a business bristling with physical and financial risk.

We hadn't even made our own wine yet, but everyone kept reminding us that the problem wasn't making the wine, it was selling the wine.

Selling the wine we had bought with the property would help to fill the hole created by the unexpected expenses. Despite the success of our Christmas campaign, Sean was pessimistic. 'The first campaign was supported by a lot of people buying the wine because it was our first offer. Most of them prefer beer.'

Perhaps he was right but I forged ahead regardless.

Barry O'Brien, Aideen's husband and one of our best friends back home, forwarded me a special offer for flights. An executive in a large tech multinational by day, he transformed into our unofficial strategy advisor and official representative on the ground by night. He had negotiated the go-ahead for another wine delivery with the customs officials, although we were still waiting for his official appointment as our tax representative. It was part of the long process for making our direct shipping business official and easy to do on a regular basis.

Barry argued that I needed to be on the ground in Dublin to promote our wines if our second shipment was to be a success and wisely advised me to start promotion of our first vintage, which was still on the vines.

I booked my flight and Sean launched our second direct sales campaign via email. Miraculously, a diary I had written about our move was published in a newspaper that Saturday with a full-page cover photo. The editor had been promising to print it for months and his timing could not have been better. In less than twenty-four hours we had thirty orders through the website.

It felt strange going on a business trip after a year of DIY and babies. As I packed my case I felt disconnected and unsure of myself. In my previous life as a consultant I was sometimes on an aeroplane every week. Minutes before I left for the airport an old colleague called to say she had a radio interview for me. I was excited and delighted by the opportunity but also worried about how I would handle being back in a professional environment and being interviewed on national radio.

Leaving Bordeaux airport, I felt like I was in no-man's-land: not yet a French winegrower but no longer a high-tech city girl. It seemed like a lifetime since we left the city.

After landing I picked up my hire car. As I drove off, my hand kept reaching for the door instead of the gear shift. The oncoming car stopped dead in its tracks. The fellow inside waved me out, making sure I was well out of range before proceeding. I saw him mouth 'crazy fool' as I drove away and realised I was on the wrong side of the road.

A few minutes later I felt confident enough to turn on the radio and was transported back into city life. The discussion hadn't changed a lot: traffic, property, football. The cityscape had been transformed. In nine months old familiar streets had morphed into Euro-chic. Down-at-heel chip shops and newsagents had been replaced by coffee shops and up-market grocers. The O'Briens' home, too, had been transformed: from dark and old-fashioned to an open-plan, natural-light haven. We swapped stories over dinner, trying to cram months into one night.

I arrived for the radio interview the next morning shaking with nerves and praying for a calm voice. The show host put me at ease as the ads played. By the time the break was over I felt like we were old friends. For the next fifteen minutes we talked about our new life.

When I got back to base Aideen danced around with delight.

'You were amazing!' she said. I blushed. Aideen is a professional life coach and great at providing feedback. That week she did wonders for me, boosting my confidence that had plummeted in a year of rolling paint and changing nappies.

'How did you do it?' she asked. 'You sounded so natural. I was jumping round the room the entire time you were on air.'

It was easier than any other interview or professional talk I had done, perhaps because I was talking about our life and passion.

'The only mistake you made was using some French words without translating them.'

That evening I found myself telling them about how the *chai* was isolated instead of how the winery was insulated: I was becoming more French than I realised. We sat down to dinner and Sean phoned.

'We've got sixty orders and I haven't even sent the offer to the Christmas customers yet,' he said. So much for his worries.

When I got back, the rhythm of our new farm life felt right. Washing, labelling and capsuling wine bottles for the new order was far more comfortable in early spring than it had been in the winter. We finished the operation in a couple of days. To top the success of the trip we received a copy of a letter to Barry appointing him as our tax representative. At last we were official and could make our wine offers whenever we wished.

# Chapter 7
# Poil de Vache

Shipping wine to end customers was important but direct sales at the property were also a key part of our plan. We had to get the grounds looking more presentable for the tourist season. The region of Aquitaine and the department of the Dordogne are much-loved tourist destinations for French and foreign alike. They are renowned for history, beauty and fine food and wine. Just over an hour's drive from us could be found delights like the prehistoric cave art of Lascaux, called the 'Sistine Chapel of Prehistoric Art', and Richard the Lionheart's castle of Beynac where he lived for much of the last fifteen years of his life. Within five minutes' drive of us were ancient castles including the oldest dungeon in the Dordogne at Gageac Castle, gourmet restaurants, picturesque vineyards and even an international competition-level twenty-seven-hole golf course.

Sean bought a large brush cutter from a local DIY shop so he could tackle the places he couldn't reach with the field mower. The brush cutter worked for 50 centimetres then stopped. After dropping Sean and the girls at the E. Leclerc supermarket to do the weekly shopping I made a dash for the DIY shop on the other side of Bergerac. I waited at the counter for twenty minutes before a shop assistant appeared. He took me and the machine to the back of the shop where he verified that it was not working.

'You have to go to *service après vente*.'

'Where is it?' I asked, expecting him to point to a convenient after sales service kiosk.

'Poil de Vache.'

'*Comment?*' I said.

'Poil de Vache,' he said, a little louder.

'It's not in this shop?' I said, somewhat taken aback and beginning to wonder if he was swearing at me for being a foreigner rather than telling me where to go. I had a vague recollection that *vache* meant cow but could also be used in a less savoury context.

'No, it's on the road to Sarlat about ten minutes from here,' he said even louder.

'*Quoi?*' I said, certain I had misheard despite the amplification.

'You need to take it to Agnostini Garage in Poil de Vache,' he yelled. 'He will fix it for you. He's our *service après vente*. It's near the road to Sarlat about ten minutes from here. Look, I'll draw a map so you can find it.'

Too dumbfounded to reply I took the scruffy map and set off. About ten minutes later, a tiny laneway announced the hamlet of Poil de Vache. Having explored the entire hamlet in half a second and found nothing, I was about to give up my quest when I saw a faded sign half hidden by a tree, saying 'Agnostini 500 m'. The road led to a car garage in the backyard of a house. Monsieur Agnostini, an unkempt version of Monsieur Bonny, came out of the dingy interior.

'Ah, another brush cutter. Don't tell me, it's the starter motor,' he said, waving his arm into the darkness where fifteen brush cutters of the same brand were lined up.

'When will it be ready?' I asked. 'I need it by the weekend.'

'*Pas possible*. It will take ten days to order the part then a few days to do it. *Une quinzaine de jours minimum*.'

That little '*quinzaine de jours*', nominally fifteen days, normally meant infinity. I did not have the time to argue as I knew that Sean and the two girls would be wondering if I was in Bergerac Hospital, having taken two hours to return the faulty machine. When I got back to the shopping centre, the two girls were happily playing on the toys near the entrance and Sean appeared relaxed. They were getting onto French time.

Fifteen days later I phoned to see what had happened to the brush cutter.

'The part still hasn't arrived,' said Monsieur Agnostini. 'I apologise for the manufacturer. *Normalement* it should be here by Monday.'

The little word '*normalement*' meant 'not a chance'.

On Monday Agnostini was fiercely apologetic but the part still had not arrived. 'It will be ready in a few days. I will call you. Don't worry to call back. As soon as it's ready I will call you.'

He didn't call. By the following Monday my French was remarkably good. He remained calm, apologising for the manufacturer's tardiness and promising the same promise I got on the last call. I hung up before he finished and called the shop. I explained to the store representative that I wanted a new brush cutter.

'Madame,' he said imperiously, 'if I gave everyone with a problem machine a new one I would have no margin.'

I offered to contact the European director of consumer affairs to discuss this statement and he promised that Agnostini would have the machine fixed by the following afternoon. I felt like he had done me a huge favour and thanked him profusely.

When I picked up the machine Agnostini was so affable I couldn't be furious. I left thinking how great it was that a nationwide DIY chain supported a tiny garage like Agnostini operating in a backwater like Poil de Vache. I was succumbing to the frustrating but wonderful eccentricities of France.

At last the garden could be transformed into a manicured haven of tranquillity. I needed one. *Vachement.*

Sean was still recovering from his 'shark bite' and unable to do physical work apart from driving the tractor so we swapped roles for a while. My first job in the vineyard was *épamprage*.

*Épamprage* is the removal of unwanted shoots on the trunk and head of the vine. We didn't have a machine so our vineyard required doing the equivalent of 25,000 slow, deep squats in the space of a few weeks. That's about 2,000 a day accompanied by a long, steep hike. This needs to be done at least twice a season. We had done one pass working together early in the spring.

Sean had not finished the mechanical weeding so I had to hack through a thorny wall to get to the shoots. Long-sleeved shirts and long pants, while not ideal in 35 degrees, were a necessity.

My day started at five in the morning to beat the heat. One golden, misty morning as I worked in lower Garrigue a snort announced a dainty deer a metre from me. She curved her graceful neck to get a good look at me then cantered away. Later I bent down to push aside some weeds and a brown hare leapt out. He bounded off, all legs and ears. Soon after I saw a snake as I walked back up to the house. I asked Myreille, a neighbour, about snakes. She and Olivier, her husband, owned the vineyard that ran along our border. They were similar in age to us and had a large family. Myreille had a job off the farm like many of our neighbours' wives.

'*Oui, c'est vrai,*' she said. 'There are many. One type is so poisonous, if you get bitten you must get to the hospital within twenty minutes, or *c'est fini. Et,*' she said conspiratorially, '*il faut absolument ne pas avoir peur*. If you are afraid, that will raise your heartbeat and then, *c'est fini*, even faster.'

I wondered how one did not have fear when faced with a potentially fatal snakebite and a journey to the nearest hospital of slightly more than twenty minutes but nodded sagely and decided to be more careful with my *épamprage* in future. There would be no more diving in hands first. Now I stomped with my well-shod foot around the base of the vine before bending down to do the necessary. One day I caught Sean watching me from the window, laughing uncontrollably. I gave him the one-finger salute, which made him laugh even harder.

Some days I wondered when it would end. The vines multiplied into never-ending rows on our steep slice of paradise. As my morale sank to an all-time low, and the heatwave rose to an all-time high, two friends arrived in a vintage Porsche with the top down, armed with tea, crisps and craic.

John and Sam were keen to get their hands dirty. Sam had worked with Sean in the bank and John was his eccentric, hilarious and Porsche-fanatic brother. They had been in Le Mans for the race and were now enjoying a footloose trip around France.

'Come on, Sammy Boy, let's go,' said John as I came downstairs the second morning. It was 5.30 a.m. and they were already heading out into the vineyard while I hadn't even had my breakfast.

'Caro, darlin', you need a good cup of tea you can walk on,' said John. 'That was Mum's advice when I left Limerick for London twenty years ago. Make sure you have a good cup of tea to start the day, she said, you'll be amazed at what you can do.'

I followed John's advice, brewing my Barry's Tea Gold Blend as the dawn crept across the sky each morning. Soon I was so addicted I ratcheted up to two bags. Tea I could walk on became my saviour.

With the vines well into their season we also had to think about the next phase after the growing: the winemaking. We were looking for a young, keen, modern wine scientist, or oenologist. Lucille Deneuve appeared to fit the bill.

Lucille could speak English but she always spoke to us in French. Our French dictionary was always within reach. We liked her. Well, Sean really liked her. She was a blonde bombshell, someone you would have expected to find in St Tropez rather than in the vineyards of Bergerac: pretty but bright, with a luscious body that made men look rather too closely at certain wording – those in a particular area – on the Bergerac wine T-shirt she often wore.

She recommended that we talk to and taste the wines of other local winemakers so we could tell her what style of wine we wanted to make. Her suggestions included a name I recognised as the young fellow I'd sat next to at lunch on Cécile's training course several months before.

A few days later we visited Château Court-les-Mûts, the property of the Sadoux family. Their vineyard was just over a kilometre from us on the main valley slope going towards Sainte-Foy-la-Grande. From our house we could follow a rural route that took us past the mayor's vineyard down to the D14, the Route des Coteaux, offering the most stunning westerly views down the Dordogne valley all the way. The unassuming Pierre was a third-generation winegrower and their farm was the largest independent wine operation in the Saussignac appellation. We tasted his wines and talked about what had happened in the different vintages and how they made their wines. I was stunned at his openness. We would be direct competitors but despite this he shared his passion and knowledge without hesitation.

Lucille returned for another visit sporting a slightly different Bergerac wine T-shirt that meant that Sean had to carefully check the new words printed in a strategic area. Despite my misgivings – how could someone so good-looking and so well endowed also be gifted at winemaking? – she seemed thorough and genuine. To top it all, she had worked at one of the top estates in Médoc, a favourite of ours, before becoming a consultant. It was serendipity. We decided to appoint her as our oenologist.

Lucille did a tour of the winery and promised to let us know what we needed to buy before the *vendange*. The word *vendange*, harvest, struck excitement and terror deep within me. It was months away but I already felt my nerves tighten at its mere mention. There again, the little word 'buy' also gave me a frisson of fear as we had completely emptied the coffer for equipment.

As we walked around the dingy interior of the winery I felt dread. It was dark and dirty. I had déjà vu to our arrival in the shuttered kitchen the first day at Garrigue but I could tell that this would take a lot more work than the stainless steel sink and kitchen cupboards. We needed to service the presses, clean and sterilise the winery from top to toe and purchase some small pieces of equipment. Still, the 'wish list' from our oenologist was not as daunting as I had expected.

The following morning my brain churned through our precarious financial position as I watched the dawn creep across the vineyard over my steaming cup of two-bag brew, now a well-installed habit that offered me a deep sense of comfort in this unfamiliar world. I had finished an entire pass of the vineyard in three weeks. My fingers absent-mindedly stroked the mass of scratches on my right hand, testament to the thorny walls around our vines. It was almost time to start the weeding and shoot removal again but Sean was back on form and I could bow out of the vineyard and get back to my renovations.

# Chapter 8

# Summer

Summer was upon us. With the long, hot days the fruit progressed at a rapid rate from hard, green peas to soft, sweet grapes in a few short months. Sean worked all hours.

A party of AOC 'police' arrived including Joel, the vigneron with the mass of greying-blonde hair who had scared me the first time I met him, and our old friend from the Chamber of Agriculture, Monsieur Ducasse. They were on site for yet another *contrôle* (check) of the vineyards that we had declared for Saussignac production. This time they were checking the development of the fruit, the yield, the vineyard health and cleanliness – no weeds – to ensure they met appellation standards. Sean was out working in the merlot so I showed them the five rows below the *pressoir* that he had ear-marked for Saussignac, our dessert wine.

'These vines are too loaded,' said Monsieur Ducasse, his eyebrows frowning to underline his point.

'The grapes are too big and not ripening fast enough,' said Joel, adding salt to the wound.

Sean would be furious if we were stopped from making Saussignac because of a few observations by this inspection team.

'We only want to do five rows,' I said. 'Maybe we should look at the other vineyard Sean declared. Perhaps it will be better for the Saussignac.'

Ellie was asleep safe in her cot so I locked the house and took them down to Lenvège, where there was a mix of ancient sémillon, sauvignon blanc and muscadelle white grapes. With foresight Sean had declared more vineyard than we wanted to do.

'These are far better,' said Joel. 'But you need to do some green harvesting and some de-leafing.'

Green harvesting is the removal of some of the grapes a month or two before harvest so there are fewer grapes per vine and hence less for the vine to mature, which is thought to result in better quality. De-leafing is the removal of leaves around the fruit zone so the fruit has sun directly on it, thought to aid the ripening.

'You can harvest half of the grapes when you harvest your dry white so you won't have to waste them,' said Mr Ducasse, his eyebrows working overtime. 'And it's better because you don't want to leave the grapes here on the ground as they will attract bad rot.'

A few days later, taking their instructions to the letter to ensure that we would have Saussignac in the range, Sean removed leaves on the rows we had chosen while Ellie and I meticulously ate the grapes that fell to the ground to make sure we didn't encourage any bad rot in the vineyard.

With most of the house dating back to 1737 we were guaranteed a few surprises of the kind that inevitably accompany the renovation of an antique.

The drains in our new kitchen stank and with the rising heat the stench had increased. A neighbour explained a drain 'fix' to me: force a hosepipe running water back and forth in the blocked drain until the hose appears on the other side and the water runs clear. It sounded easy so I found a hosepipe, rolled up my sleeves and donned hermetic gloves.

Lifting the drain covers offered instant olfactory confirmation of the problem.

After some exploration I found the best arrangement was lying on the ground with my arm buried in the drain. This was closer to the drain than I liked but effective and unexpectedly satisfying. I dislodged a bald tennis ball almost the size of the drain itself.

The next section of the drain was not as obvious. I could find no sign of a cover so I assumed it went directly to the septic tank. A neighbour, Pascal, who lived in the house in front of Sonia and Fred, arrived to say hello. He was a wiry, handy man who loved dropping by to see how our renovations were progressing. He pointed out grains of rice in a pool of water on the track at the corner of the house.

'Perhaps it comes out here,' he said.

The pool of water was constantly full, even with no rain. Sean and I assumed that it was a bad drainage point. The water meter showed no sign of a leak.

'It's what *les anciens* used to do,' said Pascal. 'The kitchen waste water emptied down the side of the house.'

It smacked a little of the bathroom *broyeur*. I dug into the point where the trickle of water originated. A very foul whiff rose up and Pascal quickly said goodbye.

I found the end of the drain buried about a foot below the trickle. After digging, pushing, pulling and cursing, a foot-long plug of ancient muck dislodged from the end of the drain pipe I had uncovered. It seemed unbelievable but this had been the main water exit for the kitchen and it looked like it had not been cleared since its construction.

A few minutes later the water ran clear and I felt like I had conquered the world. I had solved the immediate stench problem but the longer-term solution of routing it to the used water tank would need the expertise of Jean-Marc, the plumber.

The worst heatwave of the year hit as my mother arrived for a two-week stay. She had picked up that in the aftermath of Sean's accident we were not coping at all and had decided to come and help, plus she would see her granddaughters. My mother had been with us for the coldest winter and was now experiencing the hottest summer. When I opened the door onto the courtyard, it was like stepping into a massive oven. The car thermometer registered 45 degrees in the afternoons. We stayed indoors after nine in the morning and closed all the shutters. At ten at night as darkness settled we opened the shutters and enjoyed a few hours of relative cool before the blazing sun started the bake again. The only refuge outside was the girls' paddling pool set under shady trees.

My mother could not understand why we had moved to a place with such an intolerable climate. It was either hoar frost or a heatwave and nothing in between. I tried to explain that the six months between their last visit and her current one had been delightful. It wasn't just the weather; she and my father were still unable to comprehend why we had left our 'successful' city life. Sometimes I felt the same way… but I would never have admitted that to my parents. I wanted their unconditional support. Sean found it difficult to share a house with his mother-in-law so we hardly saw him. As it was, before my mother's visit he and I didn't talk much, thanks to him working long hours. After my mother left, our ability to communicate worsened and we both withdrew into our work: house renovations for me and vineyard work for Sean. Nonetheless, I was feeling more relaxed about Sean being out on the tractor and working with farm equipment, although I still felt angst each time he got the trimmer out.

There was a broken tile and a persistent leak in the winery roof that needed fixing, and since no machinery was involved, I let Sean go up on the roof and passed the required material up to him. A few seconds later he lurched backwards, thrashing a piece of guttering around in the air.

'Hornets,' he yelled as he fell back, breaking several more tiles. He leapt up again, still whacking violently at the air, and lurched closer to the 4-metre drop.

'Climb down the ladder! Forget the hornets! Climb down the ladder!' I screamed.

I couldn't get up in time to do anything so I stood and yelled desperately. At last, he threw the pipe down and climbed down the ladder at high speed.

'They came out of nowhere,' said Sean, puffing. 'There were a bunch of them zoning in on my neck and face. Then I got stung on the leg. As soon as that fellow got me the rest pulled back.' The sting was already red, swollen and very painful. We were lucky he had only been stung on the leg.

High summer meant hornets but also bounties of fruit. We discovered the joys of eating berries directly off the trees. Ellie, who regularly refused fruit indoors, would happily position herself in a well-stocked, shady spot and shovel fistfuls of juicy delight into her mouth. We moved from cherries to early plums, blackberries, early grapes, figs, more plums and finally the wine grapes. I made jam and compote until the shelves were groaning.

The market in Gardonne, our nearest town, every Wednesday and Sunday was held in the parking lot opposite the *supérette* (minimart). It wasn't a beautiful market like Issigeac but it was real. Most of the stallholders were local producers rather than resellers. Among the producers was a strawberry man, and over the season he offered different varieties from the early Gariguettes to the late Charlottes, succulent and flavourful, as far from bland, factory-farmed strawberries as you can imagine. The melon man was similar, offering a superb mix of melons in all manner of sizes, no doubt unacceptable to supermarkets, for tiny prices. Matched with Parma-style ham, they made the perfect starter. Alongside the melons he had piles of tomatoes topped with large sprigs of fresh basil that reeked of summer.

One late afternoon I rode the bike down to Gardonne to collect the car from the garage where it was in for a minor fix. The vines on either side of the road were loaded with ripe merlot, purple-black and velvety. The *vendanges* were getting close. A little further on, a plum orchard engulfed me in its cool shade and rich fragrance. The air was heavy with the smells of summer. I was in heaven.

By the time I drove back to Garrigue it was evening. The car beams lit up the dirt track and the vineyards. There were no streetlights or sirens, just the shadow of a hare disappearing into the brush. As I got out of the car the warm night air enveloped me in a dark embrace. The huge sky, spangled with stars arched over me and I felt a deep sense of ease. It was so familiar, so right. Despite living more sparsely than we ever had, not knowing if we would be able to earn enough to feed our children, and the ongoing tension in our relationship, I had a deep sense of being where I belonged.

A week later we attended our first Saussignac producers' annual tasting and dinner at Château La Maurigne (pronounced 'more-in-ye'), a neighbouring vineyard. An old army tent sparkling with lantern lights was set in the garden. Inside were seated our fellow producers tasting golden wine from delicate glasses.

Thierry Daulhiac, the president of Saussignac appellation and in charge of the evening, came over to welcome us and greeted me with the obligatory *bisous*, kisses. Thierry was wiry and energetic, a winegrower who was a mechanical engineer at heart, farming land where his family had tended vines for at least seven generations. He was open-minded, generous and focused. When not farming his vineyards he could be found inventing viticultural equipment for a German firm or renovating part of the house under the direction of his very organised wife, Isabelle.

The magical scene was a horizontal tasting of the previous vintage. All the bottles were covered with bags; the identity would only be disclosed at the end. We were handed paper and pencils. I felt intimidated, having never done a professional tasting before. Sneaking a glance at my neighbour's notes I took a swig of wine. A starburst of flavours exploded in my mouth: orange peel, almond, pineapple, honey. I slurped the second: passion fruit. Then the third: citrus and a hint of fennel. Almost effortlessly, writing filled the page in front of me.

Grapes are unique; no other fruit can create such a rainbow of flavours depending on its terroir. They offer a palette of polyphenols or aroma compounds that runs into the thousands compared to normal fruits like oranges and apples that would only be a couple of hundred.

Combining the great range of polyphenols of each grape type or varietal with the soil, the climate and the grower gives a unique taste. This unique 'taste of place' is terroir, an emotionally charged term that is deeply part of French culture. Blending the different results from each vineyard and each varietal is a key part of taste of place. For the French it is this complex notion of terroir that determines taste rather than the type of grape: a key difference with the New World. When you taste a mineral chardonnay from Chablis compared to a hot climate chardonnay it is easy to see why: they may be the same grape but they are worlds apart in flavour.

All I knew then was that I was tasting the same style of wines from the same small area of Saussignac and yet they tasted different. Each one had its own nuance, its own secret whisper about where it came from. When the tasting was over, each wine was debated, then unveiled.

'What do you think of number eleven, Caro?' asked Thierry.

'Passion fruit and almonds. Delicious,' I said feeling nervous. Was I correct? Would I be unmasked as the complete novice that I was? It was so expressive even I could describe it and my comment was followed by approving nods around the table.

Next up was a wine that was cloudy and fizzy: I had marked it right down, not realising still-fermenting wine was regularly presented at producer tastings.

'Slightly fizzy but good balanced flavour,' said the first commentator.

'Too woody.'

The sample was unveiled as Bernard Barse's, the wine we had helped pick with Aideen and Barry a year before. I began to take the comments personally. It was an inkling of how I would feel when Sean and I made our own wine.

Joel, the man who regularly intimidated me as part of the AOC police, was sporting beautiful, long dreadlocks and bright coloured pants. That evening I realised that he was more Joel the Jolly than Joel the Gendarme. His clothes and hair told part of the story but he also had a sharp wit and a love of practical jokes, passing me a wine glass of apple juice destined for the kids instead of the white wine I had asked for as my aperitif. He lived next door to Thierry and had four grown-up children, although he didn't look much older than us. Next time he came round for an AOC *contrôle* I wouldn't feel the ball of fear in my stomach like I had the previous times.

After the tasting, we were served aperitifs – a selection of wines from all the winegrowers who were present with pâté and rillettes – and I got talking to Geoffroy Colombe and his wife Delphine. The Colombes were famous wine producers in the area.

'What possessed you to move from successful lives in the city to wine-farming?' asked Delphine. I had déjà vu to my mother's recent visit.

I explained that we were following a long-held dream.

'But wine-farming in France is so difficult,' said Delphine. 'With all the rules and our high costs of production, how can we compete with the New World winemakers?' She meant places like Chile, Argentina, South Africa, the USA, Australia and New Zealand, where winemaking is less regulated and they have a much lower cost of labour.

'I don't know,' I said, feeling a twist of fear in my stomach. If such successful farmers were struggling, how would we survive? What were we thinking? Some of these people had centuries of wine-farming experience behind them. If they were in trouble, we wouldn't have a hope.

Geoffroy and Delphine's son joined our group. Jean was working for a wine shop in England, having recently finished his studies.

'We've had twenty years of stress,' said Delphine. 'I can't believe you have given up comfortable lives in the city for this. Stress with farming and weather, stress with the harvest and winemaking and serious stress with selling. It's not easy.'

'Perhaps having many small producers will prove to be France's saviour,' I said. 'People are looking for something different. Look how California producers are creating special vineyard areas and how large producers like E. & J. Gallo are splitting up their range to cater to consumer demand for unique, small production wines.'

'Yes, I agree,' said Jean. 'Wine lovers are looking for the human touch, the artisans.'

'I hope you are right,' said Delphine, not convinced.

At that moment the first course of a feast was served. The lanterns twinkled and a gentle summer breeze flapped the side of the tent as we sat down at the long trestle table that had been speedily transformed for the banquet by Chantal Gerardin, the co-owner of Château La Maurigne, and Isabelle, Thierry's wife. Five courses followed with accelerating repartee as the night progressed. I soaked up the atmosphere. Rural France was supposed to be closed, but here it was the opposite. There was a shared history and sense of place. It was rich with generations and good humour but welcoming to newcomers like us. We had landed in an extraordinary place.

The tasting of the Saussignacs was held a week or two before harvest and it signalled the imminence of our first *vendanges*. My stomach cramped with fear and excitement at the thought. This was what we had come to France for but we could not afford to mess up. We had to produce great wine, not just any wine, to survive financially.

# Chapter 9

# Vendanges!

Lucille, our wine scientist, began her regular visits. For the next eight weeks she would visit for a couple of hours at least twice a week. Every couple of days she and Sean would disappear into the vineyard for hours to taste grapes and assess their ripeness. Stuck inside, looking after Ellie who was a year and a half, I couldn't help but feel a twinge of jealousy. Lucille was gorgeous, appeared to be single and was spending hours and hours alone with my husband in a deserted vineyard.

As the days stretched into weeks I found myself imagining them having a full-blown affair. My trust in Sean had plummeted with our stumbling relationship. I began to spy out of the windows to see what they were up to. I kept reminding myself that I would know from Sean's eyes. He couldn't pass through a border post with a single bottle of liquor undeclared he was so honest. That didn't help reduce my angst, though. I had never been jealous before but the state of our relationship left me feeling unsure.

When they returned from their promenades Lucille would field our endless questions with the patience and demeanour of a teacher. Our 'serious *oenologue*', as Sean called her, was reliable, despite her Playboy looks. I told myself to get a grip. This was my husband, Sean, a man who had felt it necessary to confess an affair he had well before our relationship started when we were playing the 'we're just friends' game back in our early twenties.

Sean's parents arrived to help with the harvest. John, Sean's father, was in his late sixties and relatively fit. He was a forester by trade and still worked part-time on forestry projects in South Africa. He quickly became a key man on the harvest team. Peta-Lynne, well-used to grandchildren thanks to Sean's siblings' progeny, took charge of the girls and delivering food to a hungry harvest team.

Sean and John commenced the mammoth task of cleaning equipment, vats and buildings. I escaped to Thierry and Isabelle Daulhiac to talk over our plans for the coming harvest. They had been very open at the Saussignac dinner and seemed like good people to ask advice given Thierry's impressive seven generations of wine history and the quality of their wines.

As I was leaving, their sons, Paul and Émilion, returned from school and a little white van pulled up behind them. It looked empty, then a familiar head of curly grey-blonde hair popped up armed with the largest water gun I had ever seen. Joel showered the boys and everyone else liberally then laughed hysterically and drove off, leaving us giggling in his wake. I would look at him through different eyes next time he came round to police our practices in the vineyard. Perhaps it was his way of coping with pre-*vendanges* stress.

With Sean's folks on hand I could tour the vineyards and sample grapes with Sean and Lucille. This helped to calm my rising angst and also offered the opportunity to see and understand the fruit of our labour.

After the year of work the vineyards were like old friends. Upper Garrigue, the vineyard that Cécile and Sean had carefully monitored every week as our indicator for the health of all our vineyards, was the most manicured and would be the highest yielding of our merlot vineyards. Cimitière merlot was concentrated like our old vines in Hillside. The two cabernet sauvignon vineyards, Gageac and Lenvège, were far less ripe, about two weeks behind the merlot, while the whites were the most advanced: sweet and aromatic.

The *'ban des vendanges'*, the name for the official opening of the harvest for our AOC Bergerac, was declared. Despite this official opening, which changed each year with the weather, the development of the grapes was slow and each laboratory maturity analysis came back with 'review in a few days'.

The waiting was excruciating but I also felt very alive. There was something about harvest time that was at once tense, exciting and invigorating. Perhaps it was that a full year of work in the vineyard depended on this critical period, or perhaps it was more profound and ancient than that: a connection with the annual cycle of life that has nurtured man since his first days on earth.

A heatwave followed by a few days of heavy rain changed everything. The heat ripened the grapes and the rain put them at risk. From 'review in a few days' the analysis came back with 'harvest tomorrow'. We were thrown headlong into the *vendanges* hurricane.

We booked the harvest machine for the next morning. Sean kicked himself for not harvesting the whites before the fresh deluge despite Lucille's hesitation. Choosing the day to harvest is a critical matter; a few extra days of 'hang time' on the vine can make a world of difference to the end product and that was the risk we took. Now Lucille was concerned that rot might set in.

I had written everything down in a flow chart but despite my preparation I was terrified. This would be our first day of working with the winery equipment. Everything was huge and dangerous. I tried to lift the lid off the press on my own and couldn't do it. Sean yelled, 'Just get on with it.' I tried again but it wouldn't budge. Sean was aggressive and had no time for someone who couldn't keep pace. I felt inadequate. John came to my aid and we successfully lifted the lid off the press together so I could do a final clean and disinfect the inside.

We had the advice of Lucille but we had to make the day-to-day decisions and do the work. We were essentially going it alone. That afternoon Ad and Lijda, a Dutch couple we met briefly the previous year when they stopped in to visit the previous owners, came by and offered to help us for a few days. They had helped with harvests in the past. Now, miraculously, we had two 'experienced' hands.

Ad, Lijda and I did a pass through the white vineyards to remove bunches with signs of rot and found less than one bunch per row. It was a good sign for the quality of the white and laid Lucille's concerns to rest.

Sean and his dad, John, worked deep into the night to get everything ready in the winery. We ran through our checklist one last time and fell into bed, exhausted. Ellie woke at midnight vomiting. I dosed her with paracetamol and changed her sheets and clothes, my mind racing ahead to our harvest day. After a prayer for her health and a kiss on her little cheek I fell back into bed. A few hours later, tired but eager, we got up to harvest our sauvignon blanc. Despite the clear forecast, it had rained in the night – far from ideal for harvesting as rain dilutes the juice. The harvest team – John, Ad, Sean, Lijda and I – gathered in the courtyard buzzing with coffee and anticipation. As we discussed methods to blow-dry the vineyard – in wealthy vineyards helicopters have been known to fly over to create the blow-drying effect – a strong wind blew in to remove the excess water. It would help significantly. Right on time the harvest machine rolled into the courtyard. It was enormous: like a giant mechanical insect preparing to ingest our white grapes. We introduced ourselves to the driver and explained what we were planning to pick. Then I ran ahead of the machine to show him the marked rows.

We checked all the pipe connections and ran through our flow chart one more time. Within what felt like five minutes, but was actually twenty, the harvest machine had picked the Hillside sauvignon blanc. Sean drove the tractors into position and I watched in awe as our first load was poured from harvester to trailer. Then he expertly backed up to the winery looking like he had been driving tractors all his life, although it had been less than a year.

John, Ad and I lifted the large pipe that connected the trailer to the press but even with three it was difficult to manoeuvre. While I cursed, Ad and John kept their cool and coaxed it into position. After checking the connections Sean started the auger that pushes the grapes from the trailer into the pipe. Nothing came up into the press. I motioned upwards to Sean and he increased the revs. Still nothing came up. I signed again and Sean increased some more. We repeated this process several times, panic rising in me with each increase. Perhaps none of this worked at all.

As I pictured myself manually bucketing grapes from trailer to press, grapes and juice exploded out of the pipe, overshooting the press and splattering our precious harvest around the freshly cleaned winery. At my frantic motioning Sean dramatically decreased the revs. Ad carefully aimed the now manageable harvest into the presses and the rest of the load went in smoothly. We had got through our first *vendanges* scare.

As each load arrived there seemed to be a million things to check and do. Carbon dioxide gas was sprayed over the juice in the press tray and into the receiving vat. Small doses of sulphur dioxide were carefully poured separately into the press tray as the juice ran through. These were measures to protect the grapes and juice from spoiling on their trip into the vat. Our vines surrounded the house and winery so they had little distance to travel. When they got to the winery they were pressed or pumped into the vat immediately rather than having to wait. The less time grapes have travelling or sitting waiting, the better the end result, so we could use significantly less sulphur dioxide than a large operation with more travel and waiting time. This was important for organic winemaking, where we aimed for lower levels of sulphur dioxide, or 'sulphites' as it is labelled on the bottle, than conventional wine. The juice level in the press tray was monitored continuously and judiciously pumped to keep air bubbles to a minimum. As soon as another load arrived we would start the frenzied round again.

Three harvest trailers and two press loads later, we had 2,000 litres of sauvignon blanc which would net us about 150 cases of finished wine. Sean started our Kreyer cooling unit using our second pump. The pump ran for a few minutes then stopped. Ad, a qualified mechanic, dismantled it and found the axel had broken. It was Sunday and Sean was doomed to juggling cooling the wine with one pump.

After lunch we raced back out to prepare for harvesting the rest of the white grapes the following day just as Lucille arrived to check how our first day had gone. It was the weekend and she was accompanied by an extremely handsome boyfriend. He clearly was a long-term item, which helped to lay my crazy suspicion finally to rest.

'We may need to bring the merlot in this coming week as well,' she said as they prepared to leave. It was not the news we wanted to hear. We were exhausted but preparations and work on the sauvignon blanc kept us up until midnight.

The 'blue monster', as John dubbed the harvest machine, could be heard approaching well before 5 a.m. The heady scents of sémillon wafting on the warm night air provided a foretaste of what was to come in our white wine blend. The moon was still high and an owl swooped down as I ran through the vines indicating vineyard markers to Jean-François, the driver, my heart racing with adrenalin. I reached the last marker and waved goodbye to the driver, then jogged back to the winery.

We were old hands that day, splurging a drizzle of precious liquid as we pumped our first load into the press. When we finished the day's harvest Sean proudly drew off jugfuls of sémillon juice for us, then turned his attention to the sauvignon blanc, which needed to be drawn off its heavy sediment before fermentation started. We drank the luxurious liquid, full-bodied and sweet, less zesty than the sauvignon blanc but with a dimension of opulence from the varietal and the old vines.

Then it was back to cleaning presses, harvest trailers and buckets. Although we had only met Ad and Lijda briefly, they were already close friends. Working in pressured circumstances helped us get to know each other.

Sophia and Ellie could feel the stress and were kicking up more than usual about going to bed and other routines. Grandma Feely had been subjected to watching the *Les Aristochats* Disney film ten times but she was coping remarkably well, despite only seeing us when we urgently needed food.

The next day I visited Monsieur Bonny with the broken pump.

'Are you sure the axel is broken?' he asked, knowing that Sean and I hadn't a clue how to find the axel let alone tell if it was broken. I explained that we had a mechanic staying with us.

The cost of repair would be equivalent to half a new pump. We had already spent too much on this ill-fated machine so we opted for the new one but it would take a week to arrive. We needed a second pump immediately to manage the wine temperatures.

'*Ne vous inquiétez pas,*' (Don't worry) said Monsieur Bonny. 'I'll lend you the pump that I use for testing refrigeration systems until the new one comes. I can do without it for a few days.'

He bundled the pump into my boot and promised to call as soon as the new pump arrived. I couldn't believe his generosity.

'*Bon courage,*' he shouted as I waved goodbye.

The following day Lucille and I toured the vineyard while Sean drew the sémillon off its heavy lees.

'I think we need to harvest the merlot as soon as possible,' she said. 'Vignerons on the valley floor are already facing *une vraie catastrophe.*' When Lucille said *catastrophe* it was serious. She had a harried look. This harvest was not for the faint-hearted.

'The grapes were damaged by the severe heat of the *canicule*. With the rain they become swollen and split, allowing rot to set in. Look,' she said, pointing to some small freckles on one of our most exposed bunches. 'The sunburnt spots are weak and burst easily. It's worst for those vignerons who de-leafed.'

I recalled Cécile's sage advice not to de-leaf most of our vineyards, in spite of the debate about it. De-leafing around the fruit zone was thought by some to aid ripening; but by de-leafing you remove some of the leaf area for photosynthesis, which is the driver of the sugar production – plus you allow the fruit to get sunburnt.

We toured the rest of the merlot vineyards tasting anxiously. The Garrigue vineyard grapes were delicious, full and sweet. Those of Hillside and Cimitiére were smaller and the bunches were more spaced than Garrigue, allowing air to pass between the grapes and concentrating the berries. There wasn't a sign of rot in any of the vineyards.

The grapes were ready but we were not. We hadn't prepared the vats required for the red. Lucille said the latest we could push out was Thursday. More rain was forecast for Friday. I called Jean-François, the blue monster's driver, and left a message. If we didn't get the machine for Thursday we might have to harvest in the rain, which was bad. If we waited for the rain to stop it could be worse as rot might get established in our vineyard. We were on a knife edge.

Before leaving, Lucille reviewed our log of the wine's progress. She checked the mustometer which we used to measure the density of the wine and hence its progress through fermentation.

'Are you adjusting for the temperature?' she asked.

'No.' I felt like an errant schoolgirl.

'You must start as you wish to continue,' said Lucille imperiously. '*Pour faire le bon travail* we must adjust and fill in the graph so it's easy to track the wine's progress.'

I promised to try harder to 'do good work'. With little time to eat or sleep in the last couple of days, filling in the graph had seemed like a nicety.

Ad and Lijda left to return to Holland, leaving us to the Harvest from Hell. John, Sean and I were dog-tired but the whites needed work and there was preparation for the merlot to be done. The sauvignon blanc and the white blend had finished their period of cold settling and were ready to start fermentation. I prepared the cultivated yeast using my cake scale, a thermometer and other sundry items from the kitchen. Once the yeast was added, the whites entered a quieter phase where the key activity was monitoring the fermentation and, of course, not to be forgotten, filling in the graph... if I didn't want my knuckles rapped by our serious *oenologue*.

It was nearly midnight when I dredged the last of the rinsing water off the winery floor. The faint hum of harvest machines could still be heard in the distance. Farmers were working all hours to get their grapes in because of the rising risk of rot.

Jean-François called to let us know it was all go for Thursday. He sounded exhausted. He was working almost round the clock. Thierry Daulhiac assured me that this was the most difficult *vendanges* he could remember. Normally, in our area, the harvest took place over about four weeks with at least a week between each grape variety. This year, because of the weather, it was all happening the same week and we were getting a baptism of fire.

Sean and John worked through the day, cleaning the vats, pipes and buckets for the merlot harvest. Around ten that evening Sean prepared to spray tartaric acid onto the cement vat we planned to use as I read the French instructions.

'This says it needed to be done at least three days before use.'

'Feck,' exclaimed Sean, 'you'd better phone Lucille.'

*'C'est vrai,'* said Lucille, thankfully answering her phone in spite of the late hour, 'the tartaric acid needs several days to dry

otherwise the wine could react with the cement of the tank. You must find another vat.'

The only option was one of the semi-underground tanks that we had in the *pressoir*. I wanted to avoid them because they were dangerous but now we had no choice. Sean quickly filled his hand pump with the required sterilisation product then squished himself through the lid in the floor of the *pressoir* and descended into the heart of the vat.

I felt like I was on a high-pressure technology project. We were working crazy hours and under intense conditions but a camaraderie was developing between the three of us. Things were going a lot better with Sean now that the harvest was in full swing. I was still being treated like the weakest link but since establishing myself as the 'expert' on the finer points of winemaking like yeasts and analysis, I was getting a little respect. Sean emerged from the underground vat and we did a final check that everything was ready. Ellie was much better and we got four hours of solid sleep.

We woke to a star-studded sky. Ten acres of merlot made it our biggest day. At five sharp the blue monster hummed into the courtyard. I climbed up to hitch a ride to show Jean-François what we were picking for the day. Riding high on the open wing of the harvest machine I felt awed by our starlit vineyards laid out peacefully under the infinite velvet sky.

Back at the winery the lights were on and it was buzzing with activity as Sean and John connected pipes and checked vats. Sean backed up the first load of merlot, a trailer of perfectly formed berries with no foreign matter to be seen. Around dawn as we hooked up the fourth trailer the church bells in Saussignac started ringing and carried on eerily all morning.

'Someone's died in the village,' I said.

'Always look on the bright side,' said Sean.

'No, I'm sure that's what it is.' I hoped I was wrong.

On the ninth load fatigue was setting in. John and I tried to get the harvest pipe onto the trailer and it took on a life of its own, reared up and whacked us around the heads. We sat down for a few minutes until the world stopped spinning. Neither of us was seriously hurt, just a little bruised.

After a total of eleven trailers we declared victory. Ravaged by the exertion and stress of the week, we were relieved that we only had one hectare of cabernet sauvignon and our Saussignac dessert wine left to do.

Later that day we heard two vignerons had been killed in a tragic accident. The father and son were suffocated by carbon dioxide in a subterranean vat in their winery that morning. They lived down in the valley a few kilometres from us; we could see their property from Garrigue. Though we didn't know them personally, after hearing the news I stood on the balcony looking at their farm with tears pouring down my cheeks. It was gut-wrenchingly sad.

We had filled one of our semi-underground vats with the merlot. The thought of it made me nauseous. That night I had nightmares about Ellie falling into it. The tank lid was in the middle of the floor of the *pressoir* and when filled with fermenting wine, the *chapeau*, the thick cap of grapes that forms over the juice, was about 40 centimetres from it.

I kept picturing Ellie leaning over to pick a grape out of the *chapeau* and falling in. This spells instant death as the carbon dioxide suffocates and the liquid drowns. I woke up in a cold sweat. It happened over and over again. I took a double dose of my sleeping remedy.

The following day I struggled to keep my eyes open but the fermenting white juice needed to be kept cool to hold the fresh fruit aromas, while the red juice needed to be kept warm, to extract the colour and the flavour from the grapes. Our Kreyer temperature control system helped us do this, but it was far from automated. Nothing was as simple as a flick of the switch. Constant pump work was required, manoeuvring heavy pipes and equipment in an endless dance. There was more work than we could handle, even with no weekend. I didn't know then that there would be no weekends for more than two months.

Lucille arrived for her Friday visit.

'More bad weather is forecast. You should harvest the cabernet sauvignon early, perhaps next week,' she said, reaching for our winery file.

I tried to snatch it back: the densities were adjusted, but the graphs were still missing.

'I haven't done the graphs,' I mumbled, expecting to be severely reprimanded.

*'C'est pas grave,'* said Lucille. 'You are in full harvest.' At least I knew our 'serious *oenologue*' would cut us some slack in 'full harvest'.

After Lucille left I prepared the yeast for the merlot. Part way through, two buckets of yeast didn't puff up in the normal way. Convinced we hadn't fully rinsed the disinfectant off the buckets I made ready to dash for more of the expensive stuff but Sean convinced me to wait. By the time the yeast was ready it had risen the same as the rest. It was a different strain, the one for our premium wine from Hillside and Cimitière vineyards, clearly a yeast of a more restrained and refined character. We knew next to nothing then about the benefits of the natural yeasts we could extract from our own organic vineyard that could offer us the unique flavour of our terroir; that first year we followed Lucille's instructions to the letter.

We stole a few moments every morning and evening to review the wines' progress, taking the temperatures and densities and tasting them. The constant tasting of the red wines left my tongue ravaged by tannins, making it difficult to drink my early morning cup of tea brewed so strong you could walk on it – but it didn't stop me.

The wines were like people, each with their own individual characteristics. Garrigue and Hillside were merlot grapes that were picked the same morning, had similar care through the year and were barely 500 metres from one another in the vineyard but they behaved and tasted totally different. Hillside was more intense and cool, while Garrigue was fruity and hot. So far our yields were well below what we had hoped for but the quality and concentration compensated.

Another weekend passed in a blur of winery work. On Tuesday, while Sean did the winery pipe dance, I ran round the cabernet sauvignon vineyards collecting sample grapes to take into the laboratory for analysis. Later Lucille arrived with the analysis and told us we should harvest the cabernet sauvignon the following day.

'We won't be ready even if we work all night,' said Sean. 'The sauvignon blanc needs to be moved out of the *garde vin* to make way for the cabernet sauvignon and that alone will take a couple of hours with the cleaning and sterilising required.' A *garde vin* is a vat with a floating lid that offers more flexibility as the volume can be adjusted by changing the height of the floating lid. This *garde vin* was nearly 4 metres tall and only about a metre wide, making it relatively unstable in comparison to fatter, shorter vats. We nicknamed it 'Tower'.

'Can't we wait until next week?' asked Sean. He had a bad cold and wasn't feeling up to another harvest day.

'We must get the grapes in,' said Lucille. 'More rain is forecast. If we wait, the rot could set in.'

We took her advice. We didn't want to risk our precious cabernet sauvignon. I called Jean-François to book the blue monster. He promised to call back as soon as he had a slot. The next day he confirmed for the following morning. We were in the harvest hurricane. There was no respite. Nature was calling the shots. Sean emptied, cleaned and sterilised the *garde vin* then we spent hours wrestling the harvest pipe onto the top of it. I was terrified that it wouldn't hold with the force of the grapes coming through, and having been whacked by the pipe once before I was nervous, but there were no other options. I was still having nightmares about Ellie and the underground vat. Sean had a bad sore throat. I went to bed totally shattered.

The blue monster arrived just after four. At 3 metres high with fiercely powerful lights it was great for game-viewing. As we drove down through the vineyards a hare loped nonchalantly down the row in front of us and veered off into the next row then a deer took off into the shadows. I pointed out the markers and waved goodbye to Jean-François.

Our first load came in and we hooked up what we called the Serpent pipe then watched nervously as Sean slowly increased the revs. The first few grapes shot over the *cuve* (vat) onto the winery wall but the pipe stayed in position and Tower remained stable. After a minor adjustment the load went in smoothly. All the cabernet sauvignon was safely in Tower before dawn. We felt a deep sense of relief that it was the last time we would see the blue monster that season. All that was left was our Saussignac to hand-harvest in a few weeks.

Sean took the *vendanges* trailer round to the side of the house for cleaning. I heard the girls crying and went inside. As I reached the top of the stairs I heard Peta-Lynne, Sean's mum, yelling full throttle for me. Both girls sensed something serious and screamed in earnest. I told them to be calm, closed the security gate firmly behind me and ran back down the stairs.

Sean was standing over the sink holding a bloody tea towel over his hand. I had nasty déjà vu.

'I've chopped my finger off,' he said.

# Chapter 10

# Of Fingers and Foresters

I grabbed a bundle of clean tea towels and the car keys and helped him into the car. Then we were flying along the Route des Coteaux. In spite of the high speed it was the longest drive to Bergerac ever. Sean was remarkably calm but cursing his mistake prolifically; he had accidently stuck his finger into the exit pipe of the harvest trailer with the auger going. It was another strike due to fatigue.

'Perhaps we shouldn't be doing this,' I said as we passed the Barses' turn-off. 'It's too dangerous. Your health is more important than making wine.'

'But I love it,' said Sean through gritted teeth. 'Now is not the time to discuss this, Carolinus.'

'But is it worth it?' I asked. Trips to Bergerac Hospital, the death of our neighbours and my nightmares about Ellie were taking their toll.

We got to the now familiar *urgences* (A&E). It was a mere three months since we were last there. Sean was taken away. Fifteen minutes later I was told to go home as he would be in hospital for the day and perhaps longer, depending on the surgery.

I felt desperate on the way home. Sean had been in charge. I didn't know how John and I would cope now Sean was off the team. The whites still needed to be cooled and the reds needed to be pumped over. I couldn't contemplate where to start. I didn't know which pump should be used for what or how the Kreyer refrigeration unit worked. I left a message for Lucille asking her to call me to prioritise the work, then I called Jamie and asked him to stop by. I walked into the *pressoir* and John said, 'So what now, chief?' which heightened my panic.

We started with the pump-over of the Hillside juice. Pumping over is the method used to extract flavour and colour from the grapes when making red wine in Bordeaux and Bergerac. A proportion of the juice is pumped from the bottom of the tank and sprayed over the top of the tank. The juice extracts the colour and tannin from the grape skins as it trickles down into the main body of juice and it keeps the cap wet, thereby preventing it from turning bad.

Hillside was in our semi-underground vat, the one I was having nightmares about. The vat lid was in the middle of the floor of our *pressoir*, presenting a hazard even when the vat was empty. Access to the underground portion, where the vat's main door and the pipe connection were, was via a wooden trapdoor located in the working zone of the *pressoir*. Rotten and dangerous, the trapdoor was earmarked as a primary target for renovation.

I opened it and climbed down the ancient oak ladder into the gloom below. Once on solid ground I attached the pipe as fast as I could, then ascended, feeling sick at the 4-metre drop. Nearing the top, I looked up and saw several gigantic spiders clustered around my only escape. There was nothing for it; I gritted my teeth and sped up through the hole to safety.

The awful truth was that this descent-ascent needed to be undertaken six times a day for an undefined period of time. We started the pump and realised there was a problem; the wine was not coming up from the tap below. Feeling sorely cheated at having to face the trip into the cavern again with nothing achieved, I descended and checked that the tap was open. John tried the pump again to no avail. We tried with the tap the other way, still no luck.

It was not going well. Nothing was smooth in our eccentric winery. It was certainly a winery with character. I was swearing loudly at the pipe by the time John cleared the blockage by reversing the flow several times.

We took turns to spray the *chapeau*. 'Spray' makes it sound like we were sprinkling liquid round with a nice light hose but this is far from the truth. The hose was industrial size, weighed a ton and needed to be carefully aimed and controlled so the jet of wine spread as evenly as possible. When we finished John valiantly offered to descend into the cavern to do the necessary and I agreed, somewhat too eagerly.

The pump-over of Garrigue went more smoothly. I climbed up another old oak ladder onto Garrigue's 3-metre-tall fibre vat with a sloping top and no safety rails and grabbed onto the rim of the chimney with one hand and the pipe with the other. John started the pump and the industrial hose carrying the equivalent of 200 litres a minute leapt to life. I tried to control it, hold on and pray all at once.

When that ordeal was over we pumped clean water through the pumps and the Kreyer before tackling the cooling of the sémillon that was now fermenting at a good pace. I hoped we would avoid this operation while Sean was in hospital but the wine was 20 degrees and needed to be between 15 and 18. We connected the Kreyer refrigeration unit to the necessary pipes and I turned the switch. The Kreyer refused to start. I imagined Sean's reaction if 6,000 litres of sémillon went wrong while I was in charge.

I was about to go inside to phone Jamie when he arrived. He quickly set about diagnosing the problem and was close to admitting defeat when he discovered that the electricians had changed the polarity on the new board so the Kreyer's fan was turning in the wrong direction. Minutes later the sémillon was cooling happily and I was beyond grateful.

It was past two o'clock when Lucille arrived as I was making my way across the courtyard to get some lunch.

'*Ça va?*' asked Lucille. 'I came as soon as I could. Did the finger land in the wine?'

An oenologist has to keep her priorities straight.

'No, it's somewhere on Garrigue in the rinsing water,' I said. John had looked for the missing bit of finger once it was light enough but it was lost – washed down the road where we did a final rinse of the trailers, into Upper Garrigue. It brought a new dimension to how much of himself Sean put into his vineyard and his wines.

'Is Sean all right?'

'I haven't heard from the hospital yet. He was in a lot of pain.'

We talked through what had to happen in the winery over the following few days. Lucille was losing her school teacher approach and becoming more of a collaborator.

'*Faites très attention à vous* and best wishes to Sean,' she said as she left; better than a rap over the knuckles.

It was mid afternoon and I hadn't eaten since four that morning. I bit into a baguette stuffed to bursting with fig jam, then into a large piece of cherry chocolate and called the hospital. Sean was out of theatre and could be collected. He had lost the top third of his middle finger on his left hand. To avoid future problems the surgeon had cut away a little more of the bone than the harvest trailer had done and removed the nail root.

'Come now,' said Sean, 'please, Carolinus.' He sounded so vulnerable. I crammed another mouthful of fig baguette and a hunk of chocolate into my mouth and grabbed the car keys.

Sean was in reasonable humour considering his *amputation traumatique* as described on his medical certificate. His hand was bandaged up to the elbow. By the time we reached Gardonne pharmacy the anaesthetic was wearing off. On the road from Gardonne to Garrigue Sean groaned in agony at each tiny bump. He took the maximum dose of morphine and went to bed. I had never seen him in such pain.

The doctor decreed that Sean should be off for six weeks and it would take six months for the finger to heal completely. All I could think was – what the feck am I going to do? I felt bad that I was worrying about myself; at least I had all my fingers.

The following day John and I tackled Hillside again. I descended into 'Halloween Horror' cavern, speeding past the spiders despite the drop of several metres and connected up the pipe. I had already returned to the joyful light before we realised that the pipe was blocked like the day before. We tried the trick of reversing the pump unsuccessfully. A minute later Sean ran into the winery, bandaged hand held high.

'What's going on?' he demanded.

I was dispatched down into the cavern. After trying almost everything Sean decided to go down himself to check the pipe. We undid the vat-to-pipe connection yet again and checked the pipe and the tap. Lodged deep inside the tap spout was a solid rubber washer that should have remained inside the tap cap when I took it off the previous day. I was the weakest link. Sean glowered at me and stomped back to bed. I felt angry and frustrated; I was out of my depth and his attitude wasn't helping. I reminded myself that he was running on morphine and recovering from a traumatic amputation.

Over the next few days the pump-overs, which had been terrifying at first, became familiar, although we constantly reminded ourselves to take care. I now judiciously checked for washers when removing caps. Our white wines, meanwhile, motored towards the end of their alcoholic fermentation. Like a nurse, I started with a ward round each day, clipboard in hand, tasting and taking temperatures and densities of each of our 'babies' then using that information to decide what needed to be done. The only wine that wasn't behaving perfectly was the rosé, which was fermenting too slowly for Lucille's liking. It tasted delicious, though.

The following day a tempest struck that brought down barns, trees and garden sheds all over south-west France. I came out of the winery dressed in wine-splattered dry-pants to take Sophia to school and could barely open the car doors in the ferocious wind. Debris flew around. It did not feel safe. When I got back I noticed a 3-metre tree in the garden had succumbed to the tornado. Our neighbour's shed had been demolished and their garden arch lifted up by the wind and smashed into their car.

Sean came out of the house and pointed to the huge oak tree that grew outside the *pressoir*. It was not as straight as usual.

We soon verified that the 200-year-old oak was now leaning ominously against the *pressoir* – the part of the winery where the grapes are pressed and fermented – which housed our precious harvest. With the aid of Sean's dad, John, a forester by trade, we considered our options. It was impossible for us to remove on our own. The precarious situation and what was inside the building meant we needed a serious professional to do it.

I looked up the French word for tree surgeon then called every *élagueuse* in the *Pages Jaunes*. Not surprisingly, given the tempest, I found all who answered already engaged in emergencies. A few called back but when they heard the details of the tree and its situation they quickly discovered other priorities.

Our entire year's work was at risk. The tree was over 20 metres high. If it smashed through the roof of the winery it could break the tanks and cause damage to equipment. Nor was it a safe place for us to work with a mighty oak balancing on it, but the winery work had to continue.

That evening as I sat down to call through the list of *élagueuses* again, Olivier Delpeuch called back. His advertisement was promising; a drawing of him hanging off a tree in climbing gear, holding onto the trunk with one hand and cutting a massive branch with an enormous chainsaw with the other. He arrived the following day and I had to pinch myself. He was a French Rambo with striking features and rippling muscles, dressed in combats and dark glasses and drawing deeply on a rolled cigarette.

He assessed the tree from all angles.

'*C'est le pire.*'

'It's the worst' was a comment I had heard from many artisans in the build-up to a *devis* but in this instance I trusted the man.

This was not because of his exceptional physique, as Sean later insinuated somewhat jokingly.

'You will have to hire a *grosse grue*,' he said.

I didn't have a clue what a *grosse grue* was, but I was happy to hire whatever he liked. A *grosse grue*, the dictionary told me later, was a large crane. Olivier promised to organise it for the job, which he could do on Monday, which was in three days' time.

'Make sure no one is in the winery if the wind blows. The tree is dangerous.'

Just what I needed to hear facing into a full day's work in the winery.

When Olivier called later to let me know the price I noticed he never referred to a tree as a tree. It was the *chêne* or the acacia or something more specific like *le vieux chêne*. I liked it: it implied respect and gave our wounded trees, the old oak and the acacia, an identity. Or was it just the way he said it? Fortunately, the cost of the removal of the oak and the repair to the small part of the roof that had been broken by it would be covered by our insurance. I had sent them photos of the tree and its situation and they had agreed that it should be removed as fast as possible to avoid further damage. The acacia was alongside the winery and it was hanging by a thread so it had to go too.

A little later Olivier called back.

'Make sure no one is in the winery on Monday afternoon,' he said.

This was essential, not merely for safety, but more particularly, for viewing. At the designated time Peta-Lynne, Ellie and I installed ourselves comfortably in garden chairs a safe distance from our French Rambo live in action.

Olivier arrived wearing his signature combats, leather boots and dark glasses, now complemented by his climbing harness and an attractive red headband. He was more good-looking than I remembered. Peta-Lynne and I exchanged a glance.

John, experienced in all things 'tree', took one look at him and said dismissively, 'He looks a bit of a cowboy.' Luckily Sean was now able to drive the car and had taken himself to the hospital for his regular amputation check-up so we didn't have to listen to any other derogatory comments.

The enormous crane arrived, bringing to mind city skylines. Olivier attached its chains to the base of the acacia. It would be the taster before the main feature. He quickly chainsawed the acacia at the base and leapt away as the crane lifted the 4-metre tree over our 6-metre-high barns and deposited it on the newly created tasting-room parking area. Sean's mum and I almost burst into applause while Ellie reposed regally in her all-terrain buggy.

Olivier 'Rambo' then moved onto *le vieux chêne*. He climbed onto the roof of the winery and removed the smaller side branches, then attached himself to the crane, which lifted him into the sky and lowered him onto the tree. Positioned about halfway between the double-storey winery roof and the top of the tree he attached himself to the trunk, attached the chains of the crane above and sawed through the wood in the classic pose displayed in his advert. He had to manoeuvre like a rock climber holding a massive chainsaw that even in the most stable situation would have been difficult and dangerous to operate. The crane operator lifted the upper section free as Olivier finished the cut, missing him by inches. I could barely watch. He gradually moved down the tree, cutting off huge sections in similar fashion. There were gasps of awe from the three generations of Feely girls in the front-row seats. John left us in disgust under the auspices of taking photos from the other side of the winery.

Oaks are notoriously difficult trees to judge because of the considerable size and weight of side branches that influence the way the tree falls or moves. Apart from his good looks Olivier was an exceptionally skilled tree surgeon, I thought. I was in awe.

When he came back into the courtyard Olivier looked exhilarated and exhausted. I could see now that the red headband was not a fashion accessory but played the important role of keeping the sweat out of his eyes in such exacting circumstances. I brought him a glass of juice. The *grosse grue* had already left. John came up to join in.

*'C'était difficile,'* said Olivier. 'Perhaps one of the most difficult I have done. At one point, on the second level of *le vieux chêne* I cut and the crane lifted but it swung because of the uneven weight and missed my foot by millimetres.'

'I don't speak French,' said John, 'but I am a forester and I just want to tell you...' John paused for a long moment as he often did. I wondered what was coming next. Perhaps 'you're a bit of a cowboy'? '... the job you did out there today was exceptionally skilful.'

Olivier was visibly moved. Despite a significant language barrier, the tree men had a long discussion about everything from the age of *le vieux chêne* to the trees John had worked with in South Africa.

Olivier sawed the beautiful oak into 50-centimetre lengths. I thanked him profusely.

Our harvest was safe and we could go back to work in the winery. But Sean's finger was still total agony if something touched the bandage. He was working again but being single-handed was slow. John and Peta-Lynne would soon be leaving us and I didn't have any idea how we would bring in our Saussignac dessert wine, let alone do the work on the wines we already had in the winery.

Sophia and Ellie were showing signs of *vendanges* stress. Sophia developed bed-wetting problems after months of being dry, Ellie was picky at mealtimes and wouldn't go to sleep at bedtime. We had not had a moment to spend with them in six weeks. Our evening meals were rushed and often in relays because of the hellish tempo dictated by the harvest. While on the face of it Sean and I were getting along OK there was a constant undercurrent of tension. We only talked to each other for business decisions and we were both stretched to our limit by the work needed to get to grips with our new business. I often worked late into the night responding to orders and sorting out direct deliveries for our fledgling online wine business while Sean did the same in the winery with John as his left hand. The finger amputation and harvest pressure didn't help. The tension was also partly due to not spending any time alone together but ironically I was not looking forward to being alone with him when the Feelys left the following week. I felt like Sean didn't have anything to say to me except 'Just get on with it'. When everyone else had gone to bed I munched my way through several rows of *touche de sérénité* chocolate, hoping it would ease my stress.

# Chapter 11

# Digging Grapes

*'Il faut le sortir maintenant,'* said Lucille urgently. Our oenologist had tasted the merlot wines that were still on their skins. They had finished fermenting a couple of days before and she had encouraged us to keep them on the skins for more extraction until her next visit. Now I could see from her face that we had gone too far. We had to run the free-run wine off and press the juice from the remaining grapes fast.

That evening Sean attacked the relatively simple first part; running the free-run wine off the must. The grape 'must' is the skins and pips – and juice that is still inside the skins, rather than the free-run juice. He ran the wine out of the fermentation vat by gravity into a giant sieve placed in a 1,000-litre bucket, then pumped it into a new vat for maturation. Once the free-run was just dripping he left the dregs to drain slowly through the night, getting up regularly to check that everything was going according to plan.

The following day we tackled the next phase; digging the grapes out to transfer them to the press so we could extract the press wine. Press wine typically represents a fifth of the total red wine produced but it can be a key part of the blend, offering more colour and tannin than the free-run wine. This step required extreme caution because killer carbon dioxide is given off during the fermentation and it lurks unseen inside the vats.

To chase the gas out I positioned two house fans above the vats. It was Heath Robinson but it worked. Then I moved the wine paddle (like a single-sided canoe paddle but made of food-grade plastic, used to stir wine), digging tools and cleaning equipment to the back wall so we had more room to work.

Like many things over that harvest period, digging grapes was more difficult than it looked. Just moving the must pump into position under the vat's front door was near impossible since it was so heavy. The must pump is like a miniature harvest trailer; about half a metre high and wide and a metre long with a wide but short auger in its metal belly. This auger is sufficiently powerful to pump hundreds of kilograms of grape must up the harvest pipe into the press. When the must pump is in motion it looks peaceful, but one false move and it could remove a hand or a foot or worse. Its powerful auger will crush and macerate anything that gets in its way – just like what the harvest trailer did to part of Sean's finger. Once it was in place we would climb inside the enormous vat and dig the grapes out of the vat directly into it. Sean and I tried to push it into position while John held the pipe and the electrical wire.

'Push,' yelled Sean.

'It's too heavy,' I said.

'Just do it,' he growled. I nearly whacked him over the head with the wine paddle.

He pushed me out of the way and gave it a massive shove, wedging it into position. John looked surprised at Sean's behaviour. He and Peta-Lynne knew something was wrong between us but they put it down to harvest stress and finger trauma. I was having serious finger trauma myself keeping my middle finger from jamming itself in front of Sean's nose. Instead I stood back and counted to ten to calm myself. We needed to work as a cohesive team for a hazardous operation like this. Next, we connected this dangerous beast to the harvest pipe that had thumped John and me a couple of weeks before. I felt skittish.

With the must pump in position we could dig the must from the vat into it then pump the must up to the press. Sean opened the door of the vat and a small avalanche of fermented grapes fell neatly into the pump. It was perfectly positioned. He dragged a little more of the must using our food-grade winery fork – enough to fill the belly of the must pump – then switched it on and pumped the mass up to the press. Each small success with equipment we had never used was a milestone. We took a moment to congratulate ourselves then took turns digging grapes out of the front door of the vat. The recent death of our neighbours was a constant reminder of how potentially deadly our new occupation was.

Too soon it was time for someone to get inside the vat. That someone was me since Sean was still effectively one-handed. I was scared stiff.

'How am I going to get in?' I asked nervously.

'Climb over it,' commanded Sean. The vicious must pump was too heavy to move out of the way each time we got in and out.

My hand, stained red with wine, was shaking as I leaned over to test the vat's air with our BiC lighter. The flame remained strong which meant that the air was probably clear enough of carbon dioxide to be safe to enter. With Sean ready to pull me out if necessary, I clambered in. Rather than killing me, it smelt like a giant Christmas pudding. I wondered for a second if that was the smell you got just before you died – I love Christmas pudding. There was no time for philosophising. I pushed my white sterilised boots deep into the 50-centimetre-thick layer of grape must so there was no chance of slipping out into the deadly pump and dug then pushed the marc (or pressed must) to Sean at the vat door. About ten minutes later Sean demanded a turn. He had decided that he could dig despite his injury, if he covered his bandaged hand with a plastic bag to protect it from splashes.

I demanded that he unplug the must pump, horrified and scared as I was of its potential to eat body parts. He scoffed at the notion saying it was turned off at its switch. Still inside the tank and not moving until he acquiesced, I explained, as calmly as I could, that someone could fall onto the switch and turn it on mistakenly. Unplugged there was no risk. John gave him a look that said 'unplug the pump' and he did. We changed places – clambering awkwardly over the must beast.

The wine from the Upper Garrigue grapes was pressed by late afternoon and the ton of leftover skins and pips moved from the press to the entrance to our property. Leftover grape skins and wine sediments are given to state-owned distilleries for production of industrial alcohol. This 'forced gifting' is an ancient tax on French winegrowers. The distillery would collect the marc from the entrance to our property with a truck equipped with a small crane.

We had done a full day's work but we still had to press Hillside; waiting was not an option now that the wine was run off.

It was in an underground *cuve* – the one I had nightmares about. We had to move the must pump down to the horror cavern. The harvest pipe had to be moved too, and now it was gorged with grapes the weight was immense. We couldn't move it.

'This can't be right,' I said.

'Stop complaining and pull,' snapped Sean.

We all heaved again but the Serpent would not budge. I pictured us working all night.

'What about pumping water through to push the grapes out?'

Sean glowered at me.

'It's worth a try,' said John.

Several litres of water and a few minutes later we had an empty pipe. My idea had worked. Sean harrumphed and I marked up a small winery success.

Grunting with exertion we got the pump onto the tractor forks and Sean took it down to the cavern. The harvest pipe was attached to the pump then pushed up to John who was waiting at the trapdoor, tied on for safety. As soon as he had the top of the pipe I ran up to help him pull it up while Sean struggled to keep it in position below. We lifted it up over the press and tied it securely. John received a tap on the head, a gentle reminder from the pipe about who was boss.

It was dark when we started the second dig. Strangely, after the nightmares I had had about it, I now found the underground vat cosy and comforting. Our lantern hung down, providing a warm yellow glow on the beautiful red walls. The smell of Christmas pudding was delicious and the exertion of the digging combined with the low-oxygen air was elating. I wanted to stay longer but Sean made me get out since it was unadvisable to work in that environment for more than ten minutes. We took turns digging while John handled the Serpent on high.

At about ten that night we finished the dig and started pressing. Sitting on old plastic crates watching the press do its work, we paused for a glass of Saussignac dessert wine and an ice cream. The endorphins from hard physical work, the successful pressing of our first vintage of red wine and the divine taste created a moment of elation that helped to ease the difficult parts of the day. Peta-Lynne, who had brought us our dinner to eat on the run a little earlier and had been monitoring progress every half-hour, joined us to savour the moment. The girls were safely asleep. Once the pressing was finished we took in the silence of the winery, enjoying the delicious smells of fermentation and the call of the barn owl. The cleaning of the press and the vats could wait.

On Lucille's visit the following day I toured the Saussignac vineyard with her. We tasted and collected sample grapes as we walked.

'Collecting samples is not something oenologists do but today it is *pratique*,' said our serious oenologist, underlining the clear delineation of roles so essential to French life. 'I think you could do your first pick at the end of next week.'

'I don't know how we will do that with Sean one-handed. His parents leave tomorrow. I couldn't do it alone.'

'*C'est vrai*. But it would be a pity to lose it. *C'est très joli*.'

The botrytis noble rot was not what the average person would call pretty. The grapes were shrivelled and mottled; grey, yellow and black; many were furry... but they tasted heavenly. The *Botrytis cinerea* attacks the grape skins, creating little perforations that allow the grape to shrivel and concentrate its juices without losing its freshness. In the process the 'noble rot' imparts delectable honey, almond and apricot flavours and creates a wine that is deliciously concentrated.

'What press will we use?' I asked, as much to myself as to Lucille.

We had planned to borrow a manual press from a neighbouring winemaker but Sean needed to collect it with the tractor – which remained out of the question given the state of his hand. To use our electric press we needed a minimum load. Saussignac has to be hand-picked selectively over a minimum of three picks. Because the botrytis develops at different rates on different bunches you pick only the grapes that are at the level of development you want – this means picking selectively multiple times through the same vineyard. For most winegrowers it is three to five picks spread over several weeks from late September to early November. I had no idea how much yield we would get from our selected rows at each pick.

'You should ask one of the other Saussignac producers. Someone experienced. I am not a specialist in *liquoreux*,' said Lucille. *Liquoreux* is the French word for a botrytis-style dessert wine like Saussignac or Sauternes.

'We want to do a light Saussignac, something around eighteen to twenty,' I said, surprising her with my knowledge on the subject. We wanted to make our wine slightly less sweet than the average Saussignac, which was around 21 or 22 potential alcohol (also known as 'must weight' – a measure of the amount of sugar in grape juice, which indicates the amount of alcohol that could be produced if it is all fermented to alcohol, rather than left as residual sugar). This meant we needed to pick to have a level of around 330 grams of sugar per litre. Of this, around 200 grams would become alcohol, creating a level of 12 per cent and the rest would remain as natural residual sugar in the wine.

'Be careful,' she said in her typical cautious manner. 'It's easy to make a mistake and land up with too little sugar to be AOC Saussignac.'

At my request Thierry Daulhiac, the president of the Saussignac appellation, came round that evening. We walked down to Lenvège and he tasted a few grapes then pulled out his refractometer. I had bought one for Sean the week of the finger amputation; we hadn't used it yet. Thierry took a bunch of grapes in his fist and squeezed the juice expertly over the screen. He looked into it then passed it to me.

'*C'est déjà au dessus de vingt-cinq. Tu vois?*' (It's already over twenty-five. Do you see?)

I nodded sagely.

'*C'est joli. Très joli.* Very pretty, yes, even more pretty than mine.'

I was getting the idea about the 'pretty' term, an indicator of the quality of the noble rot rather than physical beauty. I was taken aback by the disarming honesty that allowed him to admit this to me, an outsider without a clue. He walked along the rows looking at the grapes.

'There is enough for you to press it in the electric press, I think. Anyway, if there isn't enough there are ways to fill it.'

'How?' I asked.

'A rice bag for example, or *autrefois*, in the old days, they used straw.'

'Where would I get a rice bag?'

'I don't know. You'll have to ask someone who uses the same press, perhaps the Sadoux.'

'How should we pick to get a result of eighteen to twenty?'

'Perhaps the best way is to do a medium pick on the first pass, then check the level and on the next pass adjust the pick to compensate.' We walked down a row and Thierry showed me which bunches he would take – brown or mixed gold and brown showing good botrytis – and which he would leave – gold or green and gold – to get a medium result. I tried to imprint the images in my head. Thierry's boyish face spread into a wide ironic grin.

'*Enfin*, it's not easy.'

It looked easy for him. Dressed in jeans and a sweatshirt, he had such an easy confidence in the vineyard, a confidence that comes from years of experience. He sensed, almost by instinct, what the grapes he picked and squeezed onto the little screen of the refractometer would offer in sugar concentration.

'So, are you going to do a little Saussignac?' he asked.

'*Ça dépend*. With Sean injured it's not easy.'

'*Sans doute*. But it's very, very pretty. *Enfin*, it would be a pity to lose it.'

That evening I called Pierre Sadoux to find out about the press. Pierre-Jean, his father, answered and I introduced myself.

'We might not have enough Saussignac to fill the press,' I explained. 'I know you have the same presses so I wondered if you could suggest a solution.'

'*C'est difficile, oui,*' replied Pierre-Jean, not offering a solution.

'Do you have any suggestions?'

'You could borrow a press that can take a smaller load.'

'Hmm, but Sean is injured so moving a press won't be easy. Thierry Daulhiac mentioned straw.'

'*Oui, c'est vrai*. You can do that. But you must make sure that the straw is in perfect condition. It must be from this year and not old straw.'

I remembered the Barses kept hay for their sheep so I called Bernard. He agreed that we could collect a bale if we needed one on the day.

That Monday the Saussignac producers union held a day for wine professionals and journalists to experience picking noble rot at Château Le Chabrier. The gentle picking operation was followed by tasting of Saussignac wine from each of the producers present. As we tasted through the wines I told Richard Doughty, an organic producer we had met a few times, about Sean's finger amputation.

'He was lucky,' said Richard. 'A good friend of ours, a Saussignac producer, died when he fell into a harvest trailer ten years ago.'

I felt sick to my core, horrified that the winegrower accidents we had read about were so prevalent among people we now knew. I resolved to give Sean another lecture on taking care.

We sat down to lunch at two large tables set up in the entrance hall of Château Le Chabrier, a seventeenth-century hunting lodge. Melt-in-the-mouth pâté toasts and succulent figs with Roquefort blue cheese grilled on top were served as the starter to accompany a flight of different Saussignac wines. If that wasn't enough to seduce the invited wine professionals, pork roasted with prunes and Saussignac followed. Joel the Jolly, seated next to me – fortunately unarmed – told me he had cooked it. He proudly admitted to keeping the water gun in the car at all times, and then laughed heartily as he recounted a story of leaving rotting steak under the mayor's car seat. The mayor took a week to track down the disgusting stench. Leaving aside stinking steak, this pork dish was the best pork I had ever had. I was convinced that Joel was joking about having cooked it. Thierry assured me it was true and some sleuthing in the kitchen revealed that it was.

The cheese board that followed was a voyage of flavours from the region and beyond; Échourgnac, the wonderful cow's milk cheese with walnut liquor made by nuns in the Dordogne,

Cabécou, the local goat's cheese, an enormous round of Brie de Meaux and a selection of blue cheeses. The grand finale was a luscious apricot and almond tart. I thought I had died and gone to heaven. Matched with a young Saussignac, redolent of apricot compote, it was sublime.

I went home in time to help Sean finish off the day's winery work. It was the twilight of the Feely seniors' stay. We had been through one of the most intense periods of our lives and were closer for it. The next morning I said a tearful farewell to them and Sean took them to the airport while I got on with the winery ward round.

Sean walked back into the winery just as precious cabernet sauvignon shot onto the winery wall.

'What the heck's going on here? Why didn't you wait for me to get back?' he demanded.

I had not tied the over-pipe sufficiently tightly and the pressure of the pump had shot the pipe out of the vat. I hastily switched off. Relatively little had been lost and the incident gave Sean the opportunity to step back into the driver's seat. I could have waited for him but John and I had been doing this successfully the weeks he was out of commission and I wanted to get ahead with the work.

He overreacted partly to reinstate his position as leader in the winery. Now he was able to do most of what was required as long as he protected his bandage from getting wet or dirty. I cut back my time in the winery realising that the less time we spent together the better. Working together was very different to being married. I wasn't sure if it was possible to achieve both successfully.

Sean was ambivalent about harvesting the Saussignac. He was still running on morphine and finding the wines he had in the winery tough enough to control without another baby coming into the ward. I desperately wanted to have Saussignac in the range. There was something exceptional about the wine and the group of producers that made it. Sean's hand was sufficiently healed to drive a tractor. I decided to see if a few friends would help.

After one positive response from a retired English couple in Saussignac, Sue and Ian Cameron, who had become friends, I got no more takers. Sue was a major force in the village; active on the *syndicat d'initiative*, the local tourist office and initiative committee, welcoming to newcomers and a gardening dynamo. One couple would not be enough to help us on our own. Most of our local friends and neighbours were vignerons and had enough on their plates already. The O'Briens and Rogers from Ireland were due to arrive in two weeks but they would be too late. We had to get at least one pick in before that and we couldn't afford to pay for a team of hand-pickers. Seeking consolation I tucked into a row of *touche de sérénité* dark cherry chocolate as the phone rang.

'I just heard about Sean's finger. Fiona and I can come and help harvest. Do you want us to make an open invitation to our friends?' said Bruce Kingwill.

Bruce and Fiona, his wife, were South Africans who lived a few kilometres away. A stylish couple in their fifties and dedicated Francophiles, they had moved to France to follow their passion to make wine and restore houses. For a few years they made small quantities of wine, buying grapes in from other growers. They soon realised that winegrowing was a tough business – just as we were discovering – hard work, masses of red tape and difficult to make financially viable. Their renovations were magical: they had transformed several semi-ruins into ultra-charming French country houses. They had already hand-harvested many times so

I wasn't expecting a positive response from them. Sympathy for Sean's plight must have played a part.

Relief and cherry chocolate filled me with well-being. 'That would be fantastic. If we get enough people we'll start at nine on Tuesday morning.'

'I can't promise anything,' he said.

But on Sunday Bruce confirmed ten more participants, making our team sixteen – enough to do the vineyard in a morning. Our crew of pickers was a cosmopolitan melange of nationalities and ages ranging from ten to seventy years old. I gave a demonstration based on my hour with Thierry then set them loose. Soon I was running up and down the rows checking the contents of buckets, making adjustments and fielding questions. Some were fast, others were fastidious.

At the end of the morning, we had enough grapes to go ahead with our electric press straw free. While Sean pressed the grapes I served lunch: great bowls of steaming soup, baguettes, cheese and quiche followed by luscious tarts from our local *boulangerie*. The pressed juice yielded a potential alcohol level of 24, significantly more than our target of 18 to 20. It was rich and luscious, oozing with apricot and almond flavours. With the next pick we would have to seek a less sweet – or in Thierry's terms, '*serré*' – result, which would mean picking some of the golden grapes, not just the brown.

Over the following days Sean threw himself ever deeper into winery work while I zoned into renovations, housework and children. Our friends from Ireland arrived, the constant presence of visitors helping to cover over the cracks in our relationship. With our large crew of friends staying we were once again busier than ever. We got them working on our second and third picks

– the O'Briens true experts now in their second year of picking Saussignac. The week flew by and soon the Rogers were gone.

On the last night of the O'Briens' holiday, Thierry Daulhiac came around to discuss our application to be included on the Route des Vins. We had applied as soon as we had arrived to be featured on this tourist map with contact details and locations of vineyards that sold direct to the public. It had taken us a year to get this far. To say I was frustrated with the speed of our integration into this tourism initiative would be underplaying it. In retrospect, as with many frustrations in France, I had come to appreciate it as we had needed the time to finish the tasting room renovations. The ruined outbuilding that was closest to the entrance, and that had been the seasonal Portuguese workers' house in the old days, had been transformed. An engineering friend, Tim, had helped Sean renovate the caved-in roof, install a new window and door and tile the floor while I had repainted the room and the wood ceilings.

Thierry was on the committee and a key decision maker. I showed him the newly completed tasting room. There was still a way to go, but the transformation was impressive. Our renovation skills had come a long way since our arrival.

I gave him a brief summary of our quest for a vineyard of our own and our plans for the property.

'*C'est bon*. I don't think you will have a problem with getting onto the Route des Vins but they will want to taste your wines. They will ask for a sample from this harvest.'

Isabelle, Thierry's wife, and his sons, were away in Normandy so I invited him for dinner and he readily agreed. Over a simple supper we discussed the finer points of vineyard management. Sean and he talked of tractors, mechanical hoes, mowers and vine trimmers – and tricks about combining the machinery to get the work done faster. Barry and Aideen put in the odd word as the conversation flashed back and forth, sometimes in English, sometimes in French. Thierry, who had started his conversion to organic in 2005, warned of administrative pitfalls and promised to send us relevant contacts. In the flickering candlelight we exchanged views about wine, people, marketing and life.

'You've arrived!' said Aideen as Thierry left. 'I can't believe it. This time last year you didn't have a clue, now you're chatting with other winemakers like you were born to it.'

It was a good finale to Aideen and Barry's stay, an evening with a local vigneron to feel the flavour of *'la France profonde'* that we had grown to love – and an opportunity for Aideen to buoy us up.

'You must make sure that you get time alone together,' said Aideen as we cleaned up. 'Do you ever go out for a night together?'

'No,' I said guiltily. 'Maybe we should go for lunch sometime.'

'That's not enough. You need a night out together every week or two. It's essential.'

Aideen had divined our marital rift. I said we would, then did nothing. We had two days between the O'Briens' departure and the arrival of five young Americans, some of whom were children of friends, visiting us to experience life in France in exchange for helping paint the outbuildings and remaining shutters. Managing and feeding a gang of five youngsters ranging from eighteen to twenty was demanding. Between looking after our own small children and our newly acquired teenage crew, Sean and I barely exchanged a word for three weeks. Sean, meanwhile, spent the nights partying with the college kids, subtracting points from his already low stack. We had more wine on the property than they had seen in their lives. He stumbled into the kitchen late one Saturday morning after yet another party night.

'Feck me,' he said. 'You won't believe what's happening. Diana is gay and she's hitting on Erin who is going steady with Tommy. I couldn't believe my eyes last night.'

He was more interested in gossiping about their exotic relationships than in thinking about our future or our own relationship. As the love triangle between Tommy, Erin and Diana progressed, he moved from ignoring me to being rude. The rift between us widened and was impacting our daughters. Ellie no longer played happily on her own and Sophia didn't want to catch the bus to school. They were insecure and no wonder. Things were not working out. This dream was costing us our relationship and our financial security.

My life was an endless round of washing, feeding and cleaning. As much as I loved France and Château Haut Garrigue I was not happy. We had no money and didn't have a clear notion when we would have. I had to get out.

I would go back to the city, find a job and a place to live, then get the girls. I made my plans and booked a flight.

Erin told Diana to get lost, she was sticking with Tommy, and they all left. That night after cleaning up and making sure the girls were asleep I told Sean I had to talk to him. He turned off the television.

I told him my plan. He was shocked – he had no idea it had come to this. I wondered how he could not.

'You can't go, Carolinus,' he said, tears welling in his eyes. 'I need you. We're going to make this work. We had a rough time with our first harvest and then all those young kids. That was a mistake.'

'I won't live like this, SF. The only time you have two words to say to me is when you want me to phone someone in French for you, otherwise I'm no more than a house slave. I have to go.' Tears started to stream out of me. I was leaving and the pain was killing me.

Sean went white with shock as he realised I was serious.

'I've been a bear with a sore head. I don't like being swamped by people. I'm a loner. I like my space and I haven't had any in four months. Add all the visitors to the *vendanges* and the chopped finger and you've got a caged lion.'

Sean was like most men – he needed to retreat into his cave sometimes. I had forced his agreement to take the team of youngsters so we could be sure that we would finish the painting before the next tourist season started. He hadn't wanted them. Add to that living in close quarters with his parents for two months with non-stop harvest and the situation was a pressure cooker for both of us.

'I'm so sorry, Carolinus. I love you.'

He looked so vulnerable, not like the monster I had been living with for the last few months; he looked like the Sean I had fallen in love with. The stress that had been building for almost six months boiled over. I took his good hand and we sat on the sofa, tears pouring down our faces.

Once we had control of ourselves we discussed how we could repair our relationship and make sure the same breakdown didn't happen again. I looked back on the incidents of the past months and understood what had happened but I didn't cancel the flight. I wanted to be sure that the Sean I knew was really back.

# Chapter 12

# Vineyard Rights

With our relationship stabilising, my thoughts turned to our financial future. The wine business could not follow our original plan of selling three quarters of our first year's production to a *négociant* while we built up our customer base. The costs in France were significantly higher than the American extension office figures used in the business plan. To make matters much, much worse, the yield we got was half of what we had estimated. We had to make some dramatic changes for this property to be viable.

'What are we going to do?' I asked Sean, as we scrolled through the spreadsheet.

'We have to sell our wine direct earlier. We can't afford to take the easy option of selling to the *négociant*. I couldn't do it anyway, not after the blood, sweat and tears we've put into it. I never understood that cliché as well as I do now. It's high quality wine. We're not giving it away.'

'But even if we sell direct in bottles will we make a living?'

We crunched the numbers. If we were successful at selling direct at the optimistic prices we envisaged, we would still be struggling.

'We have to increase the production. The amount we're producing isn't sustainable. We have to get closer to three hundred hectos.' A year before I didn't know what a 'hecto' or hectolitre, the equivalent of 100 litres, was. Now I knew the numbers for production and costs in a vineyard and winery operation like the back of my hand.

'You're right, Carolinus. We have to get more planting rights so we can plant the peach field.'

'But more vineyard will take a long time. We needed something that can offer more immediate cash flow. What about a cottage to rent out?'

'But where will we get the money to build one? We'd have to start from scratch. We don't have any spare buildings.'

I didn't know either. Still, we had to move forward. 'If we're successful selling all our wine direct, planting more vineyard and developing a cottage, we'll have a going concern.'

We didn't have all the answers but I felt better for having an idea of what we needed for our dream to become sustainable. The following day a brochure for a course on commercialising wine appeared. I signed up.

Increasing our production seemed nonsensical since we didn't have a shortage but planning vineyard production is long-term, particularly in France. To plant a single row of vines we had to own or acquire the rights to plant. This could take two years. Once the vineyard planting rights were in order we could plant the vines but it would be three years before they produced some grapes and five years to produce a yield worth counting. The vines needed ten years to produce wines of complexity. In France winegrowers are not allowed to buy in wine to make up a shortfall. They are only allowed to sell wine they have grown. To buy in wine you had to be a *négociant*, a different business structure to being a winegrower.

Mystified by the complexities of vineyard rights, I called Cécile. She arrived, preferring to discuss it face to face.

'I'm lost,' I said.

'*Oui. En fait*, it is complicated in France. You need to talk to the INAO and Onivins. Onivins have changed their name and I don't remember what the new name is.'

'Vinifhlor,' I said. For once, I knew more than Cécile.

'*Oui, exact*. The INAO can give you free rights if you are *jeunes agriculteurs*, up to half a hectare a year. If not, you have to go to Vinifhlor and buy the rights.'

'Fantastic.' I was getting excited.

'I think you will have trouble getting the rights for *jeunes agriculteurs* because you didn't get onto the programme at the start. Sometimes it's confusing in France. If you get in at one level you go all the way, otherwise you are excluded from everything.'

It didn't sound fair. We should be able to plant what we wanted, where we wanted. This quota system was archaic.

We moved onto the agricultural aspects of planting vines on the old peach field.

'Is the soil prepared?' asked Cécile.

Sean and I exchanged a look. 'Have you worked the soil?' said Cécile having reworked the question so we could understand it.

'Yes,' we both replied.

'But I think with all the roots from the peaches you must make sure it is well prepared. You need to plough it with a *charrue*. But make sure you don't go too deep or you could destroy the soil structure and do more damage than good.'

I turned to Sean. 'Do you know what that is?'

'Yes.'

'Do we have one?'

'No.'

'It would also be better to plant a cover crop of barley,' said Cécile, surging on regardless of my confusion. 'But to do that you need a *semi*.'

Again I turned to Sean. 'Do you know what that is?'

'Yes.'

'Do we have one?'

'No.'

We all laughed like lunatics – it was déjà vu to our first meeting when Cécile had cracked up after realising how little we knew.

*'Tant pis,'* said Cécile. 'It's not critical. If you leave it for another year and work it again in the spring it will be as good, maybe better. We don't want to agitate more limestone into the soil.'

Given the difficulties we were having getting planting rights I didn't think waiting another year would be a problem. I called the INAO and explained what we were looking for.

'If you aren't registered as a *jeune agriculteur*, we can't help you,' said Madame.

'But we are under forty and we are farmers.'

'I know, but if you don't have the *jeune agriculteur* registration there is nothing we can do.'

'So how do I get rights without the registration? Can I buy the rights?'

'You can't. As of this year there are no rights outside of the *jeune agriculteur* rights. You have to buy vineyards that are already planted or hire a vineyard that is already planted.'

This was French wine bureaucracy at its zenith. We had a field of ideal vineyard land 100 metres from our house and winery, right outside our tasting room, and we could not plant it. The only option was to find vineyards elsewhere, which was impractical as our farming equipment was not licensed for public roads, plus it went against our ecological ethos. It was crazy to go and buy land elsewhere when we had the perfect site that would bring us closer to operational equilibrium. My frustration reached fever pitch but I tried to remain calm.

'How do I become registered as a *jeune agriculteur*?' I asked.

'Call the DDAF.' She gave me the number.

What followed was the usual French business call:

Me: 'Hello, please may I speak to Monsieur X.'

Madame: 'Sorry, Monsieur X only works on Tuesday and Wednesday mornings. Please phone back then between ten and twelve.'

I would look forward in my diary to find an available slot to call at exactly the time suggested. A few weeks later I called again on the suggested day.

Me: 'Hello, please may I speak to Monsieur X.'

Madame: 'Sorry, Monsieur X is on holiday please call back next week.'

And so on. I finally got in touch with Monsieur X and discovered that the only way to get the *dotation* (official status) was to have a *jeune agriculteur* specific loan on purchase of the property or on a related investment very soon after the purchase. The doors seemed to be closed.

A few days later, however, in a chance discussion with Cécile at our weekly meeting, we realised that the previous owners had not declared their *arrachage* or 'grubbing up' of a small vineyard a few years before. Grubbing up is the removal of old vines from a vineyard no longer in production. If they had declared this grubbing up, as was legally required, the rights for the vineyard would be available to plant elsewhere on the property, for up to eight years. Cécile thought it had been grubbed up about five years before so she was hopeful we would be able to use these rights.

I called the *douanes*, the French customs department, who controlled active vineyard planting rights, and asked if there was any hope for us to declare the *arrachage* and reclaim the rights.

'*Ça dépend,*' said Madame, the same lady who had helped me through the 'you have no white vines' crisis. 'Write us a letter and we will look into it.'

A few months later two *douanes* officials arrived at the property to verify that the vineyard was indeed grubbed up. It was easy to see where the vineyard had been as the trellising poles were still in place.

'The problem is that we don't know when it was grubbed up,' said Madame. 'Unless we can verify that it was in the year you claim, we won't be able to help you.'

The future looked uncertain for the old peach field. A month later Madame from the *douanes* called me.

'We found a reference to the vineyard in a *contrôle* by one of our officials the year before you claim it was pulled up so we can permit you to do a late *déclaration d'arrachage*.'

Christmas had arrived.

'*Par contre*, the previous owners overplanted by four ares which we will have to subtract from the rights and you will have to pay a ninety-euro fine for the late declaration. You must come into our offices to do the formalities.'

(There are 100 'ares' in a hectare, and for those on the imperial system 1 hectare is equal to 2,47 acres, which are not the same as ares.)

'No problem,' I said quickly.

The reduction meant my Christmas present was down by 10 per cent but I felt like I had conquered the world. We still had to plant it and then wait five years, of course. To get aid for the planting of the vineyard we would have to plant at a higher density which meant buying a new tractor and associated machinery. That was a dilemma for another day. At least this small success meant there was hope for a portion of the old peach field getting productive again.

Sophia was going to school and enjoying it, Ellie was back to playing happily on her own even when I did such boring things – to her – as working on our direct sales campaigns. There was something about me being on the PC that generally made the kids want to interrupt. If I was doing something physical like gardening, cooking or hanging up washing they were happy to play alongside. Sean took time with the girls in the evenings playing and reading stories. I had noticed that his dad had been the same. I would often find John sitting head bowed deep in conversation with two small girls showing them something – a leaf from a tree, a ladybird, an acorn. Now that the harvest was over Sean shared the cooking duties like he used to; although washing and cleaning the house, which we had shared in Dublin, were still all left to me. He was back to being the person I knew. The four months around harvest time had been like living with a stranger. I still felt a little raw and suspicious but I cancelled my flight reservation. It would take time for the trust in our relationship to rebuild.

Sean steadily made his way through his second year of pruning. One Sunday working in Hillside he heard hunting dogs. A giant wild boar dashed up the vineyard about 20 metres away from him and made for our small oak forest, followed by dogs and hunters. Sean waved frantically and yelled full throttle.

We were a *chasse interdite* area, so no hunting should take place on our land, but it was his own survival he was worried about, expecting a shot to come flying in his direction. Before the hunters reached Sean, the boar came roaring back, leapt off the cliff above the vineyard, sailed several metres through the air and landed in the row next door. He sped past without giving Sean a glance and barrelled up the other side of the valley. By the time he reached Gageac the dogs were so far behind him Sean was sure he had got away. Having come so close to tusks that could have slashed him into small portions, never mind the gunshots, Sean took an early lunch to recover.

While Sean tackled pruning in freezing temperatures, wild boar and gunshots, I zoned in on point three in 'operation survival': assessing the viability of a holiday house, or more specifically an 'eco' holiday house. The 'eco' was for environmental but also for economic. We had to do this on a shoestring. Internet research yielded wooden cabins, composting toilets and other innovative solutions. Even if we did most of the work ourselves, a new holiday house would cost us a hundred thousand euro. Banks were not giving loans against properties with vineyards because of the risk. In addition, since it would be a new building, there was no guarantee we would get planning permission. Construction bureaucracy sounded like it could rival vineyard rights.

Helen and Derek, friends from New Zealand who were on a six-month trip to see their sons, both of whom lived in France, arrived to give Sean a hand with vineyard maintenance. I worried that retirees might not be up to jobs like pulling the wood – removing unwanted vine growth from the trellising – and was dreading another bout of 'Sean the Recluse'.

Helen was blonde with wonderful apple cheeks, the look of a happy chef and a gift for creating gourmet delights. Derek was witty and wiry, with a doctorate from MIT, but preferred to spend his days making furniture or growing olives on their smallholding. Sean showed them how to pull the wood in the sémillon vineyard then came up for a meeting with a bottle supplier. At lunch Helen and Derek returned.

'We've finished the vineyard,' said Derek. 'What can we do next?'

We had estimated two days to get through that work.

'You can relax this afternoon. I don't think Sean has finished pruning the next vineyard,' I said.

'We want to clear the brush around the cliffs near the hangar. It looks like a satisfying job. I think it will take about three days.'

'How will you do it?' Sean and I had looked at the wall of brush he was referring to and decided it was not a job for a man, but for a very large machine. The brush was 5 metres deep, 3 metres high and about 100 metres long.

'With your chainsaw that I saw in the shed. I'll cut it down with the chainsaw, Helen will help me pull it out, then we'll burn it.'

Derek had sussed out the brush and done an inventory of our tools. The next day when I went down to give them a hand they had uncovered the first section of a magnificent amphitheatre of white cliffs that had been the old quarry. Derek cut back swathes of plant matter then Helen dragged the trees and brush out to feed the bonfire. Some of the brambles were as thick as a man's arm and 50 metres long.

When Sean came up from pruning and saw what they had done he said, 'We're wimps.'

On the third day they moved up to the section on top of the cliff. This dense wall of wood ran from the tasting room to the far side of the winery. From the vineyard below we could see there was something on the back of the winery, perhaps old rabbit cages. Sean and I had tried to reach it by cutting a path through the wood a few months before, and failed. It was like Sleeping Beauty's forest, impenetrable. Or so I thought.

Sean got back that evening exploding with excitement. 'Come and look, Carolinus!'

Around the side of the tasting room, a magnificent view had opened up, and the building wasn't old rabbit cages: it was a solid stone structure on two levels of 20 square metres each. To the side of it were two tiny, low stone buildings. It was a miracle.

The following day I visited Tim, our building engineer friend who had helped Sean with the tasting room roof, armed with photos and hoping to get some ideas for how to transform this ruin into a gîte, a self-catering cottage.

'Is the building on the *cadastrale*?'

'I don't know.' We had a copy of the *cadastrale*, or commune map, of our property which included all the official buildings, but I hadn't thought to look at it.

'If it is you should get planning permission more easily. It looks solid from the photos. I'll have a look next time I'm over your way.'

As soon as I got home I checked the *cadastrale* and found the ruin on it. I was over the moon with excitement.

That Christmas, we sold the last of the stock we'd bought. Now the pressure was on to finish the new wines as we needed some to sell.

While the whites and the rosé were behaving like perfect children, the reds were unwilling teenagers. They had made it through their alcoholic fermentation but steadfastly refused to progress with their malolactic fermentation (often referred to simply as 'malos'): the process in which tart malic acid is transformed into softer lactic acid. It is a natural deacidification allowed to take place in almost all red wines save those like beaujolais nouveau, the light red wine that is bottled immediately after its alcoholic fermentation, but mostly avoided in white wines so they keep their fresh Granny Smith apple acidity. Sean diligently heated the wines to the optimal temperature, monitoring and carefully timing our equipment which, of course, was far from automated.

Meanwhile, to heat the house we bought a wood-burning stove to augment our struggling system. After the purchase the installer explained that the old exit pipe was no good as it passed through the wall horizontally so would never draw correctly. Creating a new exit would be difficult in our 300-year-old building with walls almost a metre thick. It needed a minimum of a 45-degree angle so the hole had to traverse about 2 metres of wall. We spent hours trying to find an elegant solution.

In the roof over the lounge was something that looked like a chimney. It ran through our upstairs bathroom then stopped, concreted over where it should have come out in the lounge below. Why hadn't the previous owners used it instead of cracking through the wall at right angles? It didn't make any sense. Sean climbed onto the roof and verified it had all the makings of a chimney.

We didn't want to crack through our beautiful ceiling that had taken my parents weeks to renovate without being sure so we decided to contact the family that owned the property for fifty years prior to the people we bought from. We had not met Monsieur and Madame Battistella but we had heard a lot about them. Monsieur Bonny was a close friend of theirs so I asked him for an introduction.

The Battistellas arrived in a smart new car. A fit and handsome couple, they looked like prosperous, retired bankers rather than winegrowers wizened by decades of hard work. Monsieur told us that heart problems had forced him to sell the property. I completely understood: with the quantities of chocolate I needed to manage the stress of Garrigue I was sure I would have heart problems in a few years myself.

'*Vous avez fait des travaux!*' said Monsieur Battistella. 'It's good to see Garrigue getting back its beauty. We had gardens all around the house. And down here,' he pointed to the jungle to the left of the house 'there are stone stairs down to a well. We built the chimney with the second level of the house but never used it. It will work perfectly. Now, when can I collect my two hundred litres of red wine?'

We had forgotten the *ancien droit* that meant we had to hand over 200 litres of our precious wine to Monsieur Battistella.

'The malos aren't finished,' said Sean. 'You can have some white in the meantime. We'll call you when it's ready.'

Monsieur Battistella took a few litres of dry white but he wanted red. After the sweat that had gone into it, handing the wine over for free was difficult. But the chimney meant our flue would remain inside the house, providing more warmth than if it had gone up the exterior wall, and the bathroom would be toasty in winter. That was worth at least 200 litres, if the malos ever finished. We regularly did a malo paper test and intermittently a laboratory test but we had heard that it was possible to tell just by looking at the wine: little bubbles would appear and it would become lively, plus if we put an ear to the barrel we would hear a 'pop-pop' like popcorn. Sean was worried. He continued to heat the red wine but nothing was happening.

The wood stove was installed with a perfect exit through the chimney, just in time for the serious cold of December. On Christmas Eve I took the girls up to bed and returned to find Sean listening to Christy Moore with tears rolling down his cheeks. This was the third time in our lives I had seen Sean crying. The first was on Sophia's tumultuous first day of her life, the second was when I announced I was leaving.

'What's happened?' I said, worried sick that one of our parents had died.

'I miss home, Carolinus.'

I sat down and we talked about the things we both missed about Christmas in Dublin: swimming at White Rock in freezing temperatures on Christmas morning to help clear the head after too much wine, walking up the Sugar Loaf in Wicklow on St Stephen's Day, but most of all our friends and the craic.

The life of a vigneron was solitary, even though friends and family came and went. It was stressful, risky and lonely. But it was also wonderful. We were following our dream and we were working towards a new life that despite our current circumstances was full of hope. We shared a bottle of wine in front of the newly installed woodstove. With the lights off, the fire bathed the room in a warm, romantic glow. It felt like years since we had sat quietly together.

Sean's shoulder-length curls gleamed golden. He was fitter and stronger than ever. The magic of candlelight made me feel twenty-something again. We made love in front of the fire with the abandon that we had known when we first met. It was like a tsunami crashing through all the hurt of the previous six months.

'That stove was a great investment,' said Sean.

As the new year got underway Sean continued to heat the red wines for malolactic fermentation but there was no sign of progress. We decided to stop heating all except one. It was better for the wine to develop at its own natural pace.

The house boiler stopped working. It was a while since I had called Jean-Marc and it was good to hear his upbeat voice on the phone.

'A simple restart may be all that's needed. Press the red restart button on the boiler.'

I pressed but nothing happened, then I realised I was pressing the emergency light instead of the large red restart button. Lucky I was mostly just the housewife and not operating wine-related machinery. I pressed the correct button and the boiler leapt into life.

'*Ça fonctionne?*' asked Jean-Marc patiently.

'Oui.'

'*Ça fonctionne! A demain?*' (Until tomorrow?)

Three days later the boiler stopped and the restart would not work. Jean-Marc blamed our fuel provider for giving us dirty fuel and suggested his brother-in-law as a supplier. After he had fixed the boiler I showed him the ruin Helen and Derek had uncovered and asked if he could give me a quote for solar power and a bathroom.

*'Quelle vue!'* enthused Jean-Marc as we walked around the winery to the newly uncovered building, facing south up the valley of Saussignac. On our side, the peaceful winter vines were white with frost; on the opposite side a stark winter forest clung to the hillside. To the south Saussignac Castle rose like a giant keeping watch over the village.

'We could get water here no problem. I'm not an expert on solar panels but I think we could get good exposure on the roof that's facing due south.'

He promised to send his patron, the good-looking Monsieur Lambert, around to get the details so they could provide a *devis*. In true Lambert fashion I heard nothing for months.

There was still no sign of the malolactic fermentation in the red wines and the white wines had gone flat, their aromas were muted and the flavour seemed dull compared to before. Sean was worried sick but Lucille assured him it was normal for young white wines to 'close up' in winter.

# Chapter 13

# Goodbye Owl, Hello Château

Despite our fears about the wines we got on with planning our first bottling. Sean invited a bottling company to a meeting so they could explain the choices for this auspicious process. Jean-Philippe arrived in a smart suit. He talked a lot but didn't tell Sean anything.

'We need to make sure we get everything right well in advance of the bottling: bottles, corks, capsules, labels, people, machinery. We stress before the day, not on the day and absolutely not after the day.'

'But how much does it cost?' asked Sean.

'I'll send you a quote.'

'What choices do we have?'

'I'll send you the options.'

Sean told him exactly how much wine we planned to bottle and Jean-Phillippe said he could organise bottles, corks and the bottling plant; all we had to sort out were the labels.

We had been working on label ideas for months. We sent a presentation of our ideas to ten friends. I liked the image of an owl that was on a third of the label examples. I felt it gave the messages we wanted to deliver: natural, elegant, powerful; plus, we had one living in the roof. Soon responses were pouring in.

'The owl looks like an Australian brand. You need to look more French.'

'I'll be brutally frank, you cannot have a sun which conjures up images of light, alongside an owl which conjures up night-time images.' It was supposed to be a moon but client's perception is everything. 'We like the curly writing and the French look of your original label.'

'Do not use curly writing. No one can read the words.'

'The owl makes it look like Wolf Blass. Not what I would buy, but maybe you'll appeal to the average punter.'

'The owl makes it look like whiskey. You need to have a picture of a château on the label so you look French.'

'All the wines with a château on the label look the same. I can never remember what it was so I never buy it again even if I like it.'

There was no 'one size fits all' solution in wine labelling. Our first bottling was approaching fast. This was no time for confusion but we were thoroughly confused. But the feedback on the owl was clear, it would get Garrigue confused with whiskey, Australian wine and who knows what else. We axed the owl and created a new label with the outline of a roof or a mountain and a moon… or a sun depending on the client's perspective.

I sent copies of the label to the two wine buyers I had met on my marketing trip.

'I like your label. Smart.'

'Good, clean label,' said the other.

We decided to go ahead with the design. There was no time for any more trials. We'd still had no quotes or options from the smartly dressed Jean-Philippe. A few people recommended a local independent bottler so I called and he came round that evening.

Pierre de Saint Viance looked like someone out of *Asterix*. He was solid and red-haired with the air of a temper that would flare fast and be assuaged as quickly, but his keen sense of humour was to the fore. At that first meeting he gave Sean all the information he needed; his tariffs, suppliers of bottles, corks and capsules; who to contact and more.

'Make sure they give you the preferential rates they have agreed with me,' said Pierre.

In less than an hour we had all we needed. We were euphoric.

'Have you received your *agréments* yet?' asked Pierre.

'No, I need to get them this week,' said Sean.

Our labels had to state the details of our AOC so we needed our wine of origin agreements quickly. This approval was based on a laboratory analysis and panel-tasting of the wine. If the wine received the thumbs-up we would be able to call it AOC; if not, we would have to call it '*vin de table*'.

While the French AOC system is rigorously controlled and each wine appellation – there are around 400 – has their own production rules, *vin de table* or table wine has no quality controls but must comply with EU regulations. It is typically associated with large-scale industrial production, although many quality wines are appearing under *vin de table* to avoid the constraints of the AOC.

We didn't have any concerns about the wines as their analysis was perfect and their taste had changed dramatically from their mid-winter doldrums. It was hard to believe they were the same wines; they were 'absolutely delicious' as the French *Reader's Digest* magazine said in an article at the time. They had called us up out of the blue after finding us on the Internet hoping to include us in an article about farmers in the Périgord. The journalists had taken some great photos, tasted through our range of wines and written a very positive article. Feeling confident, thanks to that and what our own taste buds told us, we sent in the paperwork and a few days later the wine samples were collected.

In France there is a dedicated police force called 'the Fraud Squad' who make sure that labelling is correct and within the rules. There is no room for loose marketing statements. An error on a label can result in a fine or worse as a winegrower friend who had also been a wine merchant had recounted.

'For a small mistake on a label I spent several weeks getting to know the interior of the Sainte-Foy prison,' he said. 'It was incredible. I had no idea what I was in for; they arrested me and threw me into prison. My lawyer came round and I asked, "How long until you get me out of here?" He said, "Best case scenario, if you are innocent, six months." You can imagine what that was like.'

His wife pulled a face that said it all. In the end he was there for eighteen days for a tiny error on a label that he hadn't known was an error. He spent Christmas in jail, not knowing what he had done, as the wine was sold to him as one thing but it turned out to be another.

Clearly what we put onto the labels had to be certified to the letter.

Three weeks later the results of the AOC request arrived. Our whites had passed but the rosé had failed. The comment was 'herbaceous'. Since the failure was due to the tasting, not the analysis, we could resubmit if we wanted to, but it would cost us another full set of fees. Lucille arrived and we tasted the rosé together. It was sublime; crushed strawberries with a long finish, ideally suited to the markets we were targeting, dry but deliciously fruity.

'I can't believe they failed this wine,' I said.

'Perhaps the panel tasted a sweet rosé before yours and it made it too dry for them. There is no limit on the amount of residual sugar in Bergerac rosé,' said Lucille.

'But "herbaceous"? I get no herbaceousness on this wine.'

'Me neither,' said Lucille. 'You must resubmit.'

'No way,' said Sean. 'On principle I won't. If they fail wines like this I don't want to be part of this AOC. Anyway, it's too expensive to resubmit for such a small run. It adds a euro a case to this wine which is already expensive to produce.'

I too was beginning to doubt the AOC. When it came to Bergerac no one had heard of it. Perhaps we were better off without it. On the down side, *vin de table* was also bristling with constraints. We could not put the vintage, the varietal or the word château on the label. Most New World wines, unhindered by AOC, could use all these elements and more on their wines without tests or tasting panels.

In March I plumbed the depths of despair. Perhaps there was a seasonal element to my emotional valleys but there was also a hard reality. We continued to haemorrhage cash. We did not have enough money to pay for the bottling.

My parents arrived for a two-week visit. They were in a different zone to us; retired and living a life of comfort in North America with not a lot to worry about except their next round of golf. My dad could not understand why we were putting ourselves through so much to follow our dream. He saw the exceptional work, both physical and mental, the challenges of a new country and the financial stress, and could not fathom what had made us leave good jobs in the city.

'This house is a corridor of crisis,' he said, 'just look around.' He pointed to the chaos that accompanies two small children with time-starved parents. 'You can't carry on at this pace. You'll be dead before you reach retirement. You'll be old before your time.'

I explained that life in a start-up is always tough and more so for us with a new language and culture as well. He ignored me and continued his tirade.

After two weeks of his harrying and repeating 'this house is a corridor of crisis', I wondered if we were completely mad. But one evening, momentarily overcome by the exuberance of a couple of whiskeys followed by a glass of Haut Garrigue, my dad broke into a Zulu dance. Ellie, who had been sick, was ecstatic. For the first time in days she brightened up.

'Dance, Grand-père! Dance!' she commanded. Grand-père, nervous at the Napoleonic style of his granddaughter's request, continued to dance. For the next couple of days Ellie kept Grand-père away from his thoughts of the corridor of crisis with regular commands of 'Dance, Grand-père! Dance!'

Ellie was at the tail-end of an ear infection combined with a tummy bug that had left us with little clean linen. Her bedtime prayer said it all.

'Dear God,

'Thanks you for making Ellie better. Thanks you for making Sophia better. Thanks you for making Daddy better. And Dear God thanks you for making Grand-père dance.

'Amen.'

An invitation to attend a dinner hosted by one of the major cork manufacturers was perfectly timed since we needed to make our decision about which corks to use for our bottling. Bottling was a minefield and the responsibility for each of these elements was with us. We had to get to grips with it and make the right choice. I took copious notes.

Cork trees only produce enough cork to be harvested at about twenty years of age but they live for hundreds of years if managed and harvested correctly. The quality of the cork and the care of that cork after harvest are paramount to good wine. Corked wine, created by trichloranisole (TCA), a bacteria found in cork, has a nasty smell like mouldy newspaper, wet dog or a damp basement. Depending on the level of TCA, this odour can be anything from a faint hint to complete contamination, leaving the wine undrinkable. While there is no health risk, even a hint dramatically reduces the enjoyment of a wine. TCA is largely why screw caps have gained ground recently.

'Don't worry about the length of your cork, the quality is what's important,' said the presenter.

'That's what I always say. It's the structure, not the length,' said Regis, a wine producer from the Pécharmant appellation. Chuckles rippled round the room.

'Make sure when you're putting the corks in you don't go too fast, and keep the bottles upright for three minutes before they are boxed.'

'Yes, but you shouldn't go too slowly either. I find you need to keep a good regular pace,' said Jean-Paul, a winemaker from Saussignac, and laughter rippled again.

A year before I would not have known a good cork if it bit me. But the never-ending debate of wine closures came up regularly at community events like the Saussignac growers' evening.

'I would not use plastic,' said Jean-Marie. 'You know, I did a test with some yogurt. I put it at the bottom of my fridge for two years. It was fine when I opened it, no mould at all, but it tasted of plastic. That's food-grade plastic, like what they use for plastic corks. I wouldn't want that in my wine.'

'And they use plastic on the interior of the screw caps,' said Thierry.

If the wine was stored for a long time with either of these options, they could leave a taste of plastic and a hormone disrupter in the wine.

Sean decided on closures made from natural cork but treated to be guaranteed free of cork taint. With the components for the bottling finalised we made our spring offer to our regular customers. We needed to plan how much wine to box. Wine that is fully dressed and boxed should be sold within six months or the labels and boxes degrade. A wrong estimate either way is costly. We expected a bumper response since it was the first wine made by us. But many customers emailed to say their cellar was stocked after massive February wine sales.

I did a quick survey of the main wine retailers and found that the wine crisis was biting hard. I had read that New World producers, whose costs were a fraction of European producers', were flooding the market and that in an effort to compete, French producers had cut prices to well below cost. My survey confirmed that good French wines were selling for 25 per cent less than when we left Dublin almost two years before. Winemakers were slashing prices to offload stock. The comfortable, secure life we had left suddenly looked very appealing.

Sean sent vat samples of our wine to our highest priority target client, a chain of about twenty-five wine shops.

The client tasted them and asked us to send samples of the finished wines when they were ready. I was totally depressed. What was I expecting? An immediate order for all the production we had? I bemoaned the situation to Fiona Kingwill.

'You sent him unfinished samples? It's suicide! Don't ever do that. We were tempted into doing it with our reds in the early days. People said "Wine buyers will be able to project forward what the wine will be like". It's not true. What a disaster. Many of the people we sent the samples to would not take calls from us after that. The wines were too raw. We ruined a host of contacts. Wine buyers are not winemakers. They are not used to tasting unfinished wine.'

I felt the familiar ball of nausea in my stomach.

'So what do we do?'

'You have to make the investment in the bottling and hope it all works out.'

With the lead times required for the dry components it was impossible to put off bottling and still fulfil demand in time. Investing in bottling was a risk we had to take. We had to have faith. Our wines were good. The bottling bills would only need to be paid two months after and we would have to have closed some sales by then.

Bottling needed a minimum of three people alongside Pierre, so my parents were co-opted into giving a hand. On the auspicious day Pierre quickly set up his bottling unit, sterilised it and charged the stations with bottling material. My dad was selected to stack the bottles onto the machine. Mum took the capsuled and labelled bottles off the machine, boxed them and pushed the box through the taping machine. Sean took the finished boxes off the line and stacked them onto pallets.

As the first finished wines came off the line I felt a surge of pride. It was like watching Sophia go to her first day of school. Those wines were part of us and had our hopes and dreams tied up inside them.

Pierre zoomed around on the forklift making sure each point in the bottling unit was stocked, stacking pallets into our storeroom and sorting out hitches along the way. I made regular batches of tea and biscuits while Ellie was a perfect angel, playing for hours in the corridor of crisis and spreading her play zone throughout the lounge and kitchen. It was a demanding two days that kept Dad too busy to make any comments about the fast-extending corridor. The tough physical work involved only served to confirm for him that we had truly gone off our trolleys.

'We've got spare time, let me give you a tour of my château,' said Pierre as we finished. We piled into his car. Having never visited the private parts of Saussignac Castle, I was ecstatic at the opportunity. The commune owned one wing and I had been there for events like the annual 'Arts au Château' and the Christmas market. The private sections were owned by a diverse cosmopolitan group: one of the two main towers by two American artists, the other by an English family who used it as their holiday house. Pierre owned the middle section while the wing opposite the one owned by the commune was split in two: one part owned by a local French family that didn't use it and a second part owned by a Kiwi man and his French wife who spent half their year selling antiques in Auckland and the other half sourcing them from their pied-à-terre in France.

Over the couple of days of bottling we had come to realise that Pierre approached life with vigour. His work was bottling but his life was his family and his passion was motor cars. He collected ancient ones and did rally driving in his spare time. When he wasn't rally driving or bottling he was with his family working on renovations to his castle. I couldn't wait to see it.

The kilometre route from Garrigue to Saussignac runs past Les Tours de Lenvège then sweeps up, surrounded by vineyards, to the village. Saussignac Castle, with its massive, perfect stones, likely cut from the quarry at Garrigue, dominates the scene.

Pierre bowed nobly at the door with a sweep of his arm as we walked in. A brocaded curtain hung across a stone entrance that led from the imposing hallway into the grand salon. In the open-plan kitchen, at the entrance to this great room, a stately woman with dark hair and fair skin was slicing fresh carrots for a salad. Pierre introduced Laurence, his wife.

The castle was beautiful outside but the interior was breathtaking. Vaulted stone ceilings soared high overhead creating immense grandeur: proportions from an age where space, labour and stone were plentiful, although even then it was possible to run out of money: the front towers of the château would have been matched by two replica towers at the back but for lack of finance.

'When we arrived this room was split into five rooms with dry walls,' said Pierre. 'All these stones were covered with mortar. We planned to put the kitchen at the far end but I pulled away the tiny 1970s fireplace to discover this.' He pointed to the massive château fireplace large enough to hold ten adults standing comfortably at full height. 'I ran to Laurence and said, "Sorry, we can't put your kitchen in!"'

'And I'm still waiting,' said Laurence drily, her hand waving over the half-installed cupboards and the oven still sitting in a box in the corner. She had been making do for three years. Pierre studiously ignored the comment.

'Removing the mortar covering the stones was the hardest job, especially where the mix was more concrete than chalk. Come, let's go upstairs.'

Pierre motioned upwards and led us up another level. Pierre and Laurence's piece of the castle was about one fifth of the total but they had enough space for a family of ten. The staircase, made of stone slabs about 2 metres wide, wound around storage rooms that formed what would have been a giant-size stairwell.

The upper section, their living area, was still in progress with skirting boards and some doors and electrical points unfinished. Pierre had split the equivalent space of their grand room, just one level up, into three comfortable bedrooms, a bathroom and a study. The stone walls, high ceilings and windows – offering spring blossom views towards our farm and the Dordogne valley beyond – provided instant grandeur.

'Now I show you the dungeon, where the real history lies,' said Pierre. We descended to the gloomy basement.

'This seventeenth-century castle is built on the site of a monastery from Celtic times.'

We followed, obediently picking our way carefully through the murk. Pierre showed us his well, which dated back at least a thousand years.

'There are no prison cells here but we do have a secret tunnel.'

He led us further into the obscurity along a wooden plank that balanced precariously over a very uneven stone floor.

*'Et voilà!'* In the castle wall was a vaulted doorway leading into a tunnel completely filled in with loose stone. 'We don't know why it is filled in. Perhaps it was a rock fall. Perhaps it was to keep some treasure secret from the Germans in the war. Folklore says that a tunnel from the castle leads to Garrigue. Maybe we'll explore it one day.' Pierre smiled conspiratorially and turned to lead us out of the basement.

Laurence was putting on running shoes as we said goodbye.

'Do you run?' I asked. Laurence looked the quintessential French lady, not one who beat the pavements.

'A leetoll.'

'We must run together. How about this Sunday?'

'Why not?'

And so, that Sunday we started our regular runs, which offered me a stress-buster, an opportunity to talk French on subjects beyond wine and a closer look at French psychology and history. Laurence was a teacher's assistant and starting preparations for a full teacher's certificate. She was a delicious fountain of French culture and was into organic food and natural remedies. We struck a chord.

On our runs we sometimes met deer and other four-legged creatures. One morning, as we were running up the road to Gageac, the sun highlighting clouds of our breath, a volley of gunshots shattered the peace. We both yelled. A hunter swaggered out of the trees swinging his gun nonchalantly on his shoulder.

'People get killed every year in hunting accidents,' said Laurence, not very reassuringly. We ran the rest of the hill at astonishing speed.

Sean and I had our first wine bottled and were beginning to realise how long a game wine was. Each of our wines took a minimum of eighteen months and sometimes, for the reds, up to six years to get from pruning to bottling. Add to that new vineyards, which need five years to reach reasonable levels of production, and a winegrower can be looking at more than ten years of patience and investment from planting to bottle. Our financial plan had not taken a sufficiently long view. We were out of money.

We glared at each other over the candle. Financial stress was not helping the recovery of our relationship. Sean was working crazy hours and getting no compensation. At times we resented each other for the position we were in. Since it was a joint decision at least we felt solidarity in our resentment.

'Perhaps we could get a short-term loan from the bank,' said Sean.

I shook my head. 'We have no track record of selling bottled wine in any volume. Anyway, one of our core tenets from the start was that we would not risk this so far that we would become indebted for it. For our sanity and the kids' future we have to stick to that. The day we have to take out a loan for the day-to-day running of the business, it's over.'

That was a fairly solid line in the sand. The candle flickered ominously and went out.

'Feck it,' said Sean. 'What are we going to do?'

'Light it again.'

'No, I mean about the bottling costs.'

'We'll have to get some wine sales fast. Our creditors will have to wait.'

We knew what we wanted to do and where we wanted to go with our business. We wanted to produce high-quality, natural wines. We knew a growing part of the wine market wanted a real taste of terroir and not a trick of additives but we were running out of time and we had no idea how long it would take us to break even, if ever.

Meanwhile, Lucille had invited me to a presentation on cultured yeasts and natural additives like tannins for winemaking. In the European Union, unnatural wine additives are illegal but in some other jurisdictions winemakers can put in chemical elixirs that will add anything from lychee to chocolate flavours to their wines. The event, which included dinner, was to be held at one of the iconic vineyards in the region. As I drove up the sun was setting over the hills beyond Château Belingard creating layers of rolling hills bathed in pink and gold light. It was so postcard perfect I took a minute to walk around the garden before my entrance and the obligatory *bisous*.

Rows and rows of red wines were set up on the table. In each instance we compared an original wine with the same wine dosed with one of the additives. By the end of the evening I was convinced that additives, even natural ones, were a bad idea. Of all the wines I tasted only one tasted better with additives and that wine was hollow to start. In all instances where the original wine was good, the additives put the wine out of equilibrium. Something did not ring true. After several flights – the term used for a set of wines in a tasting – I also learnt that wearing a white shirt to a red wine tasting is not a good idea.

Each winemaker had brought a couple of examples of his own wine to have with the meal. Our modern label stood out on the table and vignerons around me reached for the bottle to try something new. I could see from their faces they were surprised that idiots from the city with no experience in this complex métier could produce a drinkable wine. Jean-Paul, a winemaker from Saussignac, tasted his glass.

'*Bon, très bon, même. C'est plein d'espoir*. (It's full of hope.) The first vintage is always full of hope.'

# Chapter 14

# Lessons in Lunacy

The reaction from our target customer was so non-committal on the vat samples that we decided to broaden our net. Sean sent bottles of finished wine to two other buyers and I booked another marketing trip. I had no experience selling wine to trade buyers and we had no track record in the wine business. On my previous trip I had spoken to a few journalists – like the radio interview – to promote our direct sales and met a few proprietors of individual wine shops to get a feel for the market but I hadn't contacted any serious buyers. Now I had to face the music and I was scared. I organised my trip around key visits then set up to meet journalists and drop off samples. We had to sell our wine and we had to sell it at a price that could support our hand-crafted production methods.

Sean took me to Bordeaux airport, coaching me all the way about how important it was for me to close some sales and loading on unnecessary extra pressure. My flight went smoothly and once again I picked up my hire car. It was a full year since my last trip. Between my fear of selling and my new fear of city-driving

I wondered how I would last the week. I arrived at Aideen and Barry's haven and took a moment to breathe in the familiar air.

'I could move back tomorrow,' I said, tucking into Barry's delicious pan-fried salmon.

'Not really,' said Aideen recalling how she'd seen me so at home with the Saussignac winegrowers. 'Wait until you're sitting on the ring road trying to get to an urgent meeting.'

We talked until midnight. The days flew. I met wine importers, dropped off samples, offered wine tastings at friends' houses and talked to wine journalists. I almost felt confident talking about the wines that were now part of us, and yet I neared the end of my stay with no sales in sight. Sean called every evening for news. It was stressful beyond measure.

On Saturday I met with one of our target buyers, responsible for wine purchases across a chain of around twenty upmarket supermarkets. He had been open and positive when we spoke on the phone. His employer was large enough to buy all the production we had available for sale to the trade. I had high hopes for the meeting.

We ordered our coffees and sat down at a stylish two-person table near the window of the plush cafe. I talked him through the vineyard, our plans and the wines. He asked questions and actively engaged in my pitch. We discussed the quantities they would need for different promotions as compared to an annual stock item. He explained they would probably include us in their annual French wine promotion as a first trial. I told him the prices and he didn't baulk. This was just the break we needed.

I was convinced I had a sale. 'So when do you need to order for the promotion?' I asked.

'Around August but I can't commit yet. We like the wines and your story but I need to talk to our consultant before making a buying decision. If we don't go for the 2006, we'll look at the 2007.'

I tried not to show my disappointment, swallowed the rest of my coffee and prepared to leave. We couldn't work with decisions by committee; we didn't have that sort of time.

'Thierry was right. It's a long sales cycle,' I said to Sean that evening.

'Well, tough luck for them. If they don't get in on the 2006, they won't get a look in on the 2007.'

Sean sounded bullish, but he wasn't the one meeting the buyers.

That evening Aideen and Barry organised a dinner with old friends. No longer was a dinner simply a chance to socialise: our wines were on show. It was great to see old friends but I couldn't relax.

'I love this rosé,' said Doug, 'not so sure about the white.'

'It's a well-made wine,' said Conor.

Each comment was sparkles from heaven or a knife through my heart. This wine was so personal. Now wine was our life, no social occasion would ever be free of marketing or analysis if wine was involved. The next day I met a group of people I had worked with for many years for lunch. The jokes started flowing and I laughed until my sides ached. I missed this repartee. Our second bottle of New Zealand sauvignon blanc arrived and I sniffed it critically.

'That's exactly the same wine but can you pick up how smoky it is compared to the first bottle?' I asked.

'She's right, you know,' said Andrew, surprised. 'That is smoky and the first one had no smoke.'

Soon they were all sniffing and nodding, impressed that I could pick up such nuances in a wine. In the old days, as their colleague, I'd been someone who knew a bit about wine but not an expert. In the intervening two years I had become a winegrower.

The last day of my trip I met our highest priority target customer, the chain of twenty-five wine shops. Walking in with a copy of the cover story that had been published about us at the time of my previous trip, I tried to look confident. Dave had dark, somewhat unruly hair and was skinny and hyper with a disarming smile. His office was mayhem: strewn with samples of wine and marketing brochures awaiting his approval. He gave the impression of being disorganised but I realised through the meeting he was a savvy business man and a serious wine expert.

'I've seen the article. I really like your story,' said Dave. 'How did you get that coverage? If I could get half of the press coverage you've had, I would be happy.'

He was right: writing the story for the newspaper the previous year and lucky breaks through my business contacts – like the radio interview – had helped our direct business significantly. The way he spoke it was clear it was going to help us here as well. He was keen to try our wines.

I talked him through the vineyard and the white that was available and ended with some negotiation pressure.

'We need a decision fast as I have someone else who is interested in the wine,' I said, adding to myself, 'or our adventure will be over'. The statement was somewhat true since the other contact was interested, although it was clear they would never buy in time to save us. I kept a poker face despite total terror that this tactic could backfire. He looked surprised, clearly not used to buying competition in a flooded wine market and said, 'I'll taste the wines again and phone you before you leave to let you know.'

I still had no order to report back to Sean but at least I had met the decision maker, the person who had direct control over the buying decisions. I liked him. He was honest and direct.

That evening Dave called to announce his decision I tried to control the tremble in my voice. He was our only hope for a fast solution.

'I like the wines but I find them a bit light – sort of Italian style,' he said.

A dagger slashed through my heart, followed by an intense urge to remove him from our target list despite how much we needed him right then. 'But I like the story and I think your wines are only going to improve. I'm already looking forward to next year. I prefer the sauvignon blanc but the price is too high, it puts you into the price level of well-known Loire Valley sauvignons.'

'What price do you need?' I asked.

He put forward a figure that was way too low for our sauvignon.

'We can do the sémillon sauvignon for that,' I said, trying to remember the negotiation lessons I had learnt in my previous life.

Dave explained the different options for pricing and the impact they had on sales. If he promoted a wine it sold much faster and price point made all the difference.

'You see it depends on what you want to do with your wine. How fast you want it to sell determines the price you give us,' he said. He then proposed buying 250 cases at 10 per cent lower than the price I had offered.

'For that price I'll have to talk to Sean,' I said, sounding more assured than I felt.

'Talk to Sean and let us know by the end of the week.'

My hand that stretched out to put the phone on the kitchen counter was shaking like a leaf.

'Tell all,' said Aideen.

'He wants 250 cases of Château Haut Garrigue sémillon sauvignon blanc.'

'Yippee!'

Barry beamed at me. 'Well done.'

'But it's not at the price we wanted.'

'It doesn't matter. It's your first trade sale. Let's celebrate!' Aideen was over the moon.

'I got this present for you,' said Sean, handing over Nicolas Joly's book *Wine From Sky to Earth* when he collected me from the airport. He was alone: Sophia was at school and Ellie was playing with Alane at Sonia's. 'This is the path to exceptional wines.'

Nicolas Joly is one of the most famous biodynamic producers in France. His farm in the Loire Valley has been a vineyard for more than a thousand years. I had read a bit about him and his methods but I was sceptical. I felt like I had been given a school textbook as a gift. After the experiences of my trip I would have appreciated a book on how to sell wine rather than one on cow horns and lunar cycles.

'Thanks, SF. But we're going to need more than exceptional wines to make sales in this market. It's more than tough out there.'

'I know, Carolinus. But I think we have extraordinary terroir and with hard work and biodynamics we can do great things. You should read it.'

We quickly moved on to more pressing items, like following up our potential order. That evening I opened the book he gave me and started reading. Biodynamics is often called 'organics plus' or 'super organics'. We were farming organically and I was convinced, but the mystical activities like burying the cow dung in the cow horn at the autumn equinox and digging it out at the spring equinox to charge it with fertility were too much for me.

The book was so gripping, however, that I read deep into the night. Joly gave substance to the mystical elements. The dung buried in the cow horn in the right place at the right time had been proven to have hundreds of times more soil-boosting microbiological activity than the same mix buried in a clay pot.

I learnt that biodynamics consisted of two key parts: working with the calendar of the earth's position in relation to the moon and cosmos, and homeopathic-like preparations or treatments for the soil and plant.

For millennia man has used the sun, moon and stars to guide his agricultural activity. Early writers like Romans Columella (AD 4–*c.* AD 70) and Varro (116 BC–27 BC) noted elements we now think of as biodynamics. Before wristwatches we told the time via the sun, moon and stars. They determine much of what takes place on earth, although in the modern world it is easy to forget that and to think that the world revolves around us...

The moon moves the oceans; it has a major influence on water. So the moon's phases influence the way plants grow through the different levels of moisture in the environment and in the plant. The Romans noted that certain crops were more successful if planted when the moon was in a specific constellation or set of stars. The moon takes two to three days to pass through a constellation, so this offered a very specific window for different crops. This, and the location of the other planets in our solar system, is what determines the biodynamic day on the calendar and hence what a winegrower – or gardener – should prioritise for that day. They also noted that harvesting at the correct time meant the food lasted longer. This is because of how the plant stores the water in the fruit/crop at different times of the lunar cycle. Less water generally means better conservation.

The biodynamics used today has its roots in a series of lectures by Austrian philosopher-scientist Rudolf Steiner in 1924. With the onslaught of chemical agriculture after World War Two much of the agricultural wisdom of the previous two millennia was forgotten. Steiner's lectures helped to keep this knowledge safe for us.

Equally important is the overarching concept of a 'whole farm' self-sustaining system. The farm must not live on inputs from outside, it must achieve a natural equilibrium. If illness arises, the cause of the problem, not the symptom, is treated.

In a healthy, organically farmed vine, only 10 per cent of the plant is created by what it takes in from the soil. Only one tenth! The other 90 per cent is created by its complex relationship with the rest of the elements around it, particularly the sun. Plants are miraculous in their ability to take the sun's energy and transform it into energy like starch and sugar that we can eat. If a vine is offered chemical fertilisers and irrigation it becomes like a drug addict. Not required to find and create its life from natural elements around it, it takes more and more from its drip. Galileo Galilei said 'Wine is sunlight, held together by water'. What a poetic way of communicating this incredible truth.

After reading the book I was convinced that we should try biodynamics. There was significant evidence that it would contribute to our quest to make expressive wines. Sean planned his next phase of vineyard work around the biodynamic calendar.

Before he headed out to start the new season's shoot removal we talked about Dave's order, which was still up in the air.

'I need to follow up. Can we do his price?' I said.

'With our yields we need twenty per cent more,' he replied.

'But we need this sale. He won't buy our wine at that price. I think we should go at ten cents over his price. That way it's not enough to scupper the order but it's enough to show we won't roll over and take whatever price he proposed.'

'Just make sure you get the order,' said Sean putting the pressure of the decision back onto me. We had to get the order but we also had to agree a price that would keep us in business.

The next day Dave phoned back. I dropped the juice I was serving Ellie and made my proposal with a tremble in my voice. Without this sale we were finished. If he didn't proceed with the order for the sake of that ten cents I'd never forgive myself.

'I'll organise the order confirmation. You'll have it in a couple of days.'

My body flooded with the euphoria of success and an adrenalin burst akin to that of having just avoided a car crash. That evening Sean and I toasted our success with a glass of the wine we had sold.

I watched the email hungrily. Days stretched into weeks and still no confirmation arrived. I put our creditors off promising to pay in a few weeks and began to worry that he had changed his mind. We needed that confirmation.

The kitchen drain had been smelly again and I was not looking forward to 'Operation Stench 2'. We needed a long-term solution that did not involve me lying on the ground with my nose in a stinking drain and a hosepipe in my hand every few months.

'Don't worry,' said Monsieur Fracasse, a compact, energetic artisan in his fifties who had been helping Sean to finish the new terrace. The new terrace was to become our outdoor area. The original one and part of the house would become a self-catering cottage that would deliver much-needed rent long before renovating the old building that Helen and Derek had uncovered – if we could ever afford it. He was full of ideas and spoke fast. 'I work with someone who does septic tanks and drains. I'll call him to come down and have a look.'

An endless blue sky spread above the Dordogne valley. Our vineyard was awakening from its winter sleep, with tiny pink shoots running along the vine canes. On the valley floor the last of the plum blossoms had given way to green leaves.

'*Pas de problème,*' (No problem) he repeated, looking at the view and losing himself in it for a moment.

'*Tiens, autre chose* (Another thing). What about the downpipe here? What's this?'

The downpipe on one side of the terrace went straight into the ground. There was only one place that it could come from and that was the bathroom upstairs.

'It must be the *broyeur* out-pipe,' I said.

'You don't want any trouble with that,' said Monsieur Fracasse. 'We'll have to put new piping in for it.'

His contact, Monsieur Jegu, arrived a half-hour later. He was a tall, polite man who had the ability to do ferocious amounts of work in a short space of time.

'We can connect this kitchen pipe to the fosse. There should be no problems and it should solve the problem of the odours with the right angle. But to be *aux normes* you'll need a grease box at the end of the kitchen drain before we connect it up to the filter unit of the septic tank,' he said.

'How much is a grease box?' My fear of costs related to plumbing came from the hefty amount of investment we had already made.

'A couple of hundred euro.'

I felt the usual frisson of fear associated with unplanned costs.

'We have to do it. What do you recommend with the downpipe from upstairs? One day I want to get rid of the *broyeur*.'

'I'll put in a sewage pipe that you can connect up if you ever replace the small pipe,' said Monsieur Jegu. *'Pas de problème.'*

'Perfect,' I said.

Work started the next morning. A few hours later the grind of the digger stopped and I saw Messieurs Jegu and Fracasse deep in conversation near our septic tank. They motioned to me to come out to join them.

They looked embarrassed and I thought they must have broken a pipe.

'What's up?' I asked. They pointed at a little pipe that ran into the exit of the septic tank.

'The out-pipe from the *broyeur* goes straight into the final filtration unit of the septic tank and not into the tank itself,' said Monsieur Jegu.

'I don't think I understand. What do you mean?'

'They connected the upstairs toilet to the out-pipe instead of to the septic tank itself so the waste from upstairs has never gone into the treatment unit. The new pipe must be connected to the main septic tank,' explained Monsieur Fracasse.

I looked up to heaven. Our 'unusual' plumbing went a lot further than kitchen waste at the corner of the house.

'How much will it cost?'

'Don't worry, I won't change the price,' said Monsieur Jegu.

He had picked up my nervous twitch. I thanked him and went inside to follow up on the order confirmation. Once again I found Dave out and left a message. I was getting seriously worried. He was our only hope of survival. Without his order we would not be able to pay the bottling costs and our suppliers could force our liquidation.

Sophia and Ellie were growing up fast. Now four and two respectively, they were real characters. Sophia was the confident, studious type and Ellie, the rogue rock star. One spring evening, I stepped out onto the terrace into delicious warm air. The immense sky was clustered with stars. Ellie was dropping stones into her water-filled beach bucket while Sophia and Sean were deep in conversation. It was the weekend and way past their bedtime but the conversation was so interesting I sat down.

'When I grow up will I find a good man like you to marry so I can have a baby?' asked Sophia.

'Yes, you'll find a good man,' said Sean.

'I think I want to marry you.'

'But you can't marry me because I'm already married to mama. You'll find a man that can make your heart sing, like a beautiful morning.'

'I don't need a man tonight because the stars are making my heart sing.'

Later that evening Sophia called me upstairs. Ellie was already fast asleep.

'I can't sleep because the stars are too bright and noisy.'

'But the shutters are closed.'

'I know but I can still hear them. They're excited that summer is coming.'

I closed my eyes and listened. I could hear faint chattering in the distance of the still night. Perhaps it was a party in Gardonne, perhaps it was the stars.

Back in the winter we had stopped heating the red wine and elected to wait for the malo to start on its own in the spring. Spring was now well under way, even the stars were telling us about it, but there was still no sign of the malo. We had promised buyers like Dave that we'd bottle our merlot in May, but now it was out of the question.

Sean tried a malo starter culture, carefully following the instructions, making sure the temperatures were ideal and monitoring the wines like newborn babies. They remained calm and oblivious.

'Don't worry,' said Lucille when I bemoaned how harsh the red wines still were. 'They will soften as soon as the malos are finished. When do you want to bottle?'

'Before Christmas,' said Sean.

'Good. We'll make sure the malos are finished by October,' she said.

'But what else can we do?'

'Let's test them again and if there is still no activity we'll try a starter culture again.'

We were losing confidence in Lucille and we were tired of waiting. I found the wines downright disgusting and for all Lucille's assurances I found it hard to believe that the malo would make such a difference to how they tasted. I called another oenologist we had met a few months before, who specialised in organic and biodynamic winemaking. She visited to taste the reds. They were as grim as I remembered.

'It's a good wine,' she said, leaving me gobsmacked. 'It's got a high level of organic matter and flavour. It needs to do its malo. Send me your PH, SO2 and AV levels and I'll tell you what to do.'

A year before I had no idea what AV was and a faint notion from school science of PH and SO2; now I was becoming expert in sulphur dioxide (SO2), free sulphur dioxide, total sulphur dioxide, *acide volatile* (AV) and the like.

Sulphur dioxide is the preservative used in winemaking and many other products. It is strictly controlled and measured in the French appellation system. Excessive doses of sulphur dioxide explain why you sometimes wake up with a sore head, much worse than you expect relative to the amount you drank. An upside of the reluctant malolactic fermentation in our red wines was that they had now completed a full year of maturation with almost no sulphur dioxide since they could not be dosed until it was complete; but that didn't make me feel any better; they still tasted horrible.

We had to find someone to set us on the right track with our red wines. Thierry Daulhiac agreed to share his secrets with us. Château Le Payral was resplendent in a climbing apricot rose and newly painted shutters.

'Caro, Sean, to be honest, I find making red wine difficult. With the white it's straightforward, with the reds: not so simple. Each year is different. Each year we try something new to strive for better quality. This year we bought a rolling carpet so the grapes can be transported into the vat rather than pumped. Despite all these efforts, I have only made one red vintage that Isabelle likes. Can you believe it? Twelve vintages and only one that she likes!'

Isabelle, Thierry's wife, was a country girl with blonde hair and an easy, open manner. I tried to picture her spitting Thierry's red wine out in disgust and could not. I thought his red wines were delicious.

Thierry showed us round his winery.

'We developed this punch down system on the open vats; it's like the ancient way of making wine.' Punch down, or *pigeage*, is the extraction method typical of Burgundy whereas pump-over, or *remontage*, is more common in Bordeaux. When you punch down you push the cap of skins and pips into the liquid; when you pump over you pour the liquid over the cap. The punch down saves the wine from the trauma of mechanical pumping several times a day.

'It's gentler on the grapes and it saves us time. We found the tannins were softer, more supple.'

By the end of our visit we still didn't have the answer about how to make excellent red wine but with exchanges like this our knowledge was growing. The next time I was over at Pierre de Saint Viance's, our friend and bottler, I met Pierre's sister Benedicte and her husband Christophe.

'You must visit them,' said Pierre. 'They're organic too.'

And so, a couple of weeks later Sean and I arrived to visit their Château Couronneau bringing friends from New York to taste Christophe's wines. We drove up a cypress-lined avenue to the fairytale stone castle and *chai*. The castle was beautiful despite having been partially destroyed through two key periods of French history: the Hundred Years War between the English and the French which ended in 1453, and again at the time of the French Revolution in the late 1700s.

It was a dream property; manicured, restored to perfection and ticking like clockwork. Christophe was mowing the front lawn. He was a wealthy ex-wine merchant with several employees but he was hands-on, his hands stained dark red, a tell-tale sign of a hardworking vigneron.

'We have a hundred acres of merlot, most of it replanted to high density,' said Christophe. 'I have a worker responsible for every twenty-five acres. I used to use men but now I only use women. They do double the work in half the time.' He looked to me and my friend Hilary for a reaction. We all laughed. A young man joined us. 'Except, of course, Mickael. He is my secret weapon. He wrote to me saying he wanted to work on an organic vineyard. Now he runs everything.'

Mickael laughed.

Back in the winery, gleaming stainless steel vats were connected to a sophisticated temperature control system. Christophe gave us each a taste of his Château Couronneau wine.

'You know what they say? To make a small fortune in wine, start with a large fortune. But it's not the case for the grand crus. A friend of mine was visiting Ausone a few weeks ago, the premier grand cru classé A in St Émilion, and a Chinese man arrived and wanted to buy five cases. He paid €250,000 on the spot. That's good business. I heard they cleared fifteen million euros in profit last year on about twenty acres.'

Christophe's clever system for pressing allowed him to use a high quality basket press without losing much efficiency. We had picked up good ideas for the future – budget permitting – but his set-up was so modern compared to ours that there were not many parallels. We returned home to a storm warning. As organic producers, the weather controlled our every move in spring and summer. If rain was forecast, the vines had to be protected before it arrived. One missed treatment and mildew could take hold. Unchecked, the entire vineyard could be destroyed in a couple of days.

Sean prepared his biodynamic concoctions in the kitchen then disappeared into the vineyard for several hours. His preparations smelt clean, herbal and comforting. Since starting biodynamic treatments we had dramatically reduced the amount of copper we needed to fight fungal disease. Copper, the ingredient officially sanctioned for organic producers to control mildew, has been used in agriculture for over 200 years but it's expensive and it doesn't break down; excessive use creates 'copper toxicity'. We wanted to reduce it and biodynamics was helping us to do that.

The biodynamic preparations smelt so pleasant I enjoyed Sean making his concoctions in the kitchen. Systemic chemicals, on the other hand, smelt so toxic I could not be outside when farmers were spraying miles away. Favoured for their long-term effectiveness, systemic chemicals are toxic to the person applying them plus they enter the plant's system rather than operating by contact, thus leading to chemical residues in the fruit and in the resulting wine. My sceptic's heart was being convinced by hard evidence. Biodynamics smelt good and it worked.

We decided to farm organically because we believed it was the route to great wines. There again, we had to question the financial wisdom of organic. It produced cleaner wines but it was labour-intensive and offered lower yields than conventional. It was early days but we were getting despondent. Unlike organic vegetables, where people expected to pay a premium for a healthy product, it seemed that wine lovers would not pay more for organic wine.

Studies had shown that polyphenolic substances, the natural flavour compounds found in wine, were higher in the organic wines than in conventional wines. Not only was the flavour better, but organically farmed wine was also higher in antioxidants, the wonderful little critters that fight cancer. My stress-busting dark chocolate was also packed with them. Hand me another slab and a large glass of organic red wine, please.

Through our journey as a producer I realised that organic was more important than it seemed from afar as a consumer. It was more than quality, taste and health; it was fundamentally important for the well-being of the land. Farming chemically set off a series of imbalances that could only be adjusted by yet more interventions. Chemical farming leads to erosion from herbicides, toxic salinity in the soil from chemical fertilisers, long-term build-up of chemical residues and lack of biodiversity.

At the same time as Sean and I were weeping over the cost of organic farming, a number of chemical products for use in vineyards were banned in the EU because of health risks for the people spraying them and also for the final consumer. And yet these EU laws only affected farmers in the EU, not wine producers in the New World. The EU happily continued importing low-cost wines farmed with these chemicals. It was two-faced and wine farmers were rightly up in arms. A holistic policy would have banned products using these chemicals from being imported too, thus offering wine producers a level playing field.

For us it was a wake-up call about the dangers of agricultural chemicals. Sean's health was priceless. I read that the level of cancer among vineyard workers in California was four times the normal rate and it had been linked directly with vineyard chemicals. Organic farming was more labour-intensive and costly but its health benefits more than compensated. We knew the flavour of our wines was much better too, but right at that moment it didn't make the hard economic reality any easier. We had to keep the faith that the quality of our wines would shine through and help us get the prices we needed to stay in business.

As a consumer my purchasing power was a significant lever in the quest for a healthy earth so I made more effort to buy only organic products, preferring to buy less in order to meet our ever-tightening budget.

Farming organically that spring was challenging. Many farmers who were experimenting with organics threw their hands up in disgust and returned to their chemical dependence. We had rain, rain and more rain. In the small square in Saussignac where the war memorial stood opposite the castle, I bumped into Pierre Sadoux, the rake of a vigneron who smoked rolled cigarettes and flew a microlight. He was looking well.

'*Salut* Pierre!'

'*C'est au feu*. Harvest last year followed by this spring. A nightmare, and the pressure isn't letting up. How are things going for you?'

Pierre was echoing what other local winegrowers had told me: our first harvest had been one of the toughest and this growing season was continuing the trend.

'Sean's working all hours but the vines are looking good.'

'How are you finding organic? I hear some organic vineyards have lost everything to mildew.'

'Sean's vigilant – so far no problems. We know nothing different so we're lucky. We don't know how easy life would be if we were conventional farmers.'

Pierre laughed. 'We're trying out mechanical weeding this year but we can't go organic. It's too complicated for us to do with the number of acres we have.'

'Why?'

'We can plan the work more easily, we're not so dependent on the weather. With systemic fungicides we are protected for fifteen days. For you, if you spray on Wednesday then you get a downpour and a storm is forecast for Sunday night you need to treat again. Our employees don't work on Sunday. If I got on the tractor I wouldn't get round the whole vineyard in time. We need three people out there to get around all our vineyards in a day. It's too risky for us.'

Perhaps in time Pierre and his father would go organic. When we bought our property we did not realise we had fallen into an enclave of organic producers. Already almost half of Saussignac wine producers were organic or in conversion to organic, compared to a national average in France of around 3 per cent. When we arrived another wave were starting conversion and since then more farms had converted. It was a virtuous circle.

'You must come round to taste the wines again sometime soon,' I said. 'It would be good to hear your opinion on the reds.'

Pierre had visited us once the previous summer to taste the old Garrigue vintages. I was eager for him to taste our own wines to see his reaction. Perhaps he could give us some useful advice on our problem children, the reds that steadfastly refused to do their malolactic fermentation.

# Chapter 15

# In the Merde with the Merlot

The apricot dawn filled me with joy. I stood on the balcony and felt uncanny delight and weightlessness looking down onto the Dordogne valley's bountiful patchwork of plum blossoms and manicured vines. We still didn't have the order confirmation, the malos hadn't started and we were broke, but I felt positive. It defied logic. Despite working harder than ever physically and mentally for no return, our new life was strangely fulfilling.

That morning the Saturday magazine of a major newspaper that ran the cover story on us the year before called to say they were going to run my follow-on story as another cover feature. Perhaps the emotions I felt at dawn were a premonition.

I called Dave, the wine buyer, with the news and suggested they take the wine in immediately so it would be in store in time for the publication date. Within hours we had the order confirmation and a date for pickup. I didn't know why they had been delaying but right then the only important thing was that we had the official order. The chunky payment would hit our bank account in a few weeks and we'd be able to get our creditors off our backs. It was a major milestone.

Our second offer of our summer wines went out to our subscriber list. Within two weeks we had sold out of our rosé and our sauvignon blanc. Some customers bought five cases of sauvignon blanc at once. It boosted our morale. People wanted our wines.

Even with these successes, the wine business would not be able to support us on its own. We had to develop new streams of revenue. I was renovating frantically to make half of our house available as a self-catering unit. Adding a second unit would make the prospects a little more rosy, but the old building Helen and Derek had uncovered was still in its ruined state. I measured up every perspective and realised the second level was too low to be useful for human habitation.

I drew up some plans then called Monsieur Fracasse, the builder who had helped with the terrace. He arrived, tape measure in hand. We walked round the side of the tasting room.

'*Quelle vue,*' he said, whistling through his teeth. 'I can see why you want to turn this into a house. From the upper level it must be even better.' It was a tranquil piece of heaven.

'Yes, but look, it's too low for a house.'

'Hmm, I see.'

'So my big problem is how to get enough living space for two people if we take the second floor out.'

'I've an idea,' he said, scribbling urgently in his notepad. 'What if we put in a mezzanine for a double bed? That way we get access to the views from the top too.'

Now Monsieur Fracasse was talking, measuring and drawing at speed. He was full of suggestions.

'*Tiens, autre chose*, we could put the bathroom out here. Or we could put the kitchen out here then have a window here so someone working in the kitchen could enjoy the views.'

'Super idea.'

'If we put the kitchen here what will we do about the bathroom? Where will we put it?'

'We could use the winery extension on the right.' I motioned in the direction of the building. 'Perhaps we could break through the concrete vats and put the bathroom in there?'

'But what about the out-pipes? From here it won't be the right angle and also we couldn't install the sewage pipe underground since the building is built on solid rock.'

We walked across to look at the size of the extension. He measured the walls. I looked at the angle and could see his point.

'*Attends, j'ai une idée*. We could put in a *broyeur*. That would solve the problem, we could…' His voice trailed off. He could see that I did not find this particular idea super at all.

'Absolutely no *broyeur*,' I said categorically.

'*Oui, t'as raison*. A *broyeur* is not good, yes, in fact, a *broyeur* is not good at all.'

I couldn't have said it better myself.

We agreed he would do the initial quote with the bathroom on the side where sewage pipes could be safely installed and with a mezzanine for the bed. We waved at Sean who was in the vineyard below carefully removing unwanted shoots from the heads of the vines. Having all his body parts intact for once he was taking on the *épamprage*, rather than me. I yelled, 'Watch out for snakes!' He laughed and waved me off. I had seen several snakes and Sean had seen none. He doubted their presence but I knew better.

Before coming to France I had a notion that making wine was easy; the diagrams used in Wine & Spirit Education Trust (WSET)

set books and Jancis Robinson's *The Oxford Companion to Wine* made it look like a few simple steps. Our problem children, the reds, were making me appreciate how wrong I was.

A multitude of decisions go into making the final product and each decision can have a dramatic impact on the end wine. It is never as simple as 'choose A or B'; there are always several variables to consider and in many cases the formula is not fully understood, thus a large dose of artistic judgement is required. Winemaking is art and science. It is also a work of agony and ecstasy: agony on the days where the wine made us question all our decisions along the way, ecstasy when it tasted like a grand cru classé and filled us with joy akin to that of a new parent.

The red wines were still tannic, acid monsters that had not completed their malos despite much coaxing. With them representing two thirds of our production, we couldn't afford to miss a year but neither could we release a wine that was not the quality level we wanted. We spoke to Lucille, who shrugged her shoulders in Gallic style. We tried another starter culture. It did not work.

Jean-Paul, a travelling wine consultant, appeared, and we leapt upon him with glee.

'Is there any hope for this wine?' I asked.

'Of course! It has good structure and great phenolic matter. It's a good wine. It needs time. The malos will start soon, don't worry.'

But I did worry. We monitored the wines every day, praying for signs. Finally, as I prepared to fire our oenologist and to write a blistering letter to the company that produced the failed starter cultures, the malos started on their own. The wines got active, bubbling slightly and making the signature 'pop-pop' we had heard about. I listened and stroked the barrels lovingly. Sean and

I checked them morning and evening, anxious that our babies would finish this key step successfully.

Grateful beyond measure, Sean got back to work in the vineyard, which was in full growth with our grapes ripening beautifully despite the wet start to the season. Summer was back and with it the bounties of free food that I gathered eagerly. Baskets of plums from a neighbour's unfarmed orchard alongside Upper Garrigue were turned into compote, jam and tarts. Sophia's holidays meant she was home to play with Ellie and to help harvest. We set up the paddling pool my mum had bought the previous summer and spent hours outside. The girls played in the sandpit or the pool while I designed and laid out our new potager; an ambitious 100 square metres of geometric beds.

Within weeks the malos were complete. After almost a year of watching and waiting, heating and grinding our teeth, we were stunned at how simple it was. We had to trust our wines. They were living things that set their own agenda.

The timing was perfect, the end of August, giving us a couple of weeks to rack the wines before the harvest started. Racking wine is the process of removing clear wine from the vat in order to leave the sediment settled on the bottom behind. We had a meeting with Lucille to taste the wines and plan the bottling. They had softened but they were still tannic monsters.

'We can't sell this,' I said. 'How long will it take for these tannins to mature?'

'It's hard to say,' said our oenologist. 'It could take three years.'

'What? We can't wait three years!'

'Perhaps in six months it will be better.'

'It had better be,' I said bitterly taking another mouthful and spitting a long red jet into the spittoon. My spitting technique was almost professional, a great improvement on my initial attempts that left me covered in red splats after each tasting session. But our plan to bottle in time for Christmas was scuppered. It was clear that even highly educated, experienced oenologists could not accurately read young wine.

'What else can we do? We need to have some red wine ready for bottling soon.'

'If we age more of the wine in oak barrels it will round out the tannins and help to express the finesse,' said Lucille.

Wine scientists are impervious to financial realities. We already had our top red wine in barrels. Oak barrels cost around €700 new. We'd need at least ten to make any impact on the volume of pure merlot we had. We'd have to find more second-hand ones. I spat tacks. It would take time for us to be better judges of unfinished wine. For now we had to control the panic that took hold each time we tasted an acidic monster in infancy. I called Pierre and cancelled the October bottling. We had to tighten our belts and wait for March when we would bottle the new whites that were still on the vines as well. At least the payment for Dave's order had arrived. Sean began vat planning for the harvest. In a couple of weeks it would be on us again. I felt a bolt of excitement and dread.

# Chapter 16

# Vendanges Tranquilles

With *vendanges* around the corner, our Dutch friend Ad arrived, looking fit and younger than ever. He had retired a week before and was now free to roam around France at leisure. Perhaps it was retiring that had given him a flush of youth or perhaps it was returning to the Dordogne where he had spent so many happy summers. Lijda couldn't come; maybe she remembered the stress of our first year and wasn't coming back for another dose of hell.

Ad set up his campervan down in the amphitheatre. The trees were loaded with figs and the limestone cliffs shone white in the summer sun. The girls zoomed down to mob him like bees to a honeypot. Ad was becoming like a grandfather to them. A few hours later he set off on his bike to visit some friends, flying along the district road like a comet.

The next day Sean's finger tingled ominously as if it remembered the harvest the previous year. While he cleaned and sterilised equipment, Ad organised Sean's workshop. Each tool soon had its home on the wall; after years of rummaging through piles on shelves it was a revelation. He extended electricity cables and connected new lights for the new workbench. When the workshop was organised, he made the half-plough that Sean wanted attached to the oil reservoir on the tractor.

Each day Sean and I walked the vineyards and tasted the grapes. We were more confident about making our decision on when to harvest. It was tranquil; there was no rain. Ad taught Sean to weld and time slowed.

Then the sauvignon blanc grapes were ready; sweet and full of flavour, their pips brown and nutty. I called to reserve the harvest machine and got my booking without having to negotiate. Sean did a final check of the equipment.

'I'm going to do a dry run,' he said. 'We're ready and we have two days to spare.'

I went inside. A half-hour later Sean crashed through the door, his steel-toe boots clomping aggressively across the kitchen.

'Feck it,' he said, peering through the lounge door. 'The Kreyer's not working. You'd better call Bonny's.'

The Kreyer was critical for making the white wine; it cooled the white juice for cold stabilisation, then later on, if the fermentation got too hot, it would enable us to keep the fermenting juice at the cooler temperatures required to keep the fruit flavours intact.

'You can't wait,' said Lucille, who had arrived for her visit, 'but you can't harvest without the Kreyer.'

Sometimes we wanted to shake her and say, 'Wake up to the constraints of real life!' But we also knew she was right. At that moment the grapes were perfect and we wanted them to stay that way. One extra day of waiting could make a difference.

We had thirty-six hours until the harvest machine was booked to arrive. Monsieur Bonny promised to send over his refrigeration expert *tout de suite*.

Ellie had started school a week before, but her first few days were overshadowed by the looming harvest. At two and a half she had to get on with it, catch the bus and settle in. I collected the girls and got home to find the Bonny van parked outside the winery and Éric hard at work. He tried a few things and refilled the gas canister. The unit hummed back to life. I felt intense relief.

To be sure, Sean asked Éric to do a start with him before he left. Sean tried starting the Kreyer and it would not murmur. They tried again. Nothing.

*'C'est bizarre,'* said Éric. 'I will have to call a refrigeration specialist. It can't be the gas.'

*'C'est très, très urgent,'* I said, anxiety cramping my stomach.

The artisan could be with us at eight the next morning. By then we would have less than twenty-four hours before the harvest machine arrived. Benoit arrived right on time and tested the Kreyer. An hour later he came in with the motherboard of the unit.

*'C'est ça.'* His finger pointed to a large burnt-out section. 'I have ordered a replacement. It's two thousand euros.'

I felt sick to my core.

'How much would it cost to get a whole new unit?'

'They start at around twenty thousand.'

We had to do the repair. I called Sonia to book a sleepover for the girls. We needed to be up and working by four in the morning. There would be no room for little people amongst the heavy machinery of harvest time.

Benoit messaged that the part would arrive that afternoon. We were right down to the wire but we could not push the harvest out by another day. Ad and I paced up and down each row carefully, removing everything that had the slightest hint of rot. It was sunny and the vineyard was glowing with an early hint of autumnal orange on some of the leaves, but we hardly noticed. The grapes were clean; only three bunches had to be removed. On our return we found Benoit and Sean huddled over the Kreyer.

They were in the same position when I got back from fetching the girls. They ran to Sean yelling 'Papa, Papa!' and leapt into his arms. It was the first time I had seen him smile all day. He kissed them then sent them to me for their *'goûter'*, the afternoon snack of brioche and juice. Getting dinner ready, the stress was almost insupportable. As the sun set over the ancient stone barn I heard the hum of a healthy Kreyer rebound across the courtyard and ran outside, overjoyed.

*'Ça marche,'* said Benoit, giving me a relieved smile. Even the machine artisans working in the wine industry felt the pressure of the harvest. They went to extraordinary lengths to make sure equipment was fixed. I dressed the girls in their pyjamas, packed their overnight bag and walked them up to Sonia. It was their first night away from home.

'You must listen to Sonia and make sure you eat all your breakfast.' Ellie cried and Sophia comforted her with a big hug. They bravely said goodnight. I tried to control the tears welling up and gave them each a *bisou*.

Sean and Ad were finishing up. We were ready and it wasn't ten o'clock. How different it felt to the chaos of the previous year.

I slept well and woke at four the next morning to a clear sky filled with stars. After wolfing down some muesli and a cup of strong tea I stepped out into the night. Minutes later the harvest machine arrived with a fine-looking chauffeur named Jean-Louis. He was tall with dark curly hair and should have been on the cover of *Men's Health*, not driving a machine in the depths of the Dordogne at four in the morning. I got up onto the harvest machine with renewed vigour.

A short ride and we were in the first vineyard of sauvignon blanc. I indicated our markers to him and headed back up. The first load was perfect and pressing went smoothly. In an hour all the sauvignon blanc was safely up at the winery. The juice was exceptional and super-concentrated but the yields were extremely low. As long as this was unique to the sauvignon blanc, we'd be OK. We had done a yield estimate and were expecting a reduction of a third, not more than half.

That afternoon Ad disappeared over the horizon on his bike while I did a second pass through the vineyard. It was looking good. The sémillon would be our most intense harvest day. I took the girls over to Sonia again. Ellie cried even harder and Sophia tried to comfort her. She was still adjusting to school and now she was being shipped out for another night. I hugged her tight and promised it would be the last night away. We would have to find another solution for the harvest nights of the reds. I couldn't do this to Ellie again at two and a half.

A few hours later the winery was buzzing with activity and light in the cold night air. Jean-Louis hummed into the courtyard and I showed him our carefully marked sémillon. Soon the harvesting was complete and we had two trailers waiting to go into the second pressing.

We emptied the press in haste aiming the pressed grape skins carefully into our small trailer so we could carry them away to the property entrance where the government distillery would collect them. We wanted the waiting grapes to be in the press before sun filled the courtyard. Time was of the essence. With the pressings removed we started up the harvest trailer to refill the press. A third of the way through the load the trailer jammed.

'We'd better unhitch it and empty the other trailer,' said Sean.

'How will we get the grapes out?' I asked.

'We could empty it by hand,' suggested Ad.

'That could take hours. We can't have it sitting around that long.'

We moved the blocked trailer aside and covered the grapes with a layer of carbon dioxide gas followed by a large canvas sheet then emptied the other trailer.

There were about 2,500 litres of grapes left in the jammed trailer. By hand, that was the equivalent of about 250 10-litre bucketloads. A quick review of options made it clear that the manual solution was the only viable one. It was a race against the clock. Ad was like a machine, bucketing load after load across from one trailer to the other. Sean and I took turns bucketing, putting carbon dioxide into the tray and watching the press to pump the free-run juice into the vat.

In thirty minutes we had the harvest trailer emptied of its two and a half tons of grapes. As the sun crept into the courtyard we transferred them smoothly into the press. While I monitored the level of juice in the press tray, Ad and Sean carefully removed the back of the auger from the trailer. Stuck in the screw was a large metal hook, the kind we use to fix the vineyard trellising. I vowed we would stop using them.

All our whites were safely in the winery and Sean was delighted with the taste. I plugged the yields into our finance spreadsheet and discovered it was more depressing than I thought. If the yields of this harvest were the norm there was no way the farm would ever be able to pay us for our hard work. In fact, we had to pay in for the privilege of working long hours and getting no holidays. It was gutting. But if we didn't have the wine harvested and made, the situation would be worse. I closed the spreadsheet and promised I would not look at it again until the harvest period was over. I could not support the stress of the harvest and that spreadsheet at the same time.

A friend, John, arrived for a holiday thinking he would be in time to help us with the reds. He texted his mum, who had farmed all her life.

'On my way to the wine farm in France. At last, some real farm work!'

'That's not real farming, it's farming for the rich,' came his mother's reply.

The perception was reaffirmed by the wine industry with photos of winemakers seated in idyllic locations, vines and peaceful oak barrels miraculously tending themselves in the background. It gave an image of history, tradition and calm, a vision of a peaceful existence well away from the rush and chaos of modern life, something timeless. We were in the midst of the period of the year where this delusional view was most at odds with the reality: a period of extremes, of pressurised physical work.

On arrival, John was invited on a bike ride by Ad. Since it looked like we would be waiting another couple of days for the reds he agreed. John was no slouch, he played football and was lean and fit. Two and a half hours later, Ad sped into the courtyard looking fresh as a daisy followed by our wilted friend.

'Phew, my arse hurts,' said John as he climbed delicately off the bike. 'He's a bionic man. We rode all the way to Bergerac then back the other way, all the way to Sainte-Foy-la-Grande. He didn't stop, not once.' John was almost weeping as he limped into the kitchen rubbing his rump. 'I need a glass of your restorative sauvignon blanc.'

I saw Ad whistling as he wandered down to the campervan full of the joys of late summer, looking like he had spent the afternoon in the hammock. The name 'bionic man' stuck. John recovered remarkably quickly but didn't make the mistake of going for another bike ride.

The red grapes were still not ready to be picked. John cursed his misfortune. He wasn't even going to experience real 'farming for the rich'. Instead we spent our days picking the fruit that was falling off the fig trees and made countless jars of jam. John had to leave soon after another friend, Bullet, arrived. Ad invited Bullet on a cycle ride, and Bullet agreed, having received no insider information from John.

'How was it?' I asked when he returned.

'Ah, not too bad, not too bad,' he said, disappearing indoors. A few moments later I heard loud snoring from his room. That evening he appeared with a cushion for his chair.

'I think Bullet needs to lose a little bit of weight then he would take on the hills no problem,' Ad confided. Each harvest visitor was given the once over by Ad, our resident personal trainer. Fortunately I had not been on the tour of torment: heaven knows what Ad would have said about me. I pictured the scene, Ad saying confidentially to Sean, 'You know, if Caro lost a few kilos she'd be able to cycle down the hill to Gardonne.'

With the red grapes still firmly on the vines we welcomed Kerry and Anne Guy, friends of friends from New Zealand, to Haut Garrigue. They had five acres of vines and a beautiful guest house,

The Point Lodge, which nestled between their vines and the sea near the Bay of Plenty. Kerry was a mile a minute and a font of information. Early in the morning I'd see him walking the vineyards, then he would arrive back with succinct advice about something he had seen; later he would pick walnuts from our trees and a gift of half a walnut cake would appear. He was the chef at their lodge.

'He talks so much,' said Ad after Kerry had been giving us advice on labels and marketing of wine. 'How can someone know so much about so many things?'

The next morning Kerry wandered into the workshop to look at the custom-built plough Ad was creating for Sean. A few hours later Ad came in for lunch.

'Kerry came to see me today and I thought to myself: hmm – how much can he know about welding and farm machinery? But you know what? He knows so much. He told me to reinforce a section that I hadn't considered and he was correct. It was the point of the greatest pressure and the part that needed the most reinforcement on the whole plough.'

'You know Ad, at first I didn't know whether to trust him but he's the real McCoy. Someone who can make a walnut cake this good and give advice on making a farm plough is pretty unique.'

'He has got so much going on in his head it's hard to keep up. Sometimes I have to switch off to cope.'

That afternoon Kerry explained his plans for a wine tourism website to me. 'I think there is good potential in the wine tourism business. It could be something to complement your wine business. I know it's hard to make ends meet on a small farm like this.'

He had read my mind.

'I was vaguely considering offering wine classes. Most of the people who visit us have asked for an introduction to French wine. They want to get the basics and have some fun. Many are New World wine drinkers and they love sauvignon blanc but don't know Sancerre is sauvignon.'

'That's a good idea. You could also do wine tours and maybe food and wine tours.'

The next day Kerry appeared with a piece of paper.

'I have worked out a potential day tour and costing for you.'

On the page was a suggested itinerary and budget of a day tour. Kerry was a powerful force. He slept little, experimented a lot and read extensively.

I signed up for the wine course offered by our local wine organisation, the CIVRB. The training of four sessions ran over a month and was a bit technical and only about Bergerac wines. I could see how I would run a class. My background in workshops and teaching project management gave me a good base but I needed to increase my content knowledge; growing and making wine for two years was not enough. At night, I reread all Sean's Wine & Spirit Education Trust course books.

Then my night-reading was stopped by something pressing: harvesting the reds. I could not face sending the girls away for the night again so we taught Sophia to use a walkie-talkie to call us when she woke up on harvest mornings, with strict instructions to remain at the top of the steps until someone came inside. We were terrified they would walk out into the courtyard where the enormous harvest machine and the tractors were working. We explained the process and the top step rule several times and did a few test runs. Sophia and Ellie were excited about their new walkie-talkie responsibility.

The next morning the weather was fine and the first load of merlot came in and was transferred into the vat without a hitch. It was so smooth we were standing around with nothing to do. I went inside to get a cup of tea and a snack for everyone. Since the finger incident, we had installed a rule of taking a break at least every two hours.

An hour later the walkie-talkie in my pocket rang. Sophia was sitting on the top step, delighted to have successfully accomplished her mission. I made her a cup of tea and a brioche and turned on the television. Soon the buzzer went again. It was Sophia calling us because Ellie had woken up. I gave her some breakfast and they settled down to watch the French kids' television shows.

Two hours later I took a break from the merlot to take the girls and Inés-Melodie, Sonia's daughter, up to school. The day was working like clockwork. By nine o'clock all the merlot was in the winery, leaving just the cabernet sauvignon to pick. For that we'd probably be waiting at least another two weeks. It was a different world to our previous harvest.

Chandra, the tall, dark and practical daughter of Canadian friends, arrived. At first she seemed rather bristly, like a hedgehog under threat, but she was organised and our house after six weeks of intensive harvest time was extremely disorganised. Nothing except the absolute essentials were taken care of in that period. It was a true corridor of crisis. My dad would have had a heart attack on the spot. Chandra kept opening cupboards and looking at disorganised shelves and saying, 'I couldn't live like this.'

I wondered how long I could live with her given the constant commentary about my corridor of crisis. But there was a lot more to Chandra than met the eye. She was a qualified lumberjack or tree surgeon and a horticulturalist with a good knowledge of medicinal and edible herbs. For the previous two years she had worked as a fire-watcher on a tower in a remote part of Canada, accessible only by helicopter. For four months a year the only human she saw was the pilot of her monthly food drop. She had learnt to be tough and resourceful; but wolves and bears hadn't prepared her for one-on-one combat with Ellie Feely.

At two and a half Ellie was a forceful character. She would get home from school, fix me with a powerful stare and say, *'Donne moi des bonbons!'* (Give me sweets!) On getting no satisfaction she would deepen her mafia-style glare and repeat, *'Donne moi des bonbons!'* I learnt to offer up something in response like juice and a chocolate brioche, and Ellie, while not completely satisfied with the state of affairs, would deign to eat that. She was a tough act.

A *fonctionnaire* from our social services organisation came around at my request. I explained that now that Ellie had started school I wanted to work for our vineyard and wine business a couple of days a week. Up until then I had officially been a full-time mother since Ellie was at home. Now that she was at school I would be officially working for the business part-time. He explained that if I worked for our agricultural enterprise – the vineyard and wine business – even for as little as one day a month I would have to pay the social charges of a full-time worker as I would be a working shareholder. It didn't make sense to me and Ellie, who was sitting on my lap, clearly found it hard to stomach. She held her little hand up and said 'Stop!' Monsieur Bellio ignored her. Ellie held her hand up again and said more forcefully 'Stop!' Perhaps she realised that her future *bonbon* budget was at risk.

Taking advantage of his silence I thanked him for his time and wished him farewell. I was sure I had misunderstood or he had misunderstood what I wanted. There was no way that a shareholder who participated in the company, working a day a week for no pay, should have to pay the social charges of a full-time employee earning a salary. I would have to do some research.

Chandra meanwhile took a strict line with Ellie and it was naked combat. She tried some of the tactics she had used with her half-wolf dog, giving strict instructions and expecting them to be followed instantly. She found that didn't work so well.

'Give the bag of seeds back to me' meant to Ellie 'Take your time, check out the bag, have a little think and then give it back.' Chandra took a hard line and was treated with extreme suspicion and given the evil eye. Ellie was a kid who needed to be given time to respond; time to show that she was the one who had decided to do what was asked. At one point Ellie would not be left in the same room as her. Then slowly the wind changed.

Each afternoon when Sophia returned from school the girls would join Chandra in the garden. They spent hours helping her arrange the potager, pottering about with their trowels, digging weeds and planting bulbs. She caught a tiny bright green tree frog and put it on their hands so they could feel the suction pads on its feet, showed them a bird's nest tucked into the crook of a vine trunk and found a bat hanging behind a shutter on the wall of the house. They were fascinated.

Chandra's lore of nature didn't pass me by. Until her arrival I had been religiously weeding some of the tastiest morsels out of the beds. After a few educational tours I was able to identify four wild salads that would become a staple for us in the summer and autumn months.

This was particularly good since I found that conventional cultivated salads like lettuce were too delicate for me. I forgot to water them or they were carried away by snails. Rocket, a hardy salad with attitude, was the only leaf that I could cultivate. Now nature provided a range of flavours and colours to paint our salads with. My favourite was purslane, which in its native form was crunchy with red stems and succulent green leaves creating a superb colour contrast on a plate.

Ad invited Chandra on a cycle ride and she agreed with alacrity. I watched with interest as they sped out of the yard. About five hours later they cycled back looking like they had been for a stroll. Ad had finally met his match. Chandra was young and fit enough to keep up with him every step of the way. The tour had ended up double the distance of the usual tour of torture and Chandra could still come back for more. I decided I wouldn't tell John and Bullet.

We waited for extra ripeness in the cabernet sauvignon but it meant we lost a lot of the harvest, far more than we expected. Ad, Chandra and I did a pass through the vineyard taking off everything that had the slightest hint of a blemish. I was ruthless. Quality was everything. 'If you have the slightest doubt, cut it off!' By the end of our pass at least a third of the grapes were lying down the centre of the row. It was yet another blow to my finance spreadsheet.

The day before Ad left, we dug the merlot out of the vats and pressed it. It was peaceful and joyful, the smell of Christmas pudding as intoxicating as I remembered. When the pressing was finished we prepared the reds to do their malolactic fermentations, wrapping their vats in silver insulation bubble-wrap blankets to keep the heat in; a trick I had learned from a neighbour.

Ad was part of the family and we missed him when he left. He took the measurements for the terrace railings and promised to make them for us as a gift; it would save us thousands of euros.

Meanwhile, Chandra set out early each morning, hoe in hand. She had made a list of things she wanted to accomplish over her time with us, having taken stock of the place and done an inventory of the tools. Her straw hat bobbing about the potager and surrounding gardens was a comforting sight. The lawn was mown, hedges that hadn't been touched in decades were trimmed, the shed was organised, the bulbs sitting in the shed were planted, weeds removed; the outstanding beds of the potager were cleared, filled with compost and worked, then neat patterns of Garrigue limestone were arranged around the herb beds, the roses and the lilies. Slowly the potager was transformed. In the evenings, not content with a full day of gardening, Chandra organised my cupboards and bookshelves or researched plants for me to consider for the garden in the spring.

By the time Chandra left, Ellie was her best friend. Sophia missed her too and I wished I could have her back every six months to put some discipline on the corridor of crisis.

With Chandra gone and the quiet of winter looming I needed cherry chocolate more than ever but Sean had cut our shopping budget to nothing. For a while the harvest had been all-consuming and I hadn't had time to think about economic reality. Despite the negative economic signs which would have put any investor off, I felt a calling in what we were doing and

I was sure there would be a viable market niche for our organic wine farm and our biodynamic wines in the future. The new whites were exceptional and the reds promising. Our customers encouraged us with emails of congratulations and compliments. We were becoming deeply rooted winemakers. We had to find a way to make the business work.

# Chapter 17

# French Wine Adventures

Jamie, the neighbour who had rented the winery in our first year, came round for lunch.

'Have you heard that the biggest *négociant* for Bergerac wines has gone under?'

Sean and I shook our heads.

'We have a chunk of our 2006 on contract to them. Luckily it's no longer my problem. I've resigned. After fifteen years of hard labour in the French vineyards I'm heading back to the UK. I don't know what I'll do yet but vineyards are booming over there.'

Part of the reason he had decided to go was that the property had been sold. He had read about the sale through a press release: the owner hadn't even told him face to face. I was shocked. For ten years Jamie had put his life and soul into that vineyard, going far beyond the bounds of duty. The property was a small part of the sale of the owner's larger business to an enormous publically listed entity. The owner must have been under non-disclosure but still, it was hard for Jamie to stomach. He decided it was time to move on.

'We'll miss you,' I said. Jamie had been a great help to us in our first year. Since he had moved his wine back to their winery we hadn't seen him much. His news was a big surprise.

We moved on to his other bombshell about the defunct *négociant*.

'How much Bergerac wine went to him?' asked Sean.

'At least a third, maybe more.'

For the Bergerac wine-producing community the news was devastating. Financial troubles were often behind the injuries and deaths all too frequent in the industry. Winemakers were overstretched. They were working too many hours particularly at peak times because they were unable to afford help, and too constrained by bureaucracy. Only a few months before another winemaker, 3 kilometres away from us, had died falling off a vat.

Our neighbour, Olivier, husband of Myreille who warned me of snakes, assured us that everyone was up for sale, if they could only get a price that would leave them with some dignity. The wine business had become so tough that people with generations of history behind them were considering giving up.

We invited Thierry and Isabelle Daulhiac over for dinner. We had dined at their house a few times: Isabelle was a dab hand at turning out seemingly effortless gourmet dishes like truffle pasta. Thierry had a sense of humour and was a great source of information about the wine business and about our commune, leaving us guffawing at his anecdotes about colourful local personalities. He grilled us on the places we had lived and visited, finding it exotic, having never travelled outside Europe.

After serving a starter of mushrooms with goats cheese grilled on top I opened a bottle of grand cru classé Pessac-Léognan, a white wine from the Bordeaux region that Sean had given me for my birthday. We'd discovered this château on a visit to Bordeaux years before and fallen in love with the wine. It didn't live up to the memory.

'Your white wine is better than this,' said Thierry.

Thierry wasn't just being polite; our white blend was better than the grand cru classé.

'It's not fair,' said Isabelle. 'Many of our Bergerac wines are better than these wines that sell for multiple times the price.'

'I can tell from the people around the table at the wine association management meetings that things are tough,' said Thierry. 'Some people have got serious financial problems. It affects decision-making. People are closed to new ideas and tired.'

Bergerac was in a bad financial cycle. Prices were lower than they had been in ten years but costs had more than doubled.

'Look at what is happening to people,' said Isabelle. 'Jean-Paul came to Saussignac with his family to follow their dream of making wine. He and his wife worked together the first few years as they both wanted to work in the business. It soon became clear that the farm was not going to support both of them, even though there was enough work for two. His wife got a job in Bordeaux and had a daily commute of more than an hour each way. They were back in the life they had hoped to leave but with no money as compensation. Then his wife got tired of it and decided to get a serious job again so she took a career opportunity in the north of France to keep the family out of the red. Now they have to commute eight hours to see each other.'

'He bought at the peak of the positive cycle. Now he's got the property up for sale,' added Thierry.

I remembered how, at a recent winemakers' gathering, Jean-Paul had said the first vintage was always full of hope. At last I understood how loaded the comment was. Modern farming realities had ground him and their dream down. Now their wine farm was a sinker for them and he couldn't cut it loose even at a major loss. It made me more worried about us. We had followed a dream like theirs. Now they were being crushed by it. Were we going to wind up the same way, with a broken family and a massive financial burden?

'Is someone keeping an eye on him?' I asked Isabelle.

'I think so. But we have other friends in Monbazillac who left the rat race to seek a better life, and now the only way they survive is by selling direct, so one of them is on the road at wine fairs and markets the whole year. They never have time together as a family. They regularly leave their kids with friends because they have to be away constantly to survive.'

I had heard stories of burly farmers in Australia crying into their fabulous wines that they couldn't give away. They could sell their water rights for more than their wine. Here in Saussignac and Bergerac we had our share of sad tales.

'What about you? How are things going?' asked Isabelle as we tidied away the plates.

*'Pas mal,'* (Not bad) I said. 'I'm looking for part-time work. If you come across anything suitable, please think of me. I could give classes in the Internet or English or entering export markets like the UK.' Isabelle was a teacher at the local vineyard college at Monbazillac.

'I'll keep my eyes open for you but the school is cutting back too. No young people want to go into vineyards and wine. They see how hard people work for nothing in return. Student intake has plummeted in the last few years. Does Sean have anyone to help in the vineyard?'

'No, he does everything himself.'

'He's very courageous.'

Over dessert of home-made chocolate mousse, a delicious and easy recipe that the proprietors of our local restaurant, Le Lion d'Or, had given me, we chatted about places we dreamed of visiting.

That Sunday, I went for my regular run with Laurence. We usually talked as we ran, often getting into deep philosophical discussions or heart-to-hearts about our men, our children, our siblings, our parents and our innermost fears and hopes. I had discovered that not only was she a fountain of knowledge on French culture but she actively played the piano and the violin. Even in her running gear she always looked well turned out in a noble country-woman way. I mentioned Isabelle's stories.

'Pierre has lost one major client who sold up. The wine business was too tough for him. But much worse are the accidents. Two of Pierre's clients died this year. It's a tough business. No one talks about it because it's a small percentage of the population that are winegrowers but the death toll is enormous.'

I asked who they were. One was the Saussignac man who fell off his vat, the other was a winemaker in Duras.

'He turned at the end of a row and the tractor rolled into a ditch and crushed him. He left three young children.'

I felt sick. This was too close to the bone for me. Why continue this crazy fantasy? Perhaps it was winter depression but maybe this dream was not going to work out. Death and financial disaster crouched at the end of each row of vines. We never got that Friday feeling. The week blurred into the weekends well out of harvest time. We had not lifted a tennis racquet or been out to dinner on our own in years.

The following Saturday we went to Pierre and Laurence's house for dinner. The girls played happily with their three kids. They were both already fluent in French. When Sophia started her new school that year Maîtresse confessed that she was convinced Sophia was from a French home despite her foreign passport.

Pierre opened a bottle of white wine that I recognised. It was from the property of another vigneron who had left a successful career to follow the dream of making wine.

'He makes good wine. But business is tough. He's a bitter man. Life is difficult. He's in business with a partner so he can't get out. He thinks that his family would have had a better life if he had stayed in his boring but financially rewarding desk job,' said Pierre.

With a business partner it would be harder to exit, that was certain. There are so many long-term decisions in wine. There would never be a good time to sell. No wonder so many wine businesses went up for sale after the liquidator had forced the situation. I promised myself that would not be us.

If people who had been successful winemakers for decades and in some instances generations were failing, the crisis was serious. I had to come up with a way for us to diversify into a complementary business. I recalled my conversation with Kerry a couple of months before and started drafting a business plan for wine tourism. That Monday when Sean came in from pruning, we sat down to a bowl of steaming soup made from our home-grown butternut squashes that were piled high in baskets in the kitchen and I told him about my ideas. We had talked vaguely about wine tourism when Kerry was visiting but then the harvest had consumed our attention.

'I'm thinking of offering wine classes and wine tours along the lines of what Kerry suggested. We have to find other ways to make money and it seems like an obvious one for us in a region like Aquitaine with so many tourists.'

'Maybe,' said Sean. 'How will you start?'

'I'll outline my ideas for what we can offer and how to present them on a website this afternoon. I've already spoken to Kerry and he has agreed to put me onto his wine tourism site. After coding the website I'll develop the course material.'

'Is it such a good idea? How much time is it going to take to get the website up? It probably won't generate anything and it will take you weeks of work.'

I was frustrated by his attitude. I needed support and collaboration, not negative vibes. He was playing his usual devil's advocate.

'But if we do nothing we'll never know. I don't think it will take me more than a week to get my ideas together and to have a site up. I'll use the template you developed for the wine site.'

That evening I handed Sean the short plan I had worked out. 'We'll have to think about pricing but I want to start with wine courses, tours and vineyard walks.'

'That sounds like a large range. Maybe you should start smaller.'

'No, I need to start with the range we want otherwise it won't happen.'

A few days later I visited our local tourist office to find out whether anyone was offering this sort of thing already.

'I don't know of anything like that,' said the pretty young lady. 'We have the Wine Association wine course and we offer wine weekends through this tourist office.' The wine course was the one I had taken a few months before; their wine weekends were two nights' accommodation and a visit to a vineyard but no wine education. Both were different from what I was planning.

'So could you promote my classes to English tourists when I have the brochures printed?'

'We can't market your offerings through our tourist office since you are not a member. We only market accommodations and visits on behalf of members. Wine producers can't be members because there are too many of you.'

'But this is something different to our wines. I'll be offering wine courses and wine tours where I'll be the educator and translator, not the vigneron.'

'Wait a minute. You can't give tours unless you are a qualified tour guide. You can't be paid to drive people around unless you are a qualified chauffeur.'

No wonder there was little entrepreneurial activity in France compared to other parts of Europe. Thinking on my feet and swallowing my frustration I replied:

'I translate and I educate, I don't offer transport. They can walk, drive themselves or get a taxi. It's their choice, transport and "guiding" is not part of my fee.'

'OK.' She continued to scrutinise the briefing document I had given her.

'You can't offer your prices inclusive of accommodation or lunch unless you are a travel agent.'

It was becoming clear that it wasn't only wine that was smothered with red tape in France.

'OK, so let's assume I'm offering the wine classes, can you market them for me?'

'No, if we market that for you then we have to market all the other activities offered by winemakers and there won't be enough room for everyone.'

'But you told me no one else is doing what I am doing.'

'I know. But others are doing things like cheese and wine tastings and tours of their wineries. We can't promote one and not the other. Come and see me again when the class is running and I'll see what I can do. If it's a one-off event, we can take the brochures.'

There was going to be no free ride via the local tourist office. Undeterred, I continued the development of my ideas for French Wine Adventures. By Christmas the website was complete. I sent the link to Kerry asking him for comments. His reply came back within hours with ten useful points. He was an invaluable advisor; his comments got to the heart and he always had practical solutions. He placed a link to my website from his own wine tourism website.

Sean's family arrived for Christmas. It was the first time that Neal, Sean's youngest brother, and his wife Gillian had visited. They were entranced by the property and our wines. Within hours they were planning the spot for building their own house at Garrigue. I offered to test my wine course on them. For weeks I had been working like a person possessed getting the website and then the course content together. Everything got neglected, especially the housework. Gillian and Glynis, Sean's sister, took me aside and explained in the nicest possible way that they felt our house needed attention. It was time to clean it from top to bottom, sort through the kids' toys and generally get the place organised.

I pictured them and my dad shaking their heads in disappointment over the corridor of crisis. It was only two months since Chandra left and I could see they were right. I had been flat out developing French Wine Adventures. Getting our heads above water was my priority, not a tidy house. Perhaps it was a character flaw: I could concentrate regardless of my surroundings.

Gillian and Glynis went through the toys, cleaned everything and reorganised the furniture into an arrangement that was welcoming and appropriate for the new exit onto the terrace. In retribution for their words that, despite being true, were hard to swallow, I forced them to sit through the first edition of my 'Introduction to French Wine'. The two-hour class covered the history of wine, the main wine regions and varietals of France, the basics of winegrowing and how to taste wine using five samples of our own wines. It was a bit rough being my first edition and the new tasting room was too cold but I enjoyed it and resolved to buy a heater for the room before my first 'real' guests arrived.

'*Très bien*, Madame Feely,' said Bruce, Glynis' husband.

'I learnt a lot,' said Glynis.

'It's good,' said Gillian. 'But you need to work on your presentation. I don't think you should use PowerPoint: just talk freely with the map. You know what you are talking about. Get rid of the slides and do a little booklet, a pocket guide that you only give to people at the end.'

'Great idea. I want to develop vineyard walks as well. We must do some family walks to research routes.'

'I think you should focus on one thing and do it well. I don't know if you should try to offer other things. You need to make sure the place is tidy if you are going to have guests visiting. People want to find the French vineyard dream. It needs to look like that and not like a place where you haven't got enough time to water the plants.' The corridor of crisis had left a lasting impression on Gillian. 'Washing needs to be folded and put away. It needs to look French chic even if it is shabby chic.'

I wanted to develop the whole range despite Gillian's misgivings. To me it would be hard to beat doing a wine tour on foot.

The next day, a quiet afternoon offered the ideal opportunity for Sean and me to investigate the walking route. There was a path that would connect us to the Bordeaux vineyards. Neal offered to provide point-to-point cover, staying in constant contact via mobile phone since we were heading off where no man had gone before. I thought it unnecessary as we were sticking to paths marked on the IGN walking map but he insisted.

We started our walk through Elysian fields. Rolling valleys, pastures and forests gave way to vineyards, golden in the winter sunlight. It was the perfect route to follow for a vineyard walking tour, not difficult and with magical views. It also went in exactly the direction we needed. I felt good, getting to know the contours of this land that we had come to love so much. We were becoming part of it, knowing every stream and valley. Two hours later we met Neal and agreed to contact him for the pickup once we had made it across the Bordeaux border from Razac-de-Saussignac. Trying to avoid roads, we followed a walking path that took us to the next valley. We reached the crest of the hill and found ourselves in a wood.

The dense forest was dark, eerie and deathly quiet. There were strange things hanging in the trees. A complex system of pulleys and tree houses ranged through it like a weird adventure park. We were in the middle of a shooting range set up specially for the release of live pheasants and other unwitting creatures. We realised we must have wandered off the path and backed up quickly. I was rattled. The ambience and terrain were so different to what we had been in an hour before.

'Here's the path,' said Sean. 'If we follow this we'll reach the road that goes from Sainte-Foy to Coutures.' I followed closely, not wanting to be alone in the deathly forest. We skirted round the wood and started down a hill alongside a large pasture. Gunshots rang out and I grabbed Sean's arm.

'Don't leave me,' I said.

'Don't worry, Carolinus. Talk loudly. *Salut, il y a des randonneurs!*' (Hello, there are walkers!)

'Hello,' I yelled.

'Ssshhh, don't talk English or they might be tempted to shoot you,' said Sean wryly.

My stomach tensed with fear as another shot rang out. Maybe Sean was right.

*'Salut! Il y a des randonneurs!'*

A man appeared at the edge of the forest in signature hunting gear: military-style combats and waistcoat. He was smoking a rolled cigarette and had yellow, uneven teeth and a large beard.

*'N'inquiétez pas!'* he called out.

A second later a hare shot out of the forest and sprinted across the field in our direction. A shot rang out and a stab of terror ran a cold trail through my insides. I felt hunted. The hare tore across the field and made it into the other forest. It had been fast enough to see another day. The hunters appeared at the edge of the forest and waved happily at us. I scowled back. My knees were weak. I called Neal and asked him to meet us at the next crossing with the road. His Land Rover appeared below and I felt a wave of relief.

While Sean gave Neal a quick summary of our exciting hike, I traced where we had been on my walking map. The area was called *'L'homme Mort'*, 'Dead Man'. I felt a shiver down my spine. I needed to mark it 'No Go' for my vineyard walks.

# Chapter 18
# La Source

After Christmas, Bruce, my brother-in-law, Neal, and Sean took on the jungle forest to the left of the house where Mr Battistella had indicated we would find an old well. Since his visit Sean and I had hacked a trail through the brush to see it. When we reached it we thought it was empty. Then the wind rippled the water and we realised it was full and clear. The stone well, cut deep into the limestone cliff in a vaulted shape and set in an enchanting dell, deserved to be made accessible.

By New Year, the well and pond were cleared and we could gaze into the crystal water. I drew a jugful and poured glasses of pure mineral water. We toasted the project. It tasted divine. Water from a limestone source is typically very pure as the rock filters the water – on analysis it is often cleaner than rainwater and superior to town water.

It seemed longer than a year since Sean sat with tears running down his cheeks listening to Christy Moore at the kitchen table. A few days before I helped on the school stand at the Saussignac Christmas market and found myself kissing half the hall. Having both girls at school offered a host of connections. We were becoming part of the community. We were integrating. Glynis and Gillian offered to look after the girls so Sean and I could go out to dinner, our first night out alone together in more than two years. I researched options in the pocket restaurant guide that the tourist office had given me on my visit a few weeks before and settled on one that looked like it offered great food and a view at a reasonable price. It was the moment to dust off a little black dress and sheer stockings I hadn't worn in years. When Sean walked into the kitchen, clean-shaven, in a sky-blue shirt that matched his eyes and ironed chinos I hardly recognised him. Sophia grilled me on where we were going and what we would eat, her fine sense of cuisine already well developed thanks to the French school system. Ellie clung to me not wanting to see us go but eventually agreed based on a bribe of *bonbons* – not great parenting but it worked.

We arrived at Au Fil de l'Eau in Sainte-Foy-la-Grande feeling unusual and a little nervous. It was so long since we had dined out together I wondered if we would have much to say. A delicious bottle of Bergerac sauvignon blanc alongside our amuse-bouche or 'amusement for the mouth', a delectable tiny asparagus soup, helped to loosen us up. I felt like I was on a first date. Our lives had been going in different directions for a while, despite working in close quarters. We needed to get to know each other again.

As we drank and ate, we talked about our future; where we wanted to take Garrigue and our organic farming. Sean was excited about the potential for biodynamic, I about wine tourism. We reconnected by voicing our dreams for a change, not what immediate action had to be taken to ensure our survival.

Seafood melted in our mouths, smoked salmon followed by trout with almonds. Our bodies relaxed. I felt young and in love again. Our first dates more than a decade before had been less refined dinners in alternative restaurants in Johannesburg; we were serenaded by Rastafarians and were reckless with youth, drank copious amounts of wine and talked until dawn, but I felt the same: enthralled. Our minds were opening up to the possibilities of our new life.

The cheeseboard was a gastronomic voyage from the walnut liqueur cheese made by nuns in the Dordogne to a rich, yellow cheese from Burgundy. We moved from the sauvignon blanc to a half-bottle of Bordeaux red. Inspired by the journey on our plates, we talked about visiting famous biodynamic growers to learn and to explore our new profession and country, about taking a family holiday with Sophia and Ellie. Wine is a long journey but we had our whole lives ahead of us. I felt like we were just starting out, young and invigorated.

A fruit tart with a swirl of chocolate accompanied a glass of Saussignac dessert wine. Our conversation moved naturally with the flow of wine to Saussignac's high percentage of organic farms and how we could be ambassadors for the environment.

Perhaps it was the Saussignac wine, a legendary aphrodisiac, or perhaps it was the intimacy of the evening but my mind turned from dreams to sensual pleasures. I had a G-string on for the first time in years. My stockinged foot touched Sean's inner thigh surreptitiously under the table, his eyebrows lifted and he called for the bill. We left replete, refreshed and in love.

Thierry Daulhiac telephoned the evening the family left.

'I want you to join the management board of the Saussignac appellation.'

'Sorry, Thierry. I don't think I understood what you said. Can you repeat?' I pushed the lounge door closed the better to hear and sat down on the floor in the hallway.

'Yes, Caro. I want you to join the management board of the Saussignac appellation. You're full of ideas. I've spoken to the rest of the committee and they're in agreement. You'll be a breath of fresh air.'

'But I know almost nothing about making Saussignac wine.'

The group consisted of the likes of Richard Doughty and Gérard Cuisset, people who had initiated commune appellation status for the dessert wines of Saussignac. The wine had been famous for centuries but did not have appellation status until 1982.

'Don't worry. We want you for your marketing ideas.'

This would be a good opportunity to get to know the other vignerons and to gain an understanding of the inside of the complex appellation system.

'What do I have to do?'

'*Enfin*, it's not too much. You participate in the meetings, help us make decisions and then each person has a special portfolio.'

'What portfolio would you want me to take on?'

'I want you to be our representative on the Saussignac *syndicat d'initiative*. You'll be the liaison between the *syndicat d'initiative* and the winemakers. It's a difficult post because the *syndicat d'initiative* always want us to give more time than we can but I think you will be good for it. Reflect on it and let me know.'

The *syndicat* was responsible for events and promotion of the general commune but wine was often promoted through events, and the wine union and the *syndicat* ran a tourist office in the village in high season.

'I don't need time to think about it, I'd love to join the group.'

I hung up and ran through to the lounge to share the news with Sean.

'That's a feather in your cap, Carolinus. Now you can agitate from the inside... and leave me in peace.' He laughed and turned back to watching his television show. We only had French channels and they were doing wonders for his language skills.

A few weeks later I joined a group of vignerons who were gathered outside the mayor's office in Razac-de-Saussignac waiting for the appellation committee meeting. The topic of conversation was the Asterix-and-Obelix-style village politics in Saussignac; a major fight was brewing between the incumbent and the previous mayor. Blistering letters copied to all the members of the commune flew back and forth. Not a day went by without another instalment in the village scuffle for power. Joel, the wild vigneron, was particularly amused; he had been in low-level combat with one of the parties for many years.

The meeting started with a review of the appellation union's finances then moved on to the new decrees for the appellation. Significant reforms were under way across France. Debates on minutiae ensued. Most consumers would never have heard of these points. I felt like standing up and calling a halt. We were wasting time discussing things that wouldn't make any difference to sales and would create administrative headaches for already stretched growers. The final item on the agenda said it all: the INAO had reviewed the appellation boundaries based on a high-level soil analysis. Four components make up terroir but they had looked only at the soil. As important for botrytis is the microclimate. For Saussignac, the grapes are best if located on north-facing land south of the Dordogne river. The INAO had thrown out the old boundaries and made the new boundary the Route des Coteaux (the D14). Bernard Barse's excellent Saussignac was now outside the appellation. None of Bernard's customers cared if he was north of the D14, a man-made barrier which had nothing to do with the appellation; they cared that he produced exceptional Saussignac wine, which they could assess for themselves. Part way through a leading vigneron stormed out of the meeting slamming the door behind him in frustration. I was not the only one who found all this bureaucracy counterproductive.

My first wine tour customers found my website via an Internet search and Kerry's website. Sean was impressed. Sheila and Jeff were winemakers from Washington state who had followed their passion and started a small winery operation. This was their first trip to Bordeaux but they had a good knowledge of French wine from years of study. They would also be our first paying guests in our new gîte, the half of our house that had become 'The Wine Cottage', helping to prove the wisdom and synergy of this new tourism initiative to Sean.

Between their initial booking and their arrival, I spent hours researching and plotting their itinerary, planning visits, restaurants and vineyards. Wine is an endless subject. I devoured our wine books and ordered more. I wanted my tours to be different, to be deeper than your average tour, and most important, to be authentic. It was challenging and thrilling.

Our first day took us to St Émilion via a visit to a barrel-maker. The factory was rustic; an old breeze-block and corrugated-iron warehouse filled with rows of beautiful barrels. The gleaming oak, packed to perfection in plastic wrapping, was backed onto medieval-looking equipment. We were welcomed by the manager of the factory, David. I asked if we could use the toilets before starting the tour.

'With three men working here, the toilets aren't in good shape,' said David. 'Perhaps we should go to the shopping centre – it's about ten minutes away.'

'I don't want to lose that much time. I'll go first and clean the place up a bit before Sheila and Jeff come in,' I said.

'As you want,' said David, leading me to a lean-to.

It was filthy and there was no toilet. I looked around, confused. David motioned into the doorless *cabine*, or cubicle, and I spied in the gloom the ancient remains of a toilet *'à la turque'*. With *à la turque,* instead of a toilet above ground, you get a tray, like a square shower tray, in the ground. In normal circumstances, it is extremely unpleasant but it is possible to use a facility like this by squatting if it is immaculately clean. In this case there was so much dirt built up that there was no sign of the original ceramic tray. What gave it away were pipes coming out of the dirt connected to a rusted cistern hanging ominously overhead and a hole in the floor. I stepped back in horror.

'We'll have to go to the shopping centre,' I said, leading Sheila and Jeff away as fast as I could.

I kicked myself for not making a prior visit. David drove us to the shopping centre where we found normal toilets that functioned perfectly in a small cafe. Now we could begin the visit.

David explained the process of making the barrels from the drying of the wood to the final toasting of the barrel, demonstrating at each point what the coopers – the barrel-makers – were doing. Barrel-making is an ancient art still largely manual despite technical advances and coopers must do two years of training to qualify. Tacked onto the wall behind the traditional equipment was a girlie calendar that would make anyone blush.

The first step was to assemble the carefully selected and pre-cut oak staves inside metal hoops. Then the cooper wet the staves and placed the partially constructed barrel over a small wood fire. This was critical: the amount of 'toasting' over the open fire has an important effect on the wine that will be aged in the barrel, so the vigneron chooses how much 'toast' depending on the style of wine they want.

Barrel selection is a fine art. Two identical barrels from the same forest and the same barrel-maker can taste quite different. Some winegrowers even go so far as to specially select their oak tree in a specific forest. French oak from the central forests is highly sought after and expensive as it grows slowly and thus has a finer grain, offering a more refined flavour than a faster growing oak.

With the help of the heat and humidity the cooper then bent the staves using a winch to obtain the shape of the barrel. The final metal hoops were put in place and the ends of the staves were trimmed and cut to receive the barrel heads. The cooper completed the final hooping with a large mallet, reinforcing the medieval sense of the place. The barrel was then tested for impermeability and, if passed, would proceed to the sand-papering and finishing. It was an intense process requiring skill and strength.

Sheila and Jeff were charmed by seeing the whole procedure done by hand and appeared unfazed by the porn on the walls. I felt the day could only improve.

We continued to a tour of Château Belair in St Émilion. From the courtyard in front of the main house Lionel, our charming guide, pointed out many of the premier grand crus classés of St Émilion including his neighbour Château Ausone where the Roman poet consul Ausonius planted vines around AD 350.

Belair belonged to the English military commander during the period of the Hundred Years War, a war that was the ultimate result of the second marriage of a lusty woman, Eleanor, to an English king. Eleanor inherited the province of Aquitaine and ruled from 1137 to 1189. Soon after inheriting she married King Louis VII of France. She bore him children, accompanied him on a Crusade to the Holy Land and took a lover in the afternoon. On their return she decided he was too religious for her, gave him the boot and persuaded the Pope to annul their marriage.

Then she married Henry Plantagenet who became Henry II of England, so Aquitaine was in English hands. During this part of her exciting life she gave St Émilion their city rights in return for fifty barrels a year of their premium wine. For the ensuing 300 years of English rule, the only French wines exported to England, and to her trading partners, were Bordeaux. Partly thanks to this export monopoly, Bordeaux is still the most well-known wine region in the world. *Merci*, Eleanor.

We went into the Belair *caves* (cellars) to see their old vintages; wines dating back to 1802 when they were the first to do *mise en bouteille au château*, estate-bottled wine. It was a treasure trove of old vintages in ancient golden tunnels and *cave* rooms that were like something out of a film set. Bordeaux was a universe of wine stars waiting to be discovered. I felt like a child inside a sweet shop just bursting to try them all.

Sheila and Jeff were ecstatic about their stay, describing it as 'perfect' and commending my knowledge. I felt I still had a lot to learn but their comments fired me up about our new line of business.

It was six months since I spat our first vintage red wines out in disgust and the wait was paying off. Now they were strong and smooth, all black fruit and mocha. Almost everything was ordered for the imminent bottling including our new label, which featured a photo of our ancient well artfully enhanced by our printer's creative studio. It made our premium wine look grown-up, serious and delicious. The logistics for the bottling were perfectly aligned. Then the bottle supplier called to say he could not supply due to a gross bottle shortage in Europe.

In a panic I called our agricultural supply company that I knew supplied bottles too. They took the order and asked me to come in for a meeting where I was presented to the owner of the business, a cigarette smouldering in his hand despite the workplace smoking ban.

'Aren't you the one who didn't pay your bill a few months ago?' he asked, flapping my €7,000 bottle order in the air and blowing smoke in my face.

'No. We didn't pay for a faulty product last year but otherwise we always pay our bills on time.'

He berated me a little more and blew a bit more smoke in my face.

'Our supplier has cancelled all bottle deliveries for February. We can't even fulfil orders for our most loyal customers.'

It was a calamity. I pleaded and begged.

He gave me a lesson on bottle economics, the number of factories in Europe, the number that had been closed down by the three main players and more. All I cared about was our bottles and when he could deliver them. His assistant arrived and saved me from the final instalment.

'I can't believe it. They've confirmed your order. The other four in February were placed before yours, but yours is confirmed and the others cancelled. Yours must have slipped through because it's quite small and they can fill it between other orders.'

Suddenly Monsieur grabbed the order confirmation from his assistant. I feared the worst.

'Ah, ah, ah! But I have made a mistake. You are Mrs Feely, it is another *étrangère* who didn't pay their bills.'

It was a relief to know our name was clear but nothing compared to the joy of having my bottles. I took a copy of the confirmation and asked them to bring the delivery date forward a few days to be sure.

For our previous bottling, the capsules were available off the shelf so we assumed the same would be true this time. Now we had a week to go and the FVB told me they did not have what we wanted in stock. It would be four weeks until the next lot arrived. I grovelled.

'I'll see what I can do,' said Madame.

A few days later she had found some capsules for us. I collected them. We started bottling the following day, progressing at a snail's pace. Neal and Gillian, Sean's brother and his wife, were over to help, and within an hour they were treated to a full education in French expletives from Pierre, our bottler.

'*Quel bordel! Ces merdes de capsules! *!@*!&*$%^*!&!*'

It was a Pierre I had not seen before. The culprits were my last-minute capsules. Every second one was sticking on the machine.

'These are bad, bad quality,' he said accusingly.

'Now I know why Madame at the FVB found the capsules so quickly for me. No one else wanted them.'

'We will have to put the capsules on by hand. Paul will do it.'

Paul, Pierre and Laurence's nine-year-old son, was soon positioned on top of a plastic pallet placing capsules onto bottles.

Several thousand bottles later we took a break for lunch. Paul's great work was enabling us to keep pace despite the *'capsules merdiques'*.

The following evening we all celebrated the successful bottling with Pierre and Laurence in their house, the slowly transforming middle section of Saussignac Castle. At last, after a wait of about four years, Pierre had fitted the oven for Laurence.

*'Ça avance!'* (It's progressing!) I said excitedly.

*'Oui, à pas de fourmis,'* (Yes, with ant-like steps) said Laurence patiently, stroking the new sideboard.

Ellie's voice resounded around the room. 'Mummy, I need to go to the *toilette*.'

Sean looked around. 'Where is she?' He had not come in contact with the castle's internal phone system. Through the great curved sewage pipe jutting out over the oven I told Ellie I was on my way. This natural telephone between upstairs and downstairs allowed communication between levels in the massive building. It was like being on a submarine.

Laurence served a cauliflower and apple salad that was the essence of freshness.

'How do you say it in French?' asked Neal.

*'Pommes et chou-fleur,'* replied Laurence. Neal repeated it several times.

Then we asked for translations of the words that we had heard from Pierre that week.

'You know Pierre picked up all that bad language in Marseille. It's the capital of the expletive. He always goes back to his Marseille accent when he swears.'

'I think these swear words are especially effective when you add *"espèce de"* (stupid) to the front of the word,' said Pierre. 'When you see an idiot on the road you roll down your window and yell *"espèce de gros con!"* Big *%$! species!'

'I'll remember that next time I am on the road,' said Neal, trying the name out several times as I held my hand over the talking pipe so our girls weren't exposed to the lesson.

Neal tried out his new words. *'Chou-fleur, pomme, gros, con...'*

'Watch out you don't get mixed up.' Pierre made the motion of rolling down his car window. *'Espèce de gros chou-fleur!'*

# Chapter 19

# Pre-school Gourmands

After my wine class in Bergerac I waited behind two students discussing with the teacher which wines would best match each course they had planned for the weekend. Their fifty-minute debate took food and wine matching to a new level. Later, I mentioned to Isabelle Daulhiac that I was planning to cook chicken in Saussignac and to serve our dry white wine alongside the dish.

'Never, never serve a different wine to the one that went into the food,' said Isabelle in horror. 'Only use good wine for cooking and always serve the same wine that goes into the meal with the food. This is a fundamental rule.'

No longer could wine be set aside as cooking wine. If it was good enough to cook with, it was good enough to serve. Nowhere is French appreciation of food more apparent than in the schools. A typical day could be endive salad to start, pan-fried fish for a main and apple tart for dessert; or tomato soup, sausages and lentils followed by crème caramel. Children learnt to eat a variety of foods that were adult and healthy. Sophia spotted a bunch of radishes at the Gardonne market. I wasn't big on radishes so we didn't have them in the potager.

'We must buy these,' she said. 'We eat them at school.'

When we got home, standing on a chair, four-year-old Sophia presided over the preparations. I cut off the radish leaves and prepared to throw them into the compost bin.

'No, no!' she exclaimed. 'You must keep those to make a green salad.' I obeyed, feeling safe in the hands of a grand connoisseur after two years in the French school system. She then recited how to make the dressing for the radish leaves; olive oil, balsamic vinegar, sugar, a pinch of salt.

The radish heads with a spot of cold butter dabbed onto them and the radish leaf salad were absolutely delicious. It was the first time I had enjoyed radishes in my life.

A few days later, I came home with a cheap Camembert.

'That doesn't taste like Camembert, it tastes more like Brie,' said Sophia imperiously.

'Maybe,' I replied.

Minutes later Sean came in. 'That's bad Camembert. It tastes like Brie.'

There would be no more cheap, nasty, imposter Camemberts in our house.

Duck is a major part of the cuisine of the Dordogne and the Périgord. My best duck breast of all time was enjoyed al fresco at the Saussignac market from an artisanal producer who grilled it right in front of me on a medieval iron platter hung over an open fire.

Free, with music and dancing included, Saussignac night market was chock-full of the ambiance of a summer *sans soucis* (without worries). As evening fell, traders erected stalls and music began to waft through the village square where tables had been arranged by energetic village volunteers. The DJ, a dynamic extrovert with a wide smile, set up his stand right against the church. Soon he was boogying and shaking to wild rock music under the clock tower. It was loaded with all the irony I had come to expect of France.

We were selling our wines for the first time at a market. Soon I was frenetically serving people by the glass. Sean went back to Garrigue for more cold wine.

*'J'aime ce vin,'* (I like this wine) said Olivier, our winemaking neighbour, coming back to buy a second bottle of sauvignon blanc from our stall. 'It's different. It's very good.'

My heart swelled with joy. Olivier was from a winegrowing family of several generations. His comments were high praise. Olivier's return for another bottle spoke more than his words.

Sean ran after our two girls weaving between tables in their pretty pink dresses. He bought *moules et frites*, mussels and chips, and they enjoyed a finger feast standing next to our stall. Then, leaving Sean to man the stand, I took the girls to boogie with the DJ in the shadow of the church. We could have danced all night if the toilet facilities had been in better shape, but alas, they were *à la turque* and not quite spotless.

We decided to make our first foray into livestock: chickens. Animals were important to the whole farm concept of biodynamics and they would improve our self-sufficiency. Despite the pressure of early summer mowing, weeding and shoot removal Sean ordered the chickens, knowing a deadline was what he needed to build the house and run.

'What kind of chickens did you order?' I asked.

'I don't know. They're the type the co-op supply as laying hens.'

'But what colour will they be?'

'I don't know.'

This said it all about the difference between men and women. For me, our chickens needed to be the cute golden-brown ones with white undercarriage, not any old chickens. For Sean, so long as they laid eggs, he wasn't too pushed.

The auspicious day arrived and Sean collected our nine chickens from the farm supply in Gardonne. He lifted the boxes out of the car and carefully let them out into the run. They were the right colour but, horror of horrors, their necks were bare, totally feather free. They ran off, scared out of their wits. Sean and the girls spent hours watching them.

Within a few weeks the chickens had become an important part of life at Garrigue. Sean got up early to let them out. At night he closed them into their coop, safe from foxes. They loved Sean, their source of food: a mix of grain and leftovers. When they saw him they would stampede like ladies at a summer sale beating each other off to be first in line. Their running gait was hilarious: one minute genteelly pecking around the garden, the next running like mad, skirts hoicked up over their knees.

The hens started laying: first a mixed bag of erratic, tiny eggs, then a steady flow of good-sized speckled or brown eggs, often with double yolks. We ate our first home-grown omelette with relish. The yolks were a more vibrant yellow than I had ever seen and the flavour was superb.

Early one Sunday morning I heard a commotion that didn't sound like the usual egg laying. I dropped everything and sprinted onto the terrace. A hen was scrambling up the road with a monstrous dog in pursuit. I let out a blood-curdling yell and ran at the dog, forgetting my own safety in my effort to protect the hen. The dog turned tail and ran.

With my heart beating like a helicopter rotor and my adrenalin pumping I went up to the chicken house fearing the worst. A bundle of chickens were huddled in one corner. I consoled them quietly and counted. Eight. I did a circuit of the garden and the fields around the house then came back to count again. The number was the same. I was devastated. Sophia and Ellie came out. Sophia counted and burst into tears.

'Don't worry, Sophia,' said Ellie sagely, not clear on what was happening.

'Ellie's right,' I said. 'Don't worry. She is probably hiding because she's scared. We'll have a good look with Dad when he comes in for some water.'

I didn't hold out much hope. I felt sad, far more affected than I thought I would be. I hadn't realised how much a part of the family they had become with their beady eyes, pointy beaks and hilarious lacy skirts.

When Sean came in from doing his anti-fungal treatment we did another circuit looking for the missing chicken. Sean went up to the hen house and counted again. As he closed the gate, fearing she was lost for good, the hen stepped cautiously out of the thick hedge behind the coop. She had been hiding in fear since the incident. Hearing Sean's voice, she felt safe enough to come out. All of the chickens were safe and sound.

Our gourmet hens were producing enough eggs to provide much of our protein requirements. We tightened our belts and stopped buying meat. Alongside decreasing our cost of living I had to create some income. The wine tourism had to succeed.

My first reservation for a Médoc wine tour had just come in. Although it was far – almost three hours' drive – it was such an iconic part of Bordeaux I had to include it in my offerings. I read up frantically, filling in the gaps in my knowledge. It was like cramming for exams but more fun.

Winemaking is one of the most ancient arts practised by man, dating back to around 8000 BC in parts of Asia; in parts of France, including our little corner of the Dordogne, winemaking predates Roman times by a few hundred years. The Médoc, an exception, was marshland until the late 1600s, when Dutch engineers were brought in to drain it for agriculture.

Austin, my client, was a Scottish oenophile doing a grand tour of France. He was on his way through the south of France and once in Bordeaux, he was keen to visit a premier grand cru classé in the Médoc. I planned our day around a visit to Château Mouton Rothschild where they offered tasting as part of the tour. When we arrived for the tour I discovered an additional bonus was their art museum. Wine is widely depicted in ancient art. Walking around the ruins of Pompeii at twenty years old, I was impressed by the sophistication of two things: their art and their plumbing. The art depicted scenes of people enjoying wine and sensual pleasures that would make a regular Playboy-reader blush.

The museum at Mouton was filled with similar ancient treasures. We passed millennia-old Greek pottery with scenes of the grape harvest and winemaking painted on their smooth round sides, magnificently erotic and celebratory. One showed nude men with massive erections lifting baskets of grapes into a press. There were scenes with dancing, music, winemaking and mystical elements like a man with horns and goat feet. Then we entered the modern art section with lurid pink pottery tea pots and other strange collectibles.

Not a moment too soon for Austin, we left the museum and headed for the important bit – tasting wine. Before being allowed to taste the really good stuff we had the Rothschild's other two grand crus classés wines. The tour guide poured large helpings of each. They were delicious but nowhere near the greatness of the Mouton finale. It was deep, full and rich, not in a cloying overripe way, but in a structured, robust way.

'Now that's a wine for me,' said Austin, draining his glass. 'Nothing like a little Pauillac for breakfast.'

By the end of the day Austin had a selection of grand crus classés in his boot. He was a true bon vivant, someone who drank for pleasure and could afford to drink the really good stuff. I hoped all my clients would be as much fun.

Alongside the tours I offered wine classes in our newly completed tasting room: the two-hour session that I called 'Introduction to French Wine'. It was an idea we hoped would bring clients to our tasting room door. My knowledge and my tasting and teaching skills were on a massive learning curve.

The old friends of Garrigue, the mice, continued to be part of the landscape. As I pulled the flat-pack boxes off a pallet to prepare a new wine order, a mouse leapt off the stack like a small, grey flying saucer and scampered across the room. I screamed and ran in the opposite direction, my heart beating like a runaway train.

I could not help my reaction of 'scream and run'. This one had created a beautiful nest out of shreds of paper from some of the packing around the boxes. Fortunately there were no baby mice in it. Mice are tiny but I was scared witless by them. It was illogical but I couldn't stop it. Sean, grumbling about my lack of country wife skills, checked for the mouse and set a trap.

Once he was sure there was no sign of the intruder, I got the boxes I needed and cleaned the stockroom from top to toe to make sure there were no more unwanted guests. At every moment I expected another mouse to leap out at me.

The same week, as I was walking home from Hillside vineyard, a large snake slithered off the vineyard track into the limestone cliffs. According to Myreille's theory, I had to remain calm if I was bitten. Here I was, far from being bitten, but my heart was racing. Clearly I was one of the ones who would be DOA at Bergerac Hospital if I ever had the misfortune of receiving a snake bite.

Sean mocked me. He had never seen a snake despite being outside far more than I. A little while before, I had nearly stood on a snake in my flip-flops. The racket the snake made slithering clumsily across the gravel path was like tambourines but Sean, a couple of metres away, heard nothing. I leapt a metre into the air and ran away screaming, proving to Sean what a wimp I was.

The next mouse episode took place during a course by the Syndicat des Vignerons Bio d'Aquitaine (SVBA), the organic wine producers' association.

The instructions to find the first class in Entre-Deux-Mers were typically French. I had a farm name in a *lieu-dit* in an obscure village and no phone numbers. All communes are made up of many *lieu-dits*, the old name of the place, almost like a street name. Our area in Saussignac was La Garrigue so that was the address for all the houses on our road including ours, which was the final property at the end of the cul-de-sac. I found the village but could not find the *lieu-dit*. Panicked at running a few minutes late, I called the association to see if they could help but got the answering machine. After circling the village several times I stopped at a winery that looked open.

Finding no one inside I paced around hoping for a call back or for the appearance of life. Five minutes later two burly farmers came out of the nearby house. They were taken aback to find a mobile-phone-packing foreign woman in their yard but they knew the property and quickly explained how to get there. Soon I was flying along vague roads in the middle of nowhere.

At Château Ferran a small group of people consisting of the owner, the oenologist giving the course and the woman who ran the organic union were talking in the courtyard. I was fifteen minutes late but the first attendee to arrive.

A half-hour later when the other vignerons, mostly handsome young men, arrived, there were no introductions. I thought perhaps everyone else knew each other but later realised most of them didn't. The course was aimed at experienced winegrowers looking to extend their knowledge and would offer a solid grounding on principles of organic and biodynamic winemaking. The eight sessions would take place over a full year so we could chart the progress of the wines through a full winemaking cycle. It was another step on the road to understanding the mysteries of winemaking. At the end of the session the other attendees gave me a familiar kiss on each cheek. It was strange having good-looking men whose names I didn't know kiss me but it was a French habit I knew I could get used to.

The next class, a month later, was at a St Émilion grand cru property. I had learnt my lesson about timing and arrived a half-hour late as the class was starting. This time there were many new people but again no introductions. Halfway through the class a little mouse ran along the shelf a few metres from our table. I would have been screaming had I not lost my voice from the shock. The mouse looked relaxed and not put off by the human voices in his domain. I was ready to leap onto the table but noting the calm demeanour of the other farmers I remained frozen in my chair. Anne, the owner of the property said fondly 'There's our little mouse.'

If I was to be a true farmer's wife, I would have to overcome my insane fear of tiny rodents. I didn't want them in my house but after experiencing the calm of all those vignerons in that converted barn my reaction to mice was transformed. If they could remain calm, I could too.

A few days later, Sean prepared some bottles for a Friday evening mystery wine session for the two of us. It was a game we had started to play a few months before. He poured a glass and set it down in front of me. I lifted, sniffed, swirled, sniffed again, then took a swig. The wine filled me with warmth. It was rich.

'That's delicious. What is it?'

'You tell me.'

I looked at the glass in the light. It looked quite bright but on the rim it was turning slightly tawny. All wine browns with age. Red wine goes from purplish red to brick red, and unoaked dry white wine goes from straw yellow with perhaps a hint of green, to deep gold, as it ages. Cabernet sauvignon is particularly purple when it is young. This one was well past its purple stage and into mahogany territory.

The next clue was the aroma. The wine was ripe blackcurrant with a hint of spice. Wines range from upfront fresh fruit in a young wine to complex and cooked fruit aromas in an older wine.

Finally, and most importantly, comes the third element, the taste of the wine. I reflected on my memory bank. The wine was reminiscent of a vintage I had tasted in Médoc.

'Tastes like a ripe Médoc grand cru.' My range of vision was Bordeaux-centric. 'Definitely oaked.'

Salvador Dalí said: 'Who knows how to taste wine never drinks wine again but tastes secrets.' Wine is an expression of the place and the year that it was produced, a magical journey back to the summer of its birth. As I learned more about wine tasting, I realised that with practice, one could tell what age a wine was, where it was from and the grape variety without looking at the label.

The wine whispered its secrets; messages in the form of look, smell and taste. The colour was the first clue about its style and age.

'I don't know. It seems slightly "cooked". No, I don't think it's Médoc. It seems too hot.' Sean played the wine along, not ready to give me the answer. We discussed other clues that it offered: the alcohol, the acidity, the tannins, the aromas. I named just about every place except the correct one. Eventually he relented and gave me the answer.

'It's a ripe, expensive cabernet sauvignon from Walla Walla in Washington state.'

A client who booked The Wine Cottage gîte had given it to us as a gift. The self-catering unit was paying off in more ways than one. 'That's where Jeff and Sheila have their vineyard,' I said. Jeff and Sheila were my first tour customers, the people who I almost subjected to the most disgusting toilet in the whole of France.

Many grand crus in the Médoc have a large percentage of cabernet sauvignon so I had been in the right arena with the varietal on my first guess but on the wrong continent.

'Now that I know what it is, it's reminiscent of the South African cabernet sauvignon we had a few weeks ago,' I added. 'In fact, I think I would struggle to tell the difference if they were both here. It's the globalisation of the wine industry.'

'How old?' asked Sean.

'Around four years,' I said.

*'Exact!'*

I held up my hand for a high-five.

Our Friday evening treat of opening a couple of bottles of mystery wine from our stash had become a great game. Sean gave me another to taste.

'What's this? It's delicious and spicy. There is something familiar about it. If it weren't for the spiciness, I would guess pure merlot.'

'Correct!' He had slipped one of our barrel samples into the mix, presenting it as a wine from our collection. 'It's last year's merlot in the American oak barrel – that's what gives it the spiciness.'

I held my hand up for another high-five.

When made naturally, there is no other product that expresses different land or terroir as well as wine. Once you follow vintages you see each is a different character with unique charm. They evolve like their vignerons. Each farm and vintage has a story. I had fallen in love with our new profession. Not the infatuation of our dream of going wine-farming but a deep, profound love, something that resonated in my soul. A resonance that came from the three years of hard work, the inspiration of working with nature and nurturing our farm back to health and gaining a deeper understanding of what wine truly was and how it could express a place. But was it a love that was unconditional? How far was I willing to pursue it?

This journey had taken me to a place I loved, peopled with colourful characters. I wanted to learn more; to share more. But it was early days and there was still no light at the end of the tunnel financially. A tour like the one I did with Austin would not change the economic reality that kept rearing its head.

## Chapter 20

# Goodbye Château?

Sean and I agonised about what to do yet again. My wine tourism had started but wasn't making any money. I was offering classes free to accommodation owners to build up my reputation, hoping it would pay off later in guests sent my way. The feedback was excellent but there was no return yet. The Wine Cottage gîte was bringing in much-needed money but nothing like what we needed to live on. Our wine sales were going well; Dave had ordered another 600 bottles and our direct business was growing. But even if we sold out it wouldn't cover the costs of operating the vineyard. We scrutinised our finance spreadsheet hoping for a miracle. Alas, nothing had changed.

'We have to tighten our belts,' said Sean.

'They're so tight I'm getting gangrene.'

'I know, Carolinus, but we're still in start-up mode, we have to expect the first few years to be tough.'

'We can't buy shoes for the girls. Look at poor Ellie: all she has are hand-me-downs. Hand-me-down clothes are fine, but shoes? She should have at least one good pair of shoes. Look at me – the cheapest body lotion I can find on my face.'

'But look at the life we have, Carolinus. Look how much fun the girls have being outside with the chickens. Look how fulfilling it is following our passion rather than doing a job. I'm working harder than I ever have but I love it.'

'I know, SF, but we can't live on fresh air. We have to make enough money to live and looking at these projections doesn't fill me with hope.'

Our dream was not working out the way I had expected. I knew it would be tough but not nearly this tough. At least, for all the sacrifices, I thought we would eventually begin to reap enough rewards to feed our family.

The following day the social services organisation inspector came around. I had spoken to him about wanting to work a couple of days a week when Ellie started school. At the time I was researching the wine classes and tours and put off finding out more about what he said. Now he was back for his pound of flesh. He explained that regardless of the circumstances I had to pay social charges of several thousand or 47 per cent of my income, whichever was the largest, per year.

'As soon as you start working, even if you are not being paid, you have to pay. It doesn't matter what you get from us. That's not the issue. If you are working for the farm, even if you are making no money, you have to pay,' he said.

Remembering Ellie's tough-guy 'Stop!' routine with him the last time, I considered asking him to hold on while I fetched my three-year-old bodyguard from school.

'The farm isn't making any money, not even enough to pay Sean the minimum wage. I'm looking for a job off the farm or to start another business. At the moment the farm can't support one person, let alone two.'

'You still have to pay the social charges. Unless you have a full-time job off the farm you have to pay the social charges as if you are the *exploitant*. You could declare yourself as working part-time on the minimum wage but then you have to declare exactly what you do for the business on the declared days and keep detailed records. If we find you doing something that is not on your declared activities or working out of the hours you declare, it will be bad for you. Anyway, that will land up being more expensive than the minimum charge as *exploitant* if you are making a loss.'

I wondered if I had fallen into the well in *Alice in Wonderland*. How could this be the only option? It would break us.

'If you don't agree to this, I will check you regularly and you can be sure we will catch you doing something that could be considered part of the business even if it is a bit of DIY. Then you will have to pay a fine and still pay the social charges. There is no other option for you. I highly recommend that you sign up for the full plate of charges right now.'

He held out a pen to me.

My throat was tight with stress. I felt like shouting 'Stop!' but no sound came out. Our finances were way off healthy and this would tip us over the edge.

He wasn't going to leave until I had signed the papers. It was that or be constantly hounded, unable to even paint the walls on the weekend without being caught and fined for working undeclared. The huge man loomed ominously over me with the pen. He gave me a big smile.

'Don't worry, I will write the letter saying you are now working full-time for the farm. All you have to do is sign it. Our objective isn't to put you out of business. Of course, it's important that you survive so you can pay us.'

I felt like vomiting onto his pristine white shirt. Under his pressure I signed the documents. He gave me a satisfied smile.

That evening Sean and I went through numerous scenarios. No matter what we did, with this new burden we would be working to pay our suppliers and the social charges and not even covering that.

'We have to sell the farm. We'll never make a living. We aren't going to make it through the next twelve months with this extra charge.' I burst into tears. 'I don't want to sell,' I sobbed.

'I know, Carolinus, but we can't carry on if we can't pay ourselves. We can't carry on until the bank forces us to sell.'

The writing was on the wall. We could not continue. I felt angry, sad and frustrated. We had put so much into pursuing our dream. Our wines were good, critics and clients loved them and yet we could not make a living. Since arriving, I had never seriously entertained the thought that we might fail. Now we were facing it full in the face. I wanted so badly for us to succeed, now more so than ever.

Once I got control of myself we discussed it further. After looking in every direction for a solution we agreed there was no way out. We had to sell. There wasn't enough time for us to build up the wine tourism business to make up for the shortfall.

We had to return to city lives and normal jobs. At least we would have most weekends off, holidays, sick leave and some money for our work. There was that upside. But even the idea of being paid could not help me shrug off the devastation I felt. The next day I called an estate agent and asked them to come around to look at Garrigue.

Laurence was still in the Basque country with family so that Sunday I set off on my own with my MP3 player, running along the road, my feet beating in time to U2. I turned onto the high vineyard track that runs along the ridge above Saussignac. As I crested the hill, a panoramic view of the village floating above the Dordogne valley with the castle, solid like an anchor in the sea of green vineyards and forests, engulfed me. I felt a deep love of this place. Our life, full of priceless riches, stretched out before me. Rich relationships, simple food, a passion for what we were doing and magnificent countryside.

I stopped and lifted my arms into the air in silent homage to this exceptional place into which we had haphazardly fallen. I felt part of it. I loved what we were doing. I wanted to stay. I wanted to stay so badly it was like a physical force sinking down into the ground. I felt like I was rooted to the spot. I could see my children and my children's children on this hill looking down towards our farm. It was like an ancient force. A spirit well. This was my home. This was our home. I felt at once powerless and powerful. Grief for the imminent loss of this place overtook me. Sobs racked through my body. I stood with tears flowing down my cheeks staring out at the landscape. That week I felt like I was in a bad dream. I went about my work in a mechanical daze. Thursday evening the phone rang.

'Hi, Caro. It's Andrew.'

I hadn't spoken to Andrew since my last trip home. It was great to hear his familiar tones. We worked together for more than five years and had known each other a lot longer.

'How are things?' I said. We had a chat about the new job that he had started. It sounded like a good place to work.

'They don't need more people do they? I need a job.'

I explained what had happened and how we had just put Garrigue up for sale. Andrew was incredulous. He had been a major supporter of our vineyard and a loyal direct customer.

'I don't think you should give up,' he said.

'We just can't see how we can make it work given the time frame and resources we have,' I said.

'Well, this is more than a friendly catch-up call. We've decided to wind up the company. After costs, there is some money to divvy out, including enough to cover your loan to it. That might help you to hang in there.'

'Tell me more,' I said, excitement mounting. He was referring to a loan I had made to a start-up about ten years before. I had written off the sum long ago, not expecting it ever to be repaid.

As Andrew filled me in I did a quick calculation. The money would meet our shortfall on running expenses for the next twelve months, which would give us the breathing space to develop the new business lines of tourism and holiday rental. I ran through to Sean.

'We've been saved,' I shouted.

'Calm down. What's going on?'

'We can take Garrigue off the market.' I felt a strange sense of déjà vu back to the days of 'it's on, it's off', when we tried to buy Garrigue almost three years before.

'I feel like we just won the lottery,' said Sean, a smile spreading over his face as the impact of my news sank in. Then he looked serious. 'But Carolinus, we have to decide if it's worth investing this second chance in Garrigue. We need to be sure we aren't throwing our energy into something that will deliver nothing in the long run. The farm has to be financially viable, it has to make a living for us. We've got to be rational.'

There it was, rational. We had to be rational, but I wasn't. If I had been rational, I would have walked out the first time a mouse launched itself at me or the first time my back felt broken from stacking too many cases of wine or the first time I came back from a full morning of shoot removal. No, it was not rational, but Sean was right, it needed to make enough money to feed our family and to fund a modest retirement.

Once the girls were asleep, we worked for hours on a new business plan. Going over the history of the business we could see how badly we had misjudged the time it would take to have the wine business operating as a going concern. The red wine had taken eighteen months longer than expected to be available. The costs had been much higher than estimated and we hadn't planned for the excruciating level of social charges despite our consultation with an expert accountant. Add the low yields of the organic road we had chosen to that and it wasn't pretty.

We looked at different scenarios and discussed potential income streams deep into the night. Our average wine prices had to increase considerably. We had to sell our wines for what they were worth. With optimistic projections, higher wine prices, the self-catering cottage and the wine classes, we could find sufficient income to keep the wine business going while we developed new vineyard plantings. The new plantings would then help Garrigue to pay its way. We would have to work hard to put bread on the table.

No one in their right mind would stick with this business. No investor on earth would touch it, but I had left my consulting roots long ago. I had found a discipline I loved, something that was awesome, demanding and vibrant.

'It's what I want, SF. We've come too far to give up. I love this place. I get up in the morning with energy.'

'I agree, Carolinus. We have to make it a success. There is too much potential to throw it away.'

We took Garrigue off the market. Knowing we would not be rethinking our decision again was pure release. We had decided to stay. We would pursue this dream to its end. The previous twelve months of constant questioning of the future were over. We would make it work. We were following something beyond logic, an ancient profession greater than ourselves.

We couldn't afford new things, the girls had hand-me-down clothes, as did I, Sean's gear was more hole than cloth, but we were living and feeling more deeply than ever before. We were also settling in the community. Each year the arts exhibition in the Château de Saussignac was accompanied by a lunch *à l'espagnole*, a bring and share, set out in the garden on long trestle tables. When I arrived at my third Arts au Château festival opening I found a huge photo of Sean, taken by Timothy White, a photographer who co-owned one of the towers of Saussignac Castle, at the entrance. The photo captured the essence of Sean, the vigneron. In the line-up he was alongside village powers like the mayor, the president of the *syndicat* of Saussignac and François, the chef at the Lion d'Or. Sean had arrived. With a few intensive language classes behind him he could now hold his own at a French dinner party. We were slowly transforming from outsiders to insiders.

The following evening we sat down to a dinner 100 per cent grown by us. Our own organic white wine, potatoes pulled from the earth an hour before, fresh chives, mayonnaise made from our own eggs, a salad made from edible weeds, herbs and hardy greens like rocket that survived erratic gardening. It was a meal that beat a grand feast, bursting with flavour, truth and freshness.

I pushed my chair back from the table and proposed a toast to Garrigue and Sean's green fingers. I felt humble and grateful for what we had, instead of harassed about what we didn't have. We were taking a risk but we were living. This was not the safe option but it was our option. It was more than a job. It was our lives. Yes, there were no weekends off but there was also fulfilment that you could not put a price on. Not only that, we were living our philosophy, contributing to what we believed in through our organic practices.

I prepared to depart for a sales and marketing trip that was long overdue and we received news that our merlot that had put us in the *merde* had won a medal in the Concours de Bordeaux, the Bordeaux wine competition. It was perfectly timed. A few days before, an unexpected article had appeared in a major newspaper: the writer, Sandra Mooney, declared Château Haut Garrigue La Source to be her favourite red wine saying, 'It's gorgeous.' I thought she was gorgeous. These were the red wines that had given me so many sleepless nights and cost Sean a third of a finger. Now they were winning accolades.

Sean took me to Bordeaux airport. We said goodbye and automatically kissed each other on either cheek *à la française*. We realised at the same moment what we had done and cracked up, giggling uncontrollably on the set-down pavement. We were becoming French. At least I knew his name.

On arrival as I drove through the city, I was filled with memories. Aideen and Barry were waiting for me with a plate of fresh salmon on the table. The butter I slathered onto the potatoes was beyond heaven. Everything was calm and ordered. My bed was made and Aideen had put out slippers for me. A new copy of *Food and Wine* magazine was on the table with a two-page feature article about us and our wines. It felt good.

Andrew gave me the use of his boardroom in the city centre for the evening wine classes I offered to our direct customers. Before my first session I made a dash into a specialist cheese shop to buy Cashel Blue, a delectable Irish blue cheese that would be matched with our Saussignac dessert wine as the finale to the class. Like the butter I had had the night before it melted on the tongue and left a long memory. My appreciation of all food had been transformed in the years at Garrigue.

A radio crew arrived to tape part of the class. I had a full house with chairs packed around the edges of the room. Everyone was in great spirits and the class was super-interactive. The years of knowledge from Garrigue poured out of me. Our organic ethos and my love of wine combined to form a powerful message. It was so much more than work. At the end of the class, Dorothy, the radio journalist, pulled me aside.

'You were great, Caro, great!'

'Thanks, Dorothy. It's easy to talk about something you love.'

'You should have your own TV show.'

I laughed and thanked her. A few minutes later everyone was gone and I was left alone with the chaos remaining after a fifteen-person wine tasting. Between trips carrying glasses down the two flights of stairs to the kitchen I read the comments on my feedback forms.

'Your passion for organically produced wine is inspiring. You make great wine and have a zest for life and knowledge. I hope to be able to attend your classes more often.'

'Thanks for taking the fear out and adding some mystery to the art of wine appreciation. We really enjoyed the class.'

'Excellent class. What clarity.'

'Awesome wines.'

I attacked my clean-up with renewed vigour. In the background, the sounds of Bruce Springsteen floated through the square. He was giving a live concert and his poignant songs filled the room. The streets were quiet with the odd couple wandering back from dinner in town. I returned Andrew's boardroom to a pristine state and let myself out through the massive door of their Georgian building.

Stepping onto the pavement I was transported back to my mid twenties and my arrival in the city. A decade of memories washed over me in a delicious wave. I carried the tools of my new trade – wine glasses, wine bottles, corkscrew and wine education booklets – back to my car and prepared to head back to Aideen and Barry. Before taking off I opened the window of the car and paused for a few minutes to listen and soak up the place. It was one of those moments in my life I would never forget. A turning point, the moment where I felt comfortable in my new professional skin. I had made the transition from consultant to wine professional.

The classes were window dressing; selling our wines to wine shops was critical. Dave, our largest wine buyer at the time, was my most important meeting of the week.

I went in to his offices with a hammering heart. After fifteen minutes of waiting he invited me in to meet one of their Australian winemakers, known as the 'Baron of Barossa', from one of the oldest winegrowing families in Australia. I felt sidelined, shoehorned in alongside a famous winegrower. We tasted his sémillon sauvignon blanc blend alongside our own, then his merlot alongside our merlot.

'That's a lovely sém-sauv,' said the Baron. My heart swelled with pride.

'Yours is delicious too,' I said.

'So how much wine do you produce, Caro?' he asked.

'We're small: 20,000 bottles.'

'Oh, yeah, small like us. We produce 25,000.' He choked on his wine. 'Did you say bottles? We produce 25,000 cases.'

For him 25,000 cases, almost fifteen times what we produced, was a small producer. It gave me a sense of the difference in scale between Australian and French producers. In France, we were close to the norm with many of our neighbours a similar size to us. In neighbouring St Émilion, the average farm was around 15 acres, about half our size. The Baron was called to go to lunch with the directors. Perhaps in a few years I'd be fortunate enough to be invited but for now I was a little-known producer with no market clout. The wine buyer and I got down to business.

'Caro, we have a new category management system. It forces us to focus on successful wines,' said Dave.

I felt my blood drain from my body. It was about six months since he had ordered from us.

'Your white wine now has a permanent place on our shelves. It is one of our core range that we want to have in stock on a permanent basis,' he said. 'We want to order all your stock of the new vintage sémillon sauvignon blanc.' Inside I was jumping for joy but I kept a cool exterior.

'What about the merlot?' I asked.

'I like it but it may be too tannic for our customers,' said Dave, then took another swig and spat a clean, high-pressure jet into the spittoon.

'It won a medal in the Bordeaux Wine Competition. We'll have the medals on the bottles in a few weeks.'

Dave looked through his stocklist.

'I haven't got much pure merlot at the moment. We'll try 1,200 bottles.' Then he offered me a price that was well below what we needed. I was desperate to have a foothold for our red wine so I agreed. It wasn't the 4,800-bottle order I had hoped for or the price I wanted, but it was better than nothing.

I called Sean that evening.

'Well done, Carolinus.'

'It's nothing to do with me. It's your great wines.'

When I hung up I was despondent. The price I had agreed on the merlot was so far from what we needed to cover the running costs as to be laughable.

'But look how far you've come,' said Aideen. 'How much does the reduction represent?' She did a quick calculation on her mobile. 'Look, you made more than that on wine sales at your classes this week. Remember this time last year you had no retail customers and now look at you. A regular stock item for them. It's mega.'

Aideen put everything in perspective. Compared to the previous year our progress was enormous. The following day, as I was leaving, a wine importer called looking for exclusivity on two of our premium wines. It was a boost to our morale but we weren't keen to jump into an exclusive arrangement and I played for time.

Ellie spotted me coming through the doors of Bordeaux airport.

'Mummy, Mummy,' she yelled, almost leaping out of the car window in excitement with Sophia hot on her heels.

I dropped my bags and ran to hug them.

The car and trailer were stuffed to bursting with barrels from a grand cru classé in the Pessac-Léognan. We had developed a relationship with the owner during Sean's days buying the wines for the bank he used to work for. Now they sold us a few of their best second-hand barrels each year. It was a fitting sight for tourists arriving into Bordeaux airport and I could see them staring at us both because of the welcome I got and for the barrels, an icon of our ancient profession.

'Sit next to me, Mummy,' said Ellie. I sat between them in the back seat so I could be hugged and stroked all the way back to Garrigue.

It was good to be back in my French home. The community of Saussignac was something to be savoured as our mayor regularly reminded us in his letters. Sophia started real school. I drove home from the post office at midday on Sophia's first day and saw her new Maîtresse about to enter her house opposite the school. She caught my eye and gave me the thumbs-up. Sophia had settled in. I felt a wave of community warmth.

Mitch O'Sullivan, the owner of a specialist wine shop in Eymet, a bastide town near us, loved our sauvignon blanc so much she wrote an article for a local paper about us. 'It's a gem with hints of bergamot and Loire Valley sauvignon minerality,' she said, congratulating us on our success. The good news kept rolling in. I considered for a second the horror of what we would have thrown away if we had sold the vineyard. We had come so close.

As I worked the pump and Sean filled the 'new' barrels with our red wine we talked excitedly about the future; where we wanted to take our wines, biodynamic certification, a wine school and the potential for the ruin. I realised our adventure had only just begun.

# Message from the Author

When I started this book it was a way to help me through the challenges of moving country and a dramatic change of life. Through the saga of our first year I felt impelled to tell the story. Now the story also has a message about our organic transformation.

Being a producer changed my buying habits. Every cent I spend has an impact on the market. It's basic economic theory but living and feeling it personally changed my ways. The consequences of chemical farming are horrible: cancer for the workers farming the land, long-term destruction of the land, pollution in the water and chemical residues in the end product leading to potential cancer for consumers; but it's hard not to be addicted to cheap food sold beautifully dressed-up in supermarkets, especially on a tight budget.

Our bakery laughed at me when I asked them for an organic baguette. I resolved not to buy from them any more. My miniscule purchasing power would make a difference, each purchase a declaration of what we believed in.

Sean and I were in the kitchen cleaning up after the girls had gone to bed.

‘I will not support non-organic,’ I raved. ‘I have to find organic suppliers so we can buy direct. If I can’t source an organic baguette, I’m going to make my own bread. I can’t be talking organic all day then supporting something else with half my purchases because it’s the easy option.’

Sean laughed. I had never made bread in my life. I was still so far from a self-sufficient farmer’s wife, my husband thought it was a joke.

‘Don’t laugh. I’m serious.’

‘Well, don’t tell me about it. Do something about it,’ he retorted.

The annual organic fair in Bergerac offered me a chance to make him eat his words. I found suppliers of everything from organic cosmetics to a biodynamic cheesemaker with whom we could share our lunar secrets. The revolution had started. Like us, people everywhere were on similar paths, discovering not only the joy and health of organic, but the ethics of it.

A treasure was my organic flour supplier, a lively fellow with a Gallic moustache and great tufts of black hair coming out of his ears and his nose and over his glasses. He created flours and oils from his crops himself and they tasted clean and clear; like the essence of what they were. The day after the fair I made my first home-made bread. It was therapeutic and surprisingly easy. Kneading the dough gave me time to contemplate where we were and where we were going.

The first phase of the violent birth of Château Haut Garrigue was complete. Through our voyage I had been transformed; from wine lover to winemaker; from consumer to producer; from ecological spectator to activist; and from outsider to insider. Sean’s biodynamics in the vineyard and winery were at an early stage but we could already see what a difference it made. Sharing my passion for wine with wine lovers gave me a thrill.

We invite you to be part of the next episode in this sometimes terrifying ride. Sign up to our newsletter or join our wine club. Email me on caro@frenchwineadventures.com, visit us or stay at our vineyard in our ecological accommodations. See www.hautgarrigue.com and www.frenchwineadventures.com for details. We look forward to hearing from you.

*À bientôt!*
Caro

# Acknowledgements

Thank you to all the wonderful characters in this book and to the team at Summersdale. Thank you to Laurence, my good friend and running partner, for reviewing the French language used in this book; nonetheless, any mistakes are my own.

Big thanks to my friends who helped with feedback and editing in the early days of this book and encouraged me with 'tough love': Senan Molony, 'Bullet' Andrew Bolton, John Campion, Gabi Cutayar and Ian and Brigit Wilson.